Hegel on Possibility

Also Available at Bloomsbury

The Architecture of Freedom: Hegel, Subjectivity, and the Postcolonial State,
Hassanaly Ladha
From Marx to Hegel and Back: Capitalism, Critique, and Utopia,
ed. Victoria Fareld and Hannes Kuch
Hegel, Logic and Speculation, ed. Paolo Diego Bubbio, Alessandro De Cesaris,
Maurizio Pagano, and Hager Weslati
Hegel and Resistance: History, Politics and Dialectics,
ed. Bart Zantvoort and Rebecca Comay

Hegel on Possibility

Dialectics, Contradiction, and Modality

Nahum Brown

BLOOMSBURY ACADEMIC
LONDON • NEW YORK • OXFORD • NEW DELHI • SYDNEY

BLOOMSBURY ACADEMIC
Bloomsbury Publishing Plc
50 Bedford Square, London, WC1B 3DP, UK
1385 Broadway, New York, NY 10018, USA
29 Earlsfort Terrace, Dublin 2, Ireland

BLOOMSBURY, BLOOMSBURY ACADEMIC and the Diana logo are trademarks of
Bloomsbury Publishing Plc

First published in Great Britain 2020
This paperback edition published in 2021

Copyright © Nahum Brown, 2020

Nahum Brown has asserted his right under the Copyright, Designs and Patents Act, 1988, to be identified as Author of this work.

For legal purposes the Acknowledgments on p. viii constitute an extension of this copyright page.

Cover design by Charlotte Daniels
Cover image © Franckreporter / Getty Images

All rights reserved. No part of this publication may be reproduced or transmitted in any form or by any means, electronic or mechanical, including photocopying, recording, or any information storage or retrieval system, without prior permission in writing from the publishers.

Bloomsbury Publishing Plc does not have any control over, or responsibility for, any third-party websites referred to or in this book. All internet addresses given in this book were correct at the time of going to press. The author and publisher regret any inconvenience caused if addresses have changed or sites have ceased to exist, but can accept no responsibility for any such changes.

A catalogue record for this book is available from the British Library.

A catalog record for this book is available from the Library of Congress.

ISBN:	HB:	978-1-3500-8169-7
	PB:	978-1-3502-6234-8
	ePDF:	978-1-3500-8170-3
	eBook:	978-1-3500-8171-0

Typeset by Integra Software Services Pvt. Ltd.

To find out more about our authors and books visit www.bloomsbury.com and sign up for our newsletters.

Contents

Acknowledgments	viii
Abbreviations	x
Introduction	1
The modal indeterminacy problem	1
Actuality stands higher than possibility	6
Possible worlds are separate from each other	10
This one world contains every possibility	17
Hegel's two conceptions of possibility	20
Possibility and Contradiction (Chapters 1–3)	24
The Thesis from Modal Optimism (Chapters 4–6)	28
Part 1 Possibility and Contradiction	35
1 Hegel on Totality: From Being to Nothing	37
Being, nothing, becoming	39
Controversies surrounding Hegel's transition from being to nothing	45
Various interpretations of the being-to-nothing transition	46
Source Interpretations	47
Non-source Interpretations	53
The Dialectical Totality Interpretation	60
Desmond's objection to Dialectical Totality	64
Dialectical Totality is the good infinite	67
Dialectical Totality and contradiction	70
2 Hegel on Contradiction: From the Categories of Reflection to Ground	73
Qualifying Hegel's treatment of contradiction	75
The categories of reflection	81
From identity to difference	84

From difference to contradiction	86
From contradiction to ground	87
The substitution interpretation	90
Contradiction as contrariety	92
Contradiction as essence	94
Contradiction as life and vitality	98
Contradiction is productive	102

3 Hegel on Possibility: From Actuality to Absolute Contingency — 105

The two sides of possibility	109
Modality and contradiction	112
The actuality of the possible *itself*	115
Formal contingency: The indifference strategy	118
Conditional actualization: The dispersion strategy	121
Absolute modality: The substance strategy	128
Absolute necessity is contingency	134

Part 2 The Thesis from Modal Optimism — 137

4 Necessity Amplifies Possibility: Hegel's Theory of Modal Transitivity — 139

Hegel's bi-conditional account of possibility and necessity	141
"Possibility entails necessity" is not absurd	143
"Necessity entails possibility" is not trivial	146
The necessity-access model	147
The necessity-production model	149
Modal transitivity and aesthetics	151

5 Leibniz, Hegel, and Deleuze on Incompossibility — 155

Leibniz and the thesis that God has actualized the best of all possible worlds	156
Absolute and hypothetical necessity	158
Leibniz and the ontological status of unactualized possibilities	160
The compossible and incompossible relation	161
Why do other incompossible worlds seem to be better than this one?	163

Why cannot all incompossible worlds come into existence? 167
Hegelian revisions to the incompossibility problem in Leibniz 171
The objection from the inclusion of divergence 176
The objection from modal elitism 177
Deleuze and the question of the ontological status of incompossibilities 181
Hegel and the incompossibility problem in Deleuze 186

6 Totality and Transformation: More Objections and Consequences 189
The objection from determinism 191
The objection from radical transformation 197

Notes 204
Bibliography 222
Index 230

Acknowledgments

This book could not have been written without the outstanding support of friends, family, colleagues, mentors, and students, as well as generous institutional support. Many of the ideas in this book were first presented at conferences at the University of Guelph (Canada), the Chinese University of Hong Kong (CUHK), the University of Regina (Canada), Tallinn University (Estonia), National Chengchi University (Taiwan), Trent University (Canada), the National University of Singapore (NUS), the Hong Kong University of Science and Technology (HKUST), Marlboro College (USA), the University of Macau (UMAC), and National Cheng Kung University (Taiwan), in conjunction with associations including the Society for Phenomenology and Existential Philosophy (SPEP), the International Association of Philosophy and Literature (IAPL), the Ontario Hegel Organization (OHO), and the International Philosophical Seminar (IPS). I would like to thank the blind reviewers of Bloomsbury Academic Publisher, who offered insightful advice about how to revise this book. I would also like to thank Jay Lampert, Tom Rockmore, John Russon, Kelly Coble, Peter Cheyne, Edward S. Casey, and John W. Burbidge for commenting on earlier drafts. I had invaluable conversations about Hegel and related themes with a lot of amazing people, including Jerry Levy, Laura Stevenson, Ross Benjamin, Jonathan Rattner, Casey Ford, Suzanne McCullagh, Joe Arel, John Lundy, Sasa Stankovic, Mario Wenning, Stefan Deines, William Franke, Béatrice Marchet, Greg Moss, Saulius Geniusas, Eric Nelson, David Chai, Shengqing Wu, Lucas Scripter, James Batcho, John Giordano, Shang-wen Wang, Michael Clark, Kai Marchal, Hans-Georg Moeller, Ting-mien Lee, Alexei Procyshyn, Luis Cordeiro Rodrigues, Tim Beaumont, Suzanne Beiweis, Itay Shani, and Billy Wheeler. I am grateful to the University of Macau, the Hong Kong University of Science and Technology, and Sun-yat Sen University for granting research time and resources. Special thanks to my grandmother Hilary Michaud for her tremendous emotional support over these years. I would also like to acknowledge permission to reuse excerpts from the following published material: Chapter 1: "Why Is Being Nothing? An Apophatic Reading of Hegel's Opening to the *Logic*," Frontiers of Philosophy in China, 13.4, 2018, 508–34, and "Is Hegel an Apophatic Thinker?" In *Contemporary Debates* in *Negative Theology and Philosophy*, edited by Nahum Brown and J. Aaron Simmons, 107–30, Cham: Palgrave Macmillan, 2017; Chapter 2: "Why Do Contradictions Sink to the Ground? A Reexamination of the Categories of Reflection in Hegel's *Logic*" Journal of Speculative Philosophy, 33.4, 2019; Chapter 3: "Indeterminacy, Modality, Dialectics: Hegel on the Possibility *Not to Be*" in *The Significance of Indeterminacy: Perspectives from Asian and Continental Philosophy*, edited by Robert H. Scott and Gregory S. Moss, Routledge, 104–23, and *Hegel's Actuality Chapter of the* Science of Logic: *A Commentary*, Lanham: Lexington Books, 2018; Chapter 5: "Transcendent and Immanent Conceptions of Perfection in Leibniz and Hegel" in *Transcendence, Immanence, and Intercultural Philosophy*, edited by Nahum Brown and William Franke, Palgrave, 2016.

Abbreviations

CPR   Kant, Immanuel, *Critique of Pure Reason*, trans. Guyer, Paul and Wood, Allen W. (Cambridge: Cambridge University Press, 1998).

CWA   Aristotle, *The Complete Works of Aristotle*, 2 vols. (Princeton: Princeton University Press, 1984).

DM   Leibniz, G.W., *Discourse on Metaphysics and Other Writing*, ed. Loptson, Peter (Toronto: Broadview Editions, 2012).

EL   Hegel, G.F.W., *The Encyclopaedia Logic*, trans. Geraets, T.F., Suchting, W.A., and Harris, H.S. (Indianapolis: Hackett Publishing, 1991).

FLB   Deleuze, Gilles, *The Fold: Leibniz and the Baroque*, trans. Conley, Tom (Minneapolis: University of Minnesota Press, 1993).

LS   Deleuze, Gilles, *The Logic of Sense*, trans. Lester, Mark (New York: Columbia University Press, 1990).

PE   Leibniz, G.W., *Philosophical Essays*, trans. Garber, Daniel and Ariew, Roger (Indianapolis: Hackett, 1989).

PS   Hegel, G.F.W., *Phenomenology of Spirit*, trans. Miller, A.V. (Oxford: Oxford University Press, 1977).

SL   Hegel, G.F.W., *The Science of Logic*, trans. di Giovanni, George (Cambridge: Cambridge University Press, 2010).

TH   Leibniz, G.W., *Theodicy*, trans. Huggard, E.M. (Charleston: BiblioBazaar, 2007).

WL   Hegel, G.F.W., *Werke in zwanzig Bänden, 5: Wissenschaft der Logik I* (Frankfurt am Main: Suhrkamp Verlag, 1969).

WLII   Hegel, G.F.W., *Werke in zwanzig Bänden, 6: Wissenschaft der Logik II* (Frankfurt am Main: Suhrkamp Verlag, 1969).

Introduction

The modal indeterminacy problem

This book explores Hegel's theory of possibility in the *Science of Logic*, and his related conception of contradiction, by examining Hegel's solution to the problem of what I call "modal indeterminacy." The problem of modal indeterminacy comes from the recognition that every possibility cannot be said to exist in actuality without some form of qualification, either by distinguishing existence in the concept "actuality" from existence in the concept "possibility" or by separating the multiplicity of possible outcomes through the conceptual scaffolding of "worlds," typically by separating this actual world from a higher or lower world that transcends it, or by arguing that there are multiple possible worlds that extend beyond this one. Most traditions in the West wrestle to find solutions for how to acknowledge the existence of possibility while avoiding the absurdity and meaninglessness that would result from the total existence in actuality of every possibility whatsoever.[1]

The concept of possibility inherently contains negativity, in the sense that what is possible both can be and can *not be*. If it is possible to walk, it is also possible *not* to walk. To claim that all possibilities exist in actuality without further qualification is to involve oneself in contradiction, which leads in turn to a jumbled field of meaningless indiscernibles, and to vague paradoxes verging on the formless. This problem haunts Aristotle's famous account of modal reality in book *Theta* (book 9) of the *Metaphysics*, and his related account of the indeterminacy of contradiction in book *Gamma* (book 4). The problem of modal indeterminacy haunts Leibniz as well, who warns against the absolute void, which is what he thinks would result if God were to have actualized every possible world rather than lifting our actual world above the others. This is the same problem that Deleuze invokes when he asks, in relation to Leibniz, why cannot all incompossible worlds come into existence along with the actual world? If every possibility exists in actuality, without qualifying the priority of actuality over possibility, or in some way separating the possible from the actual, we end up with an absurd, imageless world of chaos verging on nihilism. Just as meaning requires determinate negation in the form of a contrast of something with another, the claim every possibility exists requires some form of qualification.

The most direct and, arguably, most naive response to modal indeterminacy comes from the followers of the Megarian School of Actualism, who claim outright that unactualized potentiality does not exist.[2] The Megarians believe that an activity exists only when it is actual. They attempt to avoid a set of thorny issues that form when we concede ontological status to anything other than direct, ostensible actuality. The Megarians' motivation lies in recognizing that, even if we do not go so far as to conclude that "every potentiality exists," but only so far as to say "some unactualized potentialities exist," we run into the danger of complicating the concept of existence either by having to concede that the category "existence" is larger than the category "actuality" or by expanding our conception of actuality to include, in a paradoxical way, our conception of unactualized potentiality. Because they worry that the existence of potentiality causes a complication in terms of its relation to actuality, with the danger of finding oneself unable to establish a clear distinction between actuality and potentiality verging on modal indeterminacy, the Megarians avoid the entire problem by dismissing the existence of potentiality outright.

The Megarians attempt to avoid the dangers of modal indeterminacy, but only at a significant cost, as Aristotle explains in the *Metaphysics* 9.3, only by embracing a comical counter-position, wherein nothing *is* that is not directly actual. To be clear, the Megarians are not claiming that actualized potentiality does not exist. That position would be truly absurd since no activity whatsoever would result. Rather, they are claiming that unactualized potentiality does not exist, and therefore that nothing inactive exists. Aristotle summarizes the Megarians' position when he writes: "There are some who say, as the Megaric school does, that a thing can act only when it is acting, and when it is not acting it cannot act, e.g. he who is not building cannot build, but only he who is building, when he is building; and so in all other cases" (CWA 1046b29–31). Aristotle rejects this thesis by explaining that if what the Megarians say were true, we would be unable to ever initiate or cease to do an activity. "For it is clear that on this view a man will not be a builder unless he is building … (CWA 1046b34). A man will not have the art when he has ceased to use it" (CWA 1047a2–3). Aristotle also points out the folly of the Megarian position with an example from perception: "Nothing will even have perception," he writes, "if it is not perceiving, i.e. exercising its perception. If, then, that is blind which has not sight though it would naturally have it, when it would naturally have it and when it still exists, the same people will be blind many times in the day—and deaf too" (CWA 1047a6–10).[3]

However, Aristotle's modal theory is not as far from the Megarians' theory as *Metaphysics* 9.3 suggests. The reason why Aristotle engages Megarian Actualism in the first place as a serious argument in need of refutation is because he also views the one-to-one correspondence of actuality and potentiality to be untenable, and he sees the Megarians' position as a natural although unintuitive reaction to this problem. The Megarians go too far in rejecting the existence of unactualized potentiality outright. And yet, what Aristotle acknowledges through his engagement with the Megarians is that potentiality cannot exist without some form of qualification, without mitigating its status and in some way separating it from the actual.

We can view most modal theories in the history of Western philosophy as falling in between the two extreme poles of modal indeterminacy and actualism. Most philosophers agree that unactualized possibility exists at least to some degree. Most philosophers also qualify the existence of possibility to avoid the conclusion that every possibility exists in actuality, thereby avoiding both the comedy of extreme actualism and the dark nihilism of extreme indeterminacy. We can view the content and signature of each modal theory from the distinct ways that each philosopher qualifies the existence of possibility to avoid modal indeterminacy, on the one hand, and actualism, on the other hand.

Beyond the Megarian solution, two of the most trenchant arguments in the history of Western philosophy that aim to dismiss the problem of modal indeterminacy are *modal priority* and *world separation*. Philosophers who claim that either actuality or possibility is the more primary modal category draw out enough of a distinction between the actual and the possible to conclude both that possibility exists and that it is distinct from actuality. The classic version of this argument comes from Aristotle, who in the *Metaphysics* 9.8 expresses his suppressed Megarian tendencies by arguing that actuality is for the most part more primary than potentiality. The notion that actuality is more primary also influenced many of the Medieval logicians, especially Saint Anselm, whose ontological argument for the existence of God relies heavily on the premise "it is better to be actual than to be merely possible." Descartes's revival of the ontological argument in the *Meditations*, which aims to prove the existence of God from the indubitable first principle *Cogito, ergo sum*, also makes use of actualism, as does Kant's criticism that "being cannot be made into a predicate."[4]

The other significant way to qualify the existence of possibility is to argue that although possibility exists in the same way that actuality exists, it is nevertheless separated by "worlds." The scaffolding of possible worlds effectively distances the possible from the actual. The ancient Atomists distance the possible from the actual by defending a theory of infinite space, wherein possible worlds exist scattered throughout the cosmos. Leibniz also establishes a significant ontological difference between actuality and possibility through his conception of God, who projects infinite possible worlds in the mind while selecting only the most perfect world as the actual. The contemporary philosopher David Lewis offers a related account of possible worlds with his theory of modal realism. He claims that every possibility exists but nevertheless avoids modal indeterminacy by defending an "indexical" separation between the actual world and alternative possible worlds. In contrast to proponents of modal priority, who view either the actual or the possible as the more primary modal category, and thereby avoid the issue of modal indeterminacy, possible world philosophers divide the possible from the actual through the compartments of "worlds." The underlying consequence of any possible world theory is that this separation is upheld.

This book focuses on Hegel's complicated but rewarding way of qualifying the existence of possibility. My objective is to contribute to popularizing a reading of Hegel as a philosopher of possibility, who presents a plausible argument for why this actual world contains infinitely rich and abundant varieties of possibilities within it, as against a tradition that has conceived of him primarily as a philosopher of necessity, rationality, and finitude. Hegel's response to the problem of modal indeterminacy is quite unique. He defends the thesis that actuality and possibility are genuinely transitional concepts. By concluding that possibility and actuality transition into each other, Hegel's modal theory is controversial in that it establishes one of the weakest qualifications of the claim "every possibility exists." Many philosophers offer much stronger qualifications, such as modal priority or world separation. But Hegel only separates actuality from possibility to the slightest degree. The qualification "transitions into" is barely a qualification at all. Analysts of Hegel's modal ontology face a significant challenge in articulating how to view actuality and possibility as transitional concepts without falling into the modal indeterminacy trap that Hegel also definitely wants to avoid. Through the support of close textual and interpretive analysis from three of the most important chapters of the *Logic* (the opening of the *Logic*, as well as the contradiction and modal passages in the *Doctrine of Essence*), this book takes up this challenge of explicating and drawing out the exciting consequences of Hegel's theory of possibility.

By claiming that possibility and actuality are transitional concepts, Hegel's modal theory comes closest to the position of modal indeterminacy, but nevertheless maintains a robust, meaningful account of modal reality that avoids Leibniz's fear of the absolute void. Why is Hegel's claim that possibility and actuality are transitional concepts significant? Because any theory that cannot reconcile possibility with actuality, and see them as at least partially transitional, threatens to misinterpret modal reality by reducing the abundance of possibility, either by claiming that most or all unactualized possibility does not exist, or by claiming that possibility exists at a lower register than actuality and reality. The rewards of Hegel's theory are as significant as they are controversial. By claiming that possibility and actuality are transitional concepts, Hegel defends what I call "modal optimism," the thesis that this actual world contains infinite sets of infinite possibilities within it.

For Hegel there is only one world. This world contains infinite varieties of other world-like composites, not as a set of exterior worlds that transcend the actual world, but as a layered, immanent part of the constitution of actuality. What other modal theorists refer to as alternative possible worlds lie, for Hegel, embedded in the determinate content of this actual world. The actual world contains infinite sets of every possible combination within it. It is, as Hegel says, of absolute necessity insofar as it includes the real existence of every possibility. However, much of what it contains remains inaccessible to itself. Most modal theorists are committed to a multi-world system of transcendence that relies on an exterior position beyond the world, on a God who chooses the best of all possible worlds at the expense of alternatives, or on a transcendent realm of heavenly ideals beyond any account of what is given in actuality. In contrast, Hegel's vision of modality makes a dialectic of actuality and possibility; an infinite variety of possible world-like composites exist as immanent to this world. The world is of absolute necessity because all possibilities whatsoever exist within it. The world is nevertheless determinate and meaningful because, although possibility and actuality are transitional concepts, possibility requires the process of emergence through dialectics to become fully present in actuality. Hegel thereby avoids the problem of modal indeterminacy by conceding to only the slightest qualification, while defending a system that allows for genuine freedom at the same time as it includes the existence of every possibility whatsoever.

Before outlining the main tenets of Hegel's one-world modal theory, his argument that actuality and possibility are transitional, and what I call his "modal optimism," that is, Hegel's conclusion that this world contains immanent but infinite sets of possibility within it, I will present a brief overview of the two primary solutions philosophers have devised to make sense of the existence of possibility. In the first of these solutions, the solution from *modal priority*, philosophers argue that the existence of possibility depends on the more fundamental existence of actuality. In the second of these solutions, the solution from *world separation*, philosophers argue that reality is divided into two or more worlds and that either the truly actual world or the totality of all possible worlds exists elsewhere.

Actuality stands higher than possibility

Philosophers who endorse actuality-primacy argue that as long as modal priority is upheld, unactualized possibility can exist without succumbing to modal indeterminacy. Indeterminacy only crops up if every possibility exists in the sense that every possibility *is actual* without further qualification. Philosophers who argue for the modal priority of actuality over possibility effectively avoid the danger of indeterminacy by limiting what it means for possibility to exist.

Aristotle's statements about actuality-primacy, which appear in book *Theta* of the *Metaphysics*, establish the classic and most influential version of the modal priority argument to date. In *Theta* 9.1, Aristotle defines potentiality (*dunamis*, δύναμις) as the source of change or movement in the actual (*energeia*, ἐνέργεια). "[Potentiality] is a starting-point of change in another thing or in the thing itself *qua* other."[5] By defining potentiality in this way, Aristotle distinguishes his position from the Megarians, who are unable to account for the change or movement between one activity and another. Because they claim that unactualized potentiality does not exist, they give no explanation for the movement between activities, nor for how an activity like building can lie dormant in an agent even when not actively engaged. Because the Megarians overreact to the problem of modal indeterminacy, they fail to accurately describe one of the salient features of modal reality, which is that actuality is in a constant process of becoming. Aristotle, in contrast, goes so far as to claim that "actuality is action" (CWA 101050a22),[6] inferring from this that potentiality and actuality are united as movement. The Megarians not only fail to describe the source of the change from one activity to another, as in the case of an active agent who becomes momentarily inactive, or in the case of a perceiver who momentarily does not perceive; they also fail to give an account of the most basic teleological movements of growth, maturity, and decay, a theme that was of the utmost importance to Aristotle (as it was also to be for Hegel).

Yet Aristotle's definition of *dunamis* as the source of change or movement in the actual also betrays his underlying tendency toward actualism. Because it is the source of change, Aristotle concludes that potentiality does in fact exist, but he also concludes that it only exists for the sake of the actual. Potentiality does not exist *for itself* but always only *for another*. Viewed on its own, it is incomplete and requires actuality as its completion. The seed exists as potential, but it is not really anything at all if it is not understood from the terms of its relation to its actuality in the oak tree. Potentiality is change or movement but it is only a change or movement that has its end in the actual.

Aristotle concludes from this that potentiality is fundamentally dependent upon actuality, while actuality is fundamentally independent of potentiality.

In what can be conceived of as his defense against modal indeterminacy, Aristotle outlines in 9.8 three arguments (from definition, one sense of time, and substance) for the primacy of actuality over potentiality. In the B section of 9.8, he also claims that eternal substances take precedence over perishable substances. This can be viewed as a fourth argument in favor of actuality-primacy. Aristotle's first argument has to do with definition (*logos*, λόγος).[7] The reason why actuality is more primary than potentiality is because it functions as the definition upon which we are able to establish knowledge claims about basic reality. Our sense of the existence of potentiality comes only derivatively in relation to the primacy of actuality, which is the true, comprehensive knowledge of the thing. Aristotle also mentions time (*chronos*, Χρόνος) as support for actuality-primacy. Actuality precedes potentiality in time because "the actual member of a species is prior to the potential member of the same species" (CWA 1049b18), in other words, because the generation or procreation of the form comes from the parent. There is, incidentally, a literal sense in which the potential does come before the actual in time, that is, in the sense that "the individual is potential before it is actual" (CWA 1049b18); in other words, the child, seed, or condition has to grow into the maturity of its form over time. But this one case of potentiality-primacy is not particularly significant. Aristotle's third argument for the primacy of actuality has to do with substance (*ousia*, οὐσία). To establish this argument, he makes two interrelated points. First, he claims that substance is the form (*eidos*, εἶδος), and that as form, it exists prior to the potential. "Man is prior," for example, "to boy and human being to seed; for the one already has its form, and the other has not" (1050a5–6). Second, Aristotle claims that it is because of substance that the potential moves in the direction of the actual and seeks out the actual as its principle or end. "Everything that comes to be moves toward a principle, i.e. an end. For that for the sake of which a thing is, is its principle, and the becoming is for the sake of the end; and the actuality is the end and it is for the sake of this that the potentiality is acquired" (1050a7–10). Substance is really at the heart of his commitment to actuality-primacy because it is in terms of substance that he is able to establish the dependency as well as the teleological movement inherent in potentiality.

Aristotle goes on to explain that these three reasons (definition, one sense of time, and substance) support the conclusion of actuality-primacy only in terms of perishable substances, but not in terms of eternal substances. The actual is the *definition* because it is the form, or archetype, of perfect knowledge, which always also appears instantiated and imperfect in potentiality. Likewise, Aristotle understands the actuality-primacy of time in terms of how the forms of life are passed on from generation to generation by way of the first-order actuality of the parent. His argument from substance is also said only from the context of perishable substances, since the potential as the for-the-sake-of-which of actuality grows, ages, and dies.

However, Aristotle claims that such support for the argument from actuality-primacy is not needed when it comes to the modal priority of eternal substances. According to Aristotle, eternal substances are more primary than perishable substances, and they are always only actual and never potential (CWA 1050b6–7). The argument for this is quite persuasive: Eternal substances are not capable of not being. But what is potential has to be capable of both being and not being (e.g., if I potentially have a hundred dollars, then this can either be or not be). Therefore, since eternal substances are not capable of not being, they cannot exist potentially, but only actually. For a substance to be perishable, there has to be a division between its actuality and potentiality. The potential is thoroughly dependent on the more primary existence of the actual, but nevertheless exists through this dependency as a fracture in the actual. The existence of the potential is the sign of the vulnerability and perishability of substances. On the other hand, eternal substances are always only actual. (Aristotle lists the sun and stars as two examples of eternal substances at CWA 1050b22). One cannot even say, along with the Megarians, that actualized potential exists while unactualized potential does not exist, since the category "actualized potential" does not even apply to eternal substances.[8]

To summarize, because his account of *dunamis* as the source of change or movement in the actual leads to the double-sided consequence that potentiality exists and yet actuality is primary, Aristotle can be construed to have successfully defended his description of modal reality against both the extreme actualism of the Megarians as well as the extreme nihilism of modal indeterminacy. By recognizing potentiality as always existing only for the sake of actuality, Aristotle thereby limits the ontological status of unactualized potentiality. He offers a plausible account of the movement between activities and of the "action" of the actual, while marginalizing the role of potentiality by recognizing it as a dependent.

One might think that the growing popularity of modal theories from the contemporary continental tradition that attempt to reverse or complicate Aristotle's argument from actuality-primacy by arguing for possibility-primacy[9] threatens to succumb to the dangers of modal indeterminacy. But this is not the case. For example, Heidegger's startling reversal of Aristotle's actualism in the Introduction to *Being and Time*, a reversal epitomized in the catch phrase "possibility stands higher than actuality,"[10] uses the same resources as actuality-primacy to defend against modal indeterminacy. Even though Heidegger reverses the order of the priority from actuality to possibility, the same strategy of separating the actual from the possible by way of modal priority remains in effect. Heidegger's existential analysis of being-toward-death and of *Dasein*'s grasping the "whole" leads to a powerful alternative conception of our teleological drive from that of Aristotle's actuality-focused drive toward the end of *eidos* (i.e., this is the difference between the fruit ripening, in Aristotle's account, and *Dasein*'s futural anticipation of the possibility of death, in Heidegger's account, which is inevitable but also impossible to reach in actuality).[11] And yet, even though noticeably different arguments for the nature of modal reality arise from conclusions about possibility-primacy, both directions of modal priority use the same strategy to avert the danger of modal indeterminacy: both conclude that one category is more primary than the other, and both thereby dismiss the threat of modal indeterminacy.

Possible worlds are separate from each other

Arguments from modal priority, such as Aristotle's four arguments for the primacy of actuality over potentiality, effectively avoid the problem of modal indeterminacy. But there is also a second, equally popular strategy, the strategy of world separation. Proponents of world separation argue that although unactualized possibilities exist as a viable ontological category, reality is compartmentalized to such an extent that the possible does not exist in the same place as the actual. While some world separationists also have modal priority tendencies, such as Plato, who views the eternal actualities as above and beyond the earth, or Leibniz, who combines world separation and modal priority through the concept of God, it is nevertheless worthwhile to recognize possible worlds and modal priority as two distinct responses to the problem of modal indeterminacy.

One of the most popular models of world separation, the two-world model, is founded upon a basic concept of transcendence. Plato, for example, who can be interpreted to recognize the true forms of reality in terms of *eidos* (ideals, εἶδος), which exist above and beyond the shadowy everyday world of *doxa* (belief, δόξα). Arguments that divide reality in this way demand that we look beyond the most obvious, sensual form of actuality toward the heavens as a higher form of actuality. Most proponents of transcendence claim that this world is really two worlds. On the one hand, there is the world that we perceive directly, a dependent, perishable world that represents and merely copies the true world. On the other hand, there is the genuine although invisible world of the forms, which admits no conception of unactualized possibility, but only the timeless actualities of the archetypes that make up fundamental reality. Aristotle, in contrast, brought *eidos* closer to the earth by presenting the forms as the essences of scientific investigation, and thereby collapsed the two-world order of Plato, defending, instead, a modal priority model that recognizes potentiality and actuality as existing on the same plane, even though divided by priority.

Plato's two-world order gave way to further developments of transcendence through the Judeo-Christian three-world order. The Judeo-Christian notion of transcendence divides reality into heaven, hell, and earth, thereby framing the unity of actuality and possibility in a three-part division.[12] While followers of Plato's two-world metaphysical system rely on epistemological arguments that establish the transcendent world beyond this world as the truer world of complete knowledge, followers of Judeo-Christian three-world metaphysical systems rely on a further, normative argument. Not only is reality divided into an above and below, but the actions we take throughout our lives are predicated on these other realms. Because when we die, we are sent above or below, the decisions we make while on earth are at least partially guided by these invisible worlds. Kant's division between a noumenal and phenomenal realm can also be viewed as a development on as well as a critique of transcendent metaphysical systems. Nietzsche's declaration that "God is dead" has largely been interpreted to signal the waning of transcendence in the West. One of the most formidable opponents of transcendent metaphysical systems, Nietzsche challenges us to quit pretending that there are other worlds beyond this world, and to strive instead to live authentically in this one world we have. He criticizes the history of Western philosophy from Plato to Kant and Schopenhauer for having created a variety of make believe, fictional worlds, which shelter us from the suffering of the real world, but also take away the gravity of being alive in this world.

In contrast to two- and three-world metaphysical systems that rely on a vertical conception of transcendence with categorically different realms above (and sometimes below) the earth, the history of Western metaphysics has also laid claim to a litany of multi-world theories of possible worlds. One of the most interesting multi-world theories comes from the ancient Atomists (a group including Leucippus, Democritus, and the Epicureans), who propose that infinite possible worlds exist, literally, on the various planets and stars of the cosmos.[13] For the ancient Atomists, because space is infinite, there exist infinite planet-like worlds scattered throughout space. The earth we live on is home to only one of an infinite variety of possible worlds, which appear in the sky above us when we look at the stars at night, but nevertheless connect together in one massively vast expanse of space. This vision of possible worlds is described quite vividly in the following:

> Democritus holds the same view as Leucippus about the elements, full and void … he spoke as if the things that are were in constant motion in the void; and there are innumerable worlds, which differ in size. In some worlds there is no sun and moon, in others they are larger than in our world, and in others more numerous. The intervals between the worlds are unequal; in some parts there are more worlds, in others fewer; some are increasing, some at their height, some decreasing; in some parts they are arising, in others failing. They are destroyed by collision one with another. There are some worlds devoid of living creatures or plants or any moisture.[14]

One of the unique features of the Atomists' theory is that every world is actual, however distant spatially. They claim not only that every possibility whatsoever exists, but also that every possibility exists somewhere out there *in actuality* in the greater cosmos. Their conception of the spatially distant is the principle defense the Atomists maintain against modal indeterminacy. Every possibility exists in actuality but not every possibility exists right here on this earth. The Atomists' concept of "worlds" scattered throughout infinite space effectively averts the threat of modal indeterminacy. We are left, instead, with a vision of modal reality, in which the immediate actuality of our everyday lives, even the physical laws and fundamental forms of organic life as we know them, is dwarfed by the real although distant presence of the most fantastic and sometimes even monstrous variations of other worlds.[15]

One might object that the Atomists' principle defense against modal indeterminacy—their concept of spatial distance—is only a viable defense as long as one does not consider the notion of intergalactic travel between worlds. Space travel probably did not occur to the Atomists, who lived in the simpler technological world of Ancient Greece. But does the revelation that intergalactic travel is possible really complicate the consistency of the Atomists' theory? Does spatial contradiction underlie their vision of modal reality? We can answer this by acknowledging that even if we were able to meet other iterations of ourselves throughout the cosmos, we need not conclude that such a rendezvous between possible selves is inherently contradictory. It follows from the Atomists' modal theory that each version of myself belongs to a separate "home planet." Even if the most diametrically opposed versions of myself were to somehow meet, these selves would nevertheless be compartmentalized by the notion of home planets and also by the fact that as separate bodies we would have to travel across spatial distance to reach each other. There is no logical inconsistency that would force us to conclude from the Atomists' theory that intergalactic space travel would lead to the indeterminacy of contradiction.[16] The reason why it is not against the law of non-contradiction to recognize infinite possible worlds as existing in actuality is because of the space separator, as with Aristotle's place qualifier (i.e., it is not a contradiction to be and not to be as long as there is a difference of time, manner, or *place*).

The multiverse of the popular animated television series *Rick and Morty* offers an extended example of the Atomists' theory of possible worlds, one filled with imaginative themes about the possible world adventures that the grandfather-scientist Rick has with his grandson Morty. Rick travels from world to world by use of his portal gun and encounters infinite variations of himself and his grandson, who populate the endless spatial multiverse of possible worlds. There is even a "Citadel of Ricks," where multiple varieties of Ricks and Mortys participate together in a strange social world of possible selves. The philosophical import of this popular cartoon series is indebted to the ancient Atomists' conception of worlds, but it is also original in that it speculates about what it would mean to travel in space between Atomists' worlds, a theme the Atomists never fully developed.

Arguably the most influential of the world separation theories comes from Leibniz, who proposes that infinite sets of infinite series of possible worlds all exist within God's mind, and that the actual world is the product of God's choosing. With his theory of possible worlds, Leibniz attempts to simultaneously avoid what he considers to be the two most dangerous misconceptions of modal reality. On the one hand, there is the danger of "Spinoza's necessarianism," the position that all possibilities are already contained and predetermined in this actual world. On the other hand, there is the danger of the "absolute void," which we have already outlined as the problem of modal indeterminacy, and which Leibniz thinks would be the consequence of God's actualizing every possible world. The relationship between these two dangers is slightly different from the relationship between the dangers of extreme actualism and extreme indeterminacy, which Aristotle anticipates in his rebuttal of the Megarians. In the first, Spinoza's necessarianism, the world is completely determined and not genuinely free. In the second, the absolute void, one could say that the world is too free and dissolves into meaningless chaos through the inclusion of everything whatsoever. The first danger comes from the claim that there are no alternative worlds whatsoever and that this is the only world that could possibly be. The second danger comes from the claim that every alternative world we can think of is already included in this actual world, leading to total indistinctness. By asserting that God is free to actualize any world whatsoever but chooses the one with the most perfection in it, Leibniz finds a narrow path between the necessarianism that he attributes, fairly or unfairly, to Spinoza, and the absolute void of total inclusion.

One of the signature features of Leibniz's conception of possible worlds is that he combines the world separation strategy with an element of the modal priority strategy. Although every world does, in a sense, exist as a projection in God's mind, these worlds do not exist in the same way or with the same priority that the actual world exists. In his book *On Leibniz*, the Leibniz scholar Nicholas Rescher helpfully distinguishes the existence of possible worlds in God's mind from the real existence of this actual world by claiming that alternative possible worlds merely "subsist" rather than fully exist.[17] Leibniz defends against the absolute void of modal indeterminacy not only by claiming that God organizes the endless multiplicity of possibility into the neat compartments of separate worlds, but also by claiming that the actual world is of a higher ontological gradation than the ontological status of alternative possible worlds. God sifts through all of the possible variations of the way things could be and uncovers that one world which produces the richest and most abundant phenomena from the simplest set of laws. This is the only world that is completely real. Because the infinite variations of infinite other worlds are of a lower ontological status and cannot be said to fully exist, Leibniz endorses a different version of modal priority than the version that Aristotle puts forward in the *Metaphysics* 9.8.

Unlike the Atomists, who conceive of alternative possible worlds as all simultaneously existing in actuality in one massive superworld of infinite space, the infinite possible worlds of Leibniz do not reside on the same plane as the actual world, nor do they reside on the same plane as each other. According to Leibniz, each world is absolutely distinct and unrelated. There is no measure of distance between the worlds.[18] A major consequence of Leibniz's Principle of the Identity of Indiscernibles (PE 41–42) is that, just as no two worlds are completely alike, no two worlds share the same space. Leibniz endorses a theory of compartmentalized multi-space. Of course, it is logically possible to conceive of a world that has within it the vast space of multiple worlds, such as the Atomists visualize. But Leibniz would identify the packed layers of worlds within worlds as simply another possible world, which is no larger than any of the others, and not necessarily more perfect.

While Leibniz claims that possible worlds exist only in God's mind and do not exist in the way that the actual world exists, David Lewis claims in his now classic book *On the Plurality of Worlds* that all possible worlds do indeed exist. Lewis endorses the theory of "modal realism": "the thesis that the world we are part of is but one of a plurality of worlds, and that we who inhabit this world are only a few out of all the inhabitants of all the worlds."[19] One of the features of Lewis's modal realism is that he makes use of the possible-world semantics of modal logic. He defines the modal categories in the following way: "Possibility amounts to existential quantification over the worlds, with restricting modifiers inside the quantifiers ... necessity amounts to universal quantification ... What is impossible is the case at no worlds; what is contingent is the case at some but not at others."[20] He claims that if we agree to the thesis of modal realism—the thesis that every possible world exists—this enables us to apply the symbols of modal logic—□ for necessity and ◊ for possibility—to quantify over multiple worlds. Lewis says that just as "the realm of sets is for mathematicians, so logical space is a paradise for philosophers."[21]

Lewis's possible world theory resembles Leibniz's in a number of ways. In opposition to the Atomists, Lewis and Leibniz both claim that infinite possible worlds do not share the same space. "The worlds are something like remote planets," Lewis writes, "except that most of them are much bigger than mere planets, and they are not remote. Neither are they nearby. They are not at any spatial distance whatever from here."[22] They also do not share a common time, and there are no causal connections between them. Actions taking place in one world cannot cause actions to take place in other worlds. Leibniz would certainly agree with all of this.

However, there are also noticeable differences between Lewis's and Leibniz's conception of possible worlds. Modal realists propose that every possible world exists, whereas Leibniz claims that possible worlds only exist, or subsist, as Rescher puts it, in God's mind. By taking God out of the picture, Lewis views the actual world and other possible worlds as existing equally. Because Leibniz is committed to the theological assumption of an omnificent, omnibeneficent God who brings only the best of all possible worlds into real existence, Leibniz is also committed to a theological version of modal priority. With his multiple attacks on modal indeterminacy, Leibniz can be construed to be the most forceful opponent of modal indeterminacy outside of the Megarians. He not only endorses the scaffolding of worlds separated from other worlds, but also upholds a clear privileging of the actual over the merely possible, while also staunchly supporting the law of non-contradiction with his Principle of the Identity of Indiscernibles. In contrast, Lewis offers a milder defense against modal indeterminacy. He does not share Leibniz's theological assumptions. He is not claiming that this actual world is any better than other possible worlds. For Leibniz, perfection is what distinguishes the actual from the merely possible. Lewis claims, instead, that the only reason why the actual world is distinct from merely possible worlds is because of what he calls "indexical reference."[23] What saves Lewis's modal realism from the danger of modal indeterminacy, and thereby upholds both the law of non-contradiction and a robust conception of worlds as distinct from other worlds, is his notion that each world is actual to itself and merely possible to all other worlds. "Every world is actual to itself, and thereby all worlds are on par."[24] Actuality is relative. It is based on a lexical distinction between "here" and "there." This, along with the basic division that comes from the concept of "worlds," is enough to separate the actual from the possible in Lewis's theory.

This one world contains every possibility

Philosophers who do not endorse some form of modal priority or world separation, but who nevertheless claim that every possibility exists, are led to a third, controversial strategy. They are led to the strategy of critically revising our common sense assumptions about the indeterminacy of contradiction. Some philosophers, such as Deleuze, propose that the multiplicity inherent in the concept of the possible need not be recognized as contradictory when it is actualized. He proposes that the concept "possibility" should be replaced by the concept "virtuality," and that, as virtuality, the multiple outcomes of the future, or of a decision, or of an activity are able to coexist simultaneously in the same field without triggering the law of non-contradiction. In contrast, Hegel argues that contradiction does not give rise to indeterminacy, as Aristotle thought. Generally, proponents who endorse this strategy embrace an immanent conception of modal reality, while rejecting both the notion that there are transcendent worlds and also the notion that either actuality or possibility has more primacy. Let's turn back to Aristotle briefly and look at why he believes that contradiction is bound together with indeterminacy, and then present Deleuze and Hegel as two philosophers who, in very different ways, undermine the modal consequences of the law of non-contradiction.

Aristotle claims that the law of non-contradiction is the first principle of philosophy. "It is impossible," he writes in the *Metaphysics* 4.4, "for anything at the same time to be and not to be … [the law of non-contradiction] is the most indisputable of all principles" (1006a2–5). Aristotle infers from this that without the law of non-contradiction, reality would be utterly indeterminate. The law of non-contradiction is a law of separation, individuation, and determination. Aristotle says this in the *Metaphysics* 4.4 when he explains that for an expression to be meaningful, it cannot mean everything at once, but only one thing at the exclusion of all other meanings (1006b5–9).[25] This same point can be applied to the relationship between actuality and possibility. For actuality to be meaningful, not everything can be included. The actual must have over against it that which does not occur in actuality. If multiple alternative possibilities were to occur in actuality, this would break the coherence of reality. The actuality of even two conflicting possibilities at once (e.g., walking and not walking) would result in the real existence of contradiction. According to Aristotle, since contradiction leads only to indeterminacy, possibilities cannot be united in this way.

Aristotle's insight about the law of the excluded middle supports this conclusion as well. "There cannot be an intermediate between contradictories," he writes in book *Gamma* of the *Metaphysics*, "but of one subject we must either affirm or deny any one predicate" (CWA 1011b23–24).[26] The modal articulation of the law of the excluded middle comes from the recognition that if walking is actual, it follows that not walking cannot also be actual for the same subject. Everything cannot occur. Only some things occur at the exclusion of others. The process of actualization is the process of the divided middle. There cannot exist an actuality of both sides at once (both the possibility *to be* and the possibility *not to be*) nor can there be an intermittent actuality where possibilities occur ambiguously together. What stands together as unified in the merely possible always diverges into the paths of actuality. Whatever does not occur stands against what does occur in actuality, and exists only in the hypothetical sense that alternative possible outcomes could have been.

But what if contradiction does not lead to indeterminacy as Aristotle thought?[27] What if the multiple sides of possibility can be united in actuality, either because this does not fully encounter contradiction, as Deleuze proposes, or because the existence of contradiction is itself meaningful and productive, as Hegel's modal theory suggests?

Deleuze takes up the strategy of critically revising our common sense commitments to contradiction. In *Difference & Repetition*, he claims that affirmative differences coexist without developing into a unity of opposites, and thereby into contradiction. With his modal concept of virtuality, he proposes a revision to Leibniz's exclusionary conception of possible worlds, a revision that allows for the equal existence of every possibility while also dissolving the separation built into the scaffolding of possible worlds. His strategy is to undermine our common sense assumption that the law of non-contradiction and its corresponding laws of identity and the excluded middle reign supreme as the most fundamental axioms of individuation.

One of the ways Deleuze articulates his modal theory is through a literary example from the Argentinean writer Jorge Luis Borges. In his short story "The Garden of Forking Paths," a magical book, written by Borges's fictional character Ts'ui Pên, contains every possibility within it, and wherein characters act out every permutation of a decision. "Fang," Borges writes, "has a secret; a stranger knocks at his door; Fang decides to kill him. Naturally, there are various possible outcomes—Fang can kill the intruder, the intruder can kill Fang, they can both live, they can both be killed, and so on. In Ts'ui Pên's novel, *all* the outcomes in fact occur; each is the starting point for further bifurcations."[28] Borges presents a world filled with the actualization of conflicting possibilities. "[Borges] wanted," Deleuze writes, " ... to have God pass into existence all incompossible worlds at once instead of choosing one of them, the best " (FLB 71). Deleuze's conception of virtuality offers a similar conjunctive relationship. Every possibility coexists in a field of virtuality. Actualizations happen across this field, but possibilities do not fall away as other actualizations occur. In a sense, everything occurs together in the virtual.[29]

I claim in this book that the clue to Hegel's theory of possibility and his response to the problem of modal indeterminacy also lie in his radical reflection on the fundamental nature of contradiction. Common thinking abhors contradictions because contradictions show the impasse and the limits of thought and reality. However, the process of dialectical thinking is, for Hegel, the process of thinking the genuine existence of contradiction. Breaking from Aristotle's assertion that the law of non-contradiction is first philosophy and that contradictions only lead to indeterminacy, Hegel recognizes contradiction as productive, rather than reductive. "Contradiction," Hegel writes, "is the root of all movement and life" (SL 382, WLII 75).[30] Far from dissolving thought in the empty dissonance of indeterminacy, contradictions are a vital, fundamental component of thought and reality.

Hegel's theory of contradiction nevertheless should be viewed under certain restraints. Even though he claims that contradictions do not lead to indeterminacy, Hegel is not thereby endorsing the completely unqualified actuality of every possibility whatsoever. Nor is he claiming that the most absurd possibilities are actual simply because we can think them. Instead, by arguing that contradictions are determinate, Hegel proposes a significantly different vision of modal reality than do those who endorse modal priority or world separation. One could say that if Hegel embraces any form of modal priority, he embraces a co-primacy model that recognizes possibility and actuality as transitional concepts. Likewise, from the terms of world separation, one can only conclude that Hegel offers a one-world metaphysical system based on immanent layers of world-like composites, rather than transcendent worlds beyond this one. Possibilities do, in a certain respect, diverge from actuality. But their divergence does not posit alternative possible worlds that transcend the actual world. According to Hegel, possibilities that diverge are reintroduced as material for further actualizations. They diverge but they nevertheless exist as an integral part of the constitution of Hegel's one-world model. Because they remain as an immanent part of the world, they not only exist as the counterfactual projections of alternative outcomes, but also become reincorporated in further processes of actualization, through the universality of essences, and as the proliferation of infinite varieties embedded in reality.

Hegel's two conceptions of possibility

To explain how Hegel avoids modal indeterminacy while subscribing to neither the strategy of modal priority nor world separation, I will present a brief overview of his modal theory as the interaction between two interrelated conceptions of possibility: (1) possibility as alternatives and (2) possibility as a degree of quantity.

Hegel's modal theory, which appears in the "Actuality" chapter of the *Logic*, begins from an initial disposition that he ultimately criticizes. He begins from a definition of possibility as the projection of alternative actualities, what I call *possibility as alternatives*. Formally, if something is possible, this expresses both the positive and the negative side of something in actuality. If A is possible, then both A and -A are possible. Because playing the piano is possible for the pianist, both playing the piano and not playing the piano are possible. Possibility is like an open container. It holds the totality of everything within it simply because it is both the positive and the negative of the actual as one unity.

To actualize possibility causes a seemingly inevitable, structural fracture of possibility to occur. When actuality emerges out of itself, it equally submerges all sorts of other possible events and determinations, which equally could have been, but which cannot be as long as what is actual is. The pianist can and can not play the piano; but in actuality, always only one or the other of these sides emerges at the expense of its other. The pianist either plays or does not play, yet if one happens, the other cannot happen at the same given moment. Actualization brings about not only actuality but equally the erasure of much of what is possible. Although his aim is ultimately to criticize this common sense disposition, Hegel can at first be interpreted to incorporate aspects of this disposition into his own argument. Typical of Hegel, the limitations and failures of a basic claim from common sense modality—that what is actual excludes alternative possibilities from actuality—become the basis of a theory of modality that includes greater amounts of possibility in one actuality.

The concept of possibility as alternatives appeals directly to common sense. If I decide to go to Tokyo, I cannot also in the same time, manner, and place, go to Vienna. Alternatives in possibility diverge in actuality. If some event or entity is possible, then a whole multiplicity of other possibilities can also become actual. Whatever happens in actuality happens against the background of a larger set of possibilities that stand against it as its remainder. The concept of possibility as alternatives does the work of dividing the possible from the actual. Most modal theories, if they assume this conception of possibility without further qualification (or further development, as in Hegel's case), view this remainder as ontologically lower in status, as with modal priority, or as categorically separated, as with alternative world theories.

Taken in isolation, possibility as alternatives leads to an inclusion of only one possible world at the exclusion of an infinite variety of other possible worlds. This exclusion is necessary for the one that is actual. And it might seem that from this initial disposition, unactualized possibilities are ontologically insignificant and do not really exist. However, Hegel's theory turns from this initial disposition of possibility as alternatives to the further, inclusive disposition of possibility as a degree of quantity. Possibilities that at first stand against the immediately actual through the division of actualization become reintroduced through dialectics as the material conditions for further actualizations. This effectively expands Hegel's conception of actuality to include the negativity inherent in possibility. Since immediate actualities are also conditions for the possibility of other actuals, a certain extent of what is excluded from actuality becomes reintroduced through conditional actualization as a higher degree of possibility. Conditions promote a second, interrelated, conception of possibility, not only possibility as alternatives, but also possibility as a degree of quantity. Although a seed is an immediate actuality that excludes counterfactual possibilities, it also contains within it the possibility of the tree, and therefore contains further layers and greater degrees of possible actualities. The tree that could grow from the seed is not the mere possibility of a counterfactual but the real possibility of itself. The existence of conditions is the existence of further possibilities, which lie embedded within what is immediately actual. These possibilities are not projections of other worlds. They are real possibilities that exist hidden within the immediately actual. They are contrary only in the sense that they have not yet and might not ever emerge in actuality. But insofar as what is immediately actual already contains them, they exist as further degrees of possibility within the actuality.

This second conception of possibility as a degree of quantity is as intuitive as the first conception of possibility as alternatives. We often find ourselves measuring possibility by weighing whether one course of actuality has more or less possibility than another. While traveling, learning a new language, and exploring other cultures can help to broaden possibility, confining oneself to one's room, sleeping for long hours in depression, and avoiding the contact of others can reduce the experience we have of possibility. In our day-to-day lives, we are often preoccupied with the idea that possibility can expand and contract. When we make decisions or evaluate our fallen positions in the world, we take for granted that more or less possibility can exist in one actuality. Utopian and dystopian visions follow from the same guiding principle. Possibility is really what is at stake when we imagine visions of paradise or apocalyptic posthuman terrains.

One benefit that comes from this analysis of Hegel on possibility is the clear demarcation of each conception's usage and application. Our everyday language sometimes mixes up these two usages of possibility, and conceptual analysis of modality sometimes refers to one or the other without noticing the distinction. While possibility as alternatives helps to establish why possibility is a basic condition for propositional validity, it is also the concept behind conjectures about other possible worlds, the contingency of this actual one, as well as our common sentiments of regret and desire for what could have been but is not. Possibility as a degree of quantity, however, marks off other regions of modal reality, from normative evaluations of the good and the bad to our basic experiences about freedom, abundance, and world-complexity.

Hegel's insight about possibility goes much further than to announce the distinction between these two conceptions. Hegel formulates an argument not only for why these two conceptions of possibility are distinct, but also for why the initial conception of possibility as alternatives entails possibility as a degree of quantity. The double movement of emerging and submerging possibility in actuality prepares the way for further actualizations, which would not have been feasible if the totality of possibility were to emerge in actuality all at once. In other words, the divergence at work in the first conception, which separates the possible into the actualized- and the unactualized-possible, also allows for the further process, as degrees of quantity, of reactivating actuality through conditions toward higher degrees of concentration and toward otherwise inaccessible regions of possible content. Conditions are the sign of this concentration because they relay between what is immediately actual and the possibilities of further actuals. By reintroducing the contraries of immediate actuality, by doing the work of satisfying conditions, what had been impossible formally—actualizing contrary possibilities—becomes possible to a certain degree. Conditions mitigate the formal contradiction of actualizing alternative possibilities by reintroducing some portion of what had been excluded from actuality. To view an immediate actuality as a condition is to estimate how much work it would take to maintain contraries without letting these become explicitly contradictory. But conditions also symbolize the great expanse of possibility. They express a modicum of the possible *qua* the possible. They are immediate, determinate actualities that also act as a gateway for the multiplicity of the possible in the actual.

The dialectical relationship between possibility as alternatives and possibility as a degree of quantity saves Hegel from the untenable position of modal indeterminacy. Because they would otherwise lead to contradiction, possibilities necessarily diverge in actuality. But because this contradiction is not indeterminate and reductive, but is instead productive and developmental, possibilities that initially diverge because of contradiction are also the material for further degrees of actualization. We end up with a one-world model that dialectically reincorporates possibilities which appear at first to be excluded from actuality. The concepts of possibility and actuality are, therefore, not identical in the way that would lead to modal indeterminacy, but are, rather, transitional, in the sense that excluded possibilities are the material for further actualizations.

Possibility and Contradiction (Chapters 1–3)

Hegel's statements about the ontological status of possibility appear primarily in the "Actuality" chapter of the *Logic* (Book 2, Section 3, Chapter 2), but I contend that the opening of the *Logic* (Book 1, Section 1, Chapter 1) and the passages about contradiction from the "Essentialities or Determinations of Reflection" chapter (Book 2, Section 1, Chapter 2) are also crucial for understanding Hegel's modal theory. To this end, the first half of this book, "Possibility and Contradiction," offers a close textual and interpretive study of Hegel's conception of possibility as it appears in the *Doctrine of Essence* by situating some of the primary consequences of dialectical modality within broader discussions of Hegel's presuppositionless starting point as well as his thesis that contradiction is more primary than identity.[31] The exegetical analysis that takes up the first half of the book is not intended to be a commentary of the *Logic* as a whole. The intention, instead, is to explore the possibility theme by presenting the Dialectical Totality conclusion (in Chapter 1) and the productive contradiction conclusion (in Chapter 2) as a necessary setup for Hegel's one-world modal vision.

In Chapters 1 and 2 of this book, I analyze two interrelated usages of contradiction, which are then applied to Hegel's modal theory. In Chapter 1, "Hegel on Totality," I outline a conception of contradiction as *totality*. A is -A forms a totality and in this way is exhaustive. Contradiction conjoins the negative with the positive in such a way that transcendence collapses into immanence. When we are presented with a contradiction, we are presented with a plurality of positions, from which there is no exterior. There is no position for A other than A *is* -A.

One popular objection to Hegel comes from the assertion that his brand of systematization leaves little room for alternative histories, alternative logical transitions, and alternative courses of life and reality. With sharp necessity, the *Phenomenology* marches along its course from the shapes of consciousness to the shapes of self-consciousness, from the early stages of reason to the full-blown realization of spirit in the state, art, religion, and philosophy. Likewise, the *Logic* turns from topic to topic with urgency in order to uncover the shapes of thought thinking itself. So also, *The Philosophy of History* projects the linear trajectory of the history of the past, not as a disconnected jumble of accidental events that happen to occur contingently and without reason, but as an intelligently designed and rigorously directed developmental path through time and society. Many interpreters of Hegel have concluded from this that his vision of a grand, complete system also leads, as a by-product, to the marginalized exclusion of other spheres of life, of alternative courses that history could have taken, of seemingly "lower" religious institutions, as well as forms of art that embody spirit to a lesser degree.

While these interpretations are plausible in their own right—after all, so much of Hegel's corpus is about the systematic, developmental progression of thought and reality—there is nevertheless another way to approach what Hegel is really doing when he explores the directions and propulsions of systematic dialectics. Chapter 1 aims to rethink Hegel's commitments about totality. Contrary to traditional connotations, Hegel consistently defines totality counter-intuitively as the coincidence of being and negativity, that is, as the complete form A is -A. Hegel's celebration of the negative side of possibility offers a specifically modal example of a theme that is prominent throughout his work. When he claims famously in the *Phenomenology* that the "true is the whole" (PH 11) or famously in the *Logic* that being and nothing are becoming (SL 59–60, WL 82–3), Hegel has the more general implications in mind of the modal claim that possibility is "the totality of form" (SL 479 and 485, WLII 204 and 212). If we define possibility not only as the positive account of itself in actuality, but also as the negative account of non-actuality, possibility then encompasses the totality of any actualization whatsoever in the sense that there is no other permutation of actuality than that it either is or is not. And yet if this recognition of possibility's negative side amounts to the exhaustion of all possible outcomes, this is a strange and unprecedented kind of exhaustion since its totalizing effect includes the possible itself, the possible *qua* the possible, and therefore amplifies possibility rather than restricts it. To include the negative side of possibility exhausts the form of actualization. Possibly A expresses the totality of actualization because it projects both A and -A. One of the primary consequences of this book, the thesis from modal optimism, comes as an inference from Hegel's insight that if possibility contains the totality of actualization, this secures the promise of infinite varieties of unactualized possibility from within this actual world.

In Chapter 2, "Hegel on Contradiction," I outline a second, interrelated conception of contradiction: contradiction as *productivity*. The reason why contradiction forms a conception of totality, in the first instance, is because there is no exterior position outside of a contradiction. Contradictions hold together every side of a matter as a unity. However, because of this, contradictions also have the specific nature of being impossible to grasp in the definite terms of thought and reality. They cannot appear in the sharp light of definitive reality. They withdraw from representation. In Chapter 2, I propose that although Hegel recognizes the impasse between thought and contradiction, he nevertheless embraces a productive conception of contradiction. Its productivity lies, specifically, in the process of its withdrawal. It produces non-contradictory concepts which stand in its place as substitutions. Concepts such as "contrariety," "opposition," and "difference" are logical representations of the underlying existence of contradiction. These seemingly non-contradictory concepts mediate and represent contradiction because contradiction cannot occur directly. Likewise, the concept of "actuality" mediates the contradiction inherent in the multiplicity of the possible. These concepts attempt to explain concrete, everyday reality in a non-contradictory way. But, at the same time, these concepts also show traces of contradiction as their substratum. Thought uses these concepts to mitigate and separate the underlying principle that things are not only themselves but also the opposite of themselves, that insofar as being becomes, being is self-contradictory. On the one hand, such concepts attempt to cover over contradiction and make it appear less than contradictory; however, on the other hand, contradiction inevitably appears through them, guides, and shapes them, in other words, produces what they are and how they function. Because it cannot appear directly, contradiction produces a range of seemingly innocuous, seemingly non-contradictory concepts to stand in its place and represent it. Actuality is one of the primary concepts produced from contradiction.

In Chapter 3, I argue that these two interrelated conceptions of contradiction form the basis for Hegel's theory of possibility. Hegel's notoriously dense chapter on "Actuality" does the work of integrating his conception of totality from the opening of the *Logic* with his subsequent conception of contradiction as primary and productive in the "Essentialities" chapter of the *Doctrine of Essence*. Hegel claims that possibility is the modal version of totality in the sense that if A is possible, then both A and not A are equally possible. The actuality of the possible *itself* (both A and not A together) is then the modal version of contradiction as *totality*. Hegel shows that this raw, unmediated actuality of possibility leads, at first, to our conception of the *impossible*, as the direct and unsustainable actuality of contradiction. Actuality can only sustain the possible *itself* through mediation. Thought covers over the underlying contradiction by dividing the possible into actualized and unactualized compartments. Thought explains the contradiction away by offering a teleological account of how something emerges into actuality by satisfying the conditions of its possibilities. Conditional actualization mitigates the otherwise unsustainable actualization of contradictory positions—of the seed, for example, that is also an oak tree. However, although this teleological account of the actuality of possibility does the service of mitigating and softening what would otherwise be a contradiction, this account also leads to growth, decay, becoming otherwise, in short, to the production and proliferation of further domains and new access points of possibility. In other words, because it is impossible to sustain the direct actualization of the possible, actuality goes through the process of developing new and otherwise inaccessible variations of possibility (new forms of life, spirit, concepts of logic, etc.). Contradiction produces these forms at the same time as it withdraws from direct actualization. Because it cannot fully emerge but must nevertheless emerge in some way, contradiction generates not only the abstract modal concepts that make up Hegel's theory in the "Actuality" chapter (i.e., formal, real, and absolute actuality, possibility, necessity, and contingency), but also the promise of the infinite variety of biological, social, and religious forms of life.

One of the most controversial Hegel claims I analyze in this book appears at the end of the "Actuality" chapter, where Hegel says that absolute necessity *is* contingency. Most commentators argue that what Hegel means is that contingency is one out of many necessary categories of his system. In this way, Hegel allows for a moment of contingency, which is, paradoxically, a necessary feature of the *Logic* as a whole. While I also think this interpretation is right, I develop the idea further in Chapter 3 by exploring the theory that by absolute necessity Hegel means the *total inclusion* of every possibility whatsoever. The reason why nothing can be otherwise is because everything has already been included, as with a contradiction, where A cannot be otherwise because A is A and -A. Contingency is the outcome of absolute necessity. I take this to mean that further contingencies are produced from the dialectical structure of totality. Total inclusion is not only the closing off of further possibilities but also the generation of further proliferations of possibilities at the same time. One of the seminal ideas of Hegel's modal theory is that necessity not only restricts possibility but also amplifies it, producing endless variations of thought and reality.

The Thesis from Modal Optimism (Chapters 4–6)

The second half of this book examines the thesis from modal optimism as a consequence of the textual analysis that takes up first half of this book. Modal optimism is the thesis that this actual world contains an infinite variety of other world-like composites within it. Proponents of modal optimism reject strategies of both modal priority and world separation. They reject the long-standing tradition of the hegemony of actuality over possibility. They also reject transcendent visions of two-world or multi-world divisions between the actual and the merely possible. Proponents of modal optimism challenge Western conceptions of transcendence and offer an immanent vision of modality, where all possibilities whatsoever exist as part of the basic constitution of modal reality, where the actual and the merely possible share the same ontological status. The second half of this book presents the tenets of modal optimism through an exploration of some of the primary insights from Hegel's "Actuality" chapter.

Common sense thinking supposes that actuality and possibility are distinct modes that can be applied variously to an object of thought, but Hegel proposes instead that the meaning of each concept is included in the meaning of the other. That actuality and possibility are transitional concepts is, for Hegel, the modal version of his statement in the *Doctrine of Essence* that "Essence must appear" (SL 418, WLII 124). The reason why immediate actuality (what Hegel calls *Schein* at the beginning of the *Doctrine of Essence*) undergoes a pressure to express the negative side of possibility is because essence does not stand against this world, as an exterior transcendent realm beyond this world but, to the contrary, *must appear* directly as the basis for the constitution of reality. One of the primary projects of the *Logic* is to expose that thought and being are completely intertwined, that essence is not something other than existence, but that the actuality of this world is at the same time the essence and totality of this world. The *Doctrine of Essence* is, in general, a fierce critique of traditional metaphysical assumptions that attempt to promote two-world or multi-world theories of reality, and the "Actuality" chapter offers a powerful attack on plurality of world axioms, which attempt to separate, categorically, actualized possibility from unactualized possibility. For Hegel that there is only one world means that the possible is in and of this world, rather than beyond this world. This single-world model is one of the profound insights of Hegel's argument, and can be seen as the modal version of Hegel's revaluation of Kant's idealism in the greater project of the *Logic* as a book.[32]

Closely related to Hegel's conclusion that actuality and possibility are transitional concepts is his equally unusual conclusion of a dialectic between necessity and contingency. While most accounts of modal ontology define necessity and contingency as opposite terms, in the sense that what is necessary cannot be otherwise but what is contingent can be otherwise, Hegel argues that necessity brings access to otherwise inaccessible possibilities and that the foreclosure of absolute necessity is the free openness of absolute contingency.

A line from Goethe's poem *Nature and Art* (1800) epitomizes Hegel's thoughts about necessity and contingency:

Wer Großes will, muß sich zusammenraffen;
In der Beschränkung zeigt sich erst der Meister,
Und das Gesetz nur kann uns Freiheit geben

[Whoever seeks greatness must gather himself together;
Only in limitation does the master distinguish himself;
And only the law can give us freedom.][33]

The "Actuality" chapter presents three speculative ways to think of the relationship between necessity and contingency dialectically. The first comes from the claim that contingency is a necessary concept of reality, that for things to be at all, they must be otherwise. This can lead to global interpretations for how to read the *Logic* as a book, in the sense that if contingency is necessary, Hegel then provides significant space for new or alterable concepts and also builds contingency directly into the transition points of the *Logic*. Hegel also presents a second version of the dialectic when he claims that it is necessary to actualize all possibilities of a given finite set. This leads to a conception of freedom in necessity, where the possibilities in one thing become dispersed in the actualities of others and are thereby propelled toward otherwise inaccessible actualizations. This can also lead to global interpretations for how to read the *Logic* as a book, in the sense that the complex stages of the *Logic* generate further possibilities from initial constraints. I also analyze a third version of the necessity-contingency dialectic, Hegel's argument that substance relies on a speculative relationship between what cannot be otherwise and what can be otherwise. Hegel's account of substance is innovative because, by defining substance in terms of this dialectic, he presents a reasonable explanation for how the immediate actuality of an individual thing is also the universality of its genus.

In Chapter 4, "Necessity Amplifies Possibility: Hegel's Theory of Modal Transitivity," I propose that "modal transitivity" is central to Hegel's conception of necessity and that productive constraint is one of the main consequences of his dialectic between necessity, contingency, and possibility. Modal transitivity shows that, while necessity restricts possibility in a superficial way, it also produces otherwise inaccessible possibilities. This entailment—from the constraints of necessity to the proliferation and abundance of possibilities—finds its most vibrant expression in the free play of artistic movements motivated by the enactment of formal and content-related constraints. In the realm of aesthetics, we see this, for example, from the formal restrictions of the English sonnet. The rhyme scheme, the iambic pentameter, the three quatrains, and the one couplet are a kind of constraint that nevertheless produce regions of aesthetic contemplation, balance, beauty, measure, which we could not otherwise have access to. Hegel's dialectic between absolute necessity and absolute contingency leads to the "optimism" of modal optimism. If immediate actualities are the conditions of other actuals, then being itself contains an immense variety of determinate possibilities within it. Yet most of what it contains either is not yet accessible from the given immediacy of factual existence or has not yet been produced from the formal structures that generate this variety in the content of things. The thesis from modal optimism has historical implications if we think of Hegel's argument as a revision of Leibniz's claim that this actual world is the best of all possible worlds. The thesis also has contemporary implications if we think of the consequences of this as sharing an ontological commitment with Deleuze's argument for why incompossible worlds all enter into existence.

Proponents of modal optimism believe that conditional actualization explains how embedded possibilities come to emerge in actuality. Conditions act as a gateway between the real, however distant, possibilities of alternative actualities and the surface of actualization. Conditions are the embodiment of possibility and actuality as transitional concepts. The actual world is one massive assemblage of conditional possibilities. These conditional possibilities stretch out in infinite ways and infinite directions. And yet since they are always anchored in terms of their entailment with what is immediately actual, their status as conditions makes them as determinate and realizable, however distantly, as they are infinite, boundless, and measureless. But conditions also place significant limitations, rules, and criteria on what can and cannot presently emerge into actuality. This is the case because conditions constrain and enable possibility with equal but opposite force.

Necessity is the demonstration of perfection, of greater degrees of possibility in actuality. Perfection comes directly from the theory that possibility and actuality are transitional concepts. What is this actual world? It is nothing other than the reality of the possible *itself*, which appears through the enabling-limiting structures of conditions. The reason why necessity is the demonstration of perfection is because conditions allow for access to further regions of possibility. Although this actual world is only immediate, since it contains the conditions for further actualizations, it contains the most perfect abundance and variety of possibilities, not only in the relative sense of greater and more complex degrees of actualization, but also in the absolute sense of the explicit coincidence of actuality and possibility.

One reason why modal optimism is an "optimism" is because proponents of the theory believe that the possibilities embedded in the process of actualization are not only infinite in number, degree, and qualitative determinateness, but also that infinite sets of infinite series exist and share the same ontological status. Modal optimists embrace the small infinity defined by the infinite possibilities of the actual world. But modal optimists also embrace the theory that there are infinite sets of infinities, and that it takes all of these infinites together to make up the total immanent inclusion of modal reality, what Hegel calls the absolute necessity of contingency. This principle of the large and the small infinite together can be viewed as a significant revision to Leibniz's "optimism," where one perfect infinite world converges (the actual) at the expense of infinite sets of infinite worlds (unactualized possibilities), which, although compossible with themselves, diverge from the actual and do not exist.

Chapter 5, "Leibniz, Hegel, and Deleuze on Incompossibility," proposes Hegelian revisions to the incompossibility problem in Leibniz and Deleuze. I claim that the incompossibility problem arises in the first place because Leibniz does not effectively distinguish between (1) possibility as alternatives and (2) possibility as a degree of quantity. Hegel's solution has to do with upgrading the ontological status of possibility to that of real existence and thereby expanding actuality to encompass what are for Leibniz diverging, incompossible worlds that do not exist.

Chapter 6, "Totality and Transformation: More Objections and Consequences," anticipates two of the most serious objections to modal optimism (from determinism and radical transformation), and thereby offers a more robust account of modal optimism. The objection from determinism claims that modal optimism leads to political and social confinement. The objection from radical transformation claims that the thesis from modal optimism leads to the absurd consequence that things can transform into entirely different things without reason. This chapter also concludes with a statement about the ontological significance of modal optimism, which is, at the same time, the conclusion of the book.

The second half of this book also explores the relationship between modality and system in Hegel. The thesis that necessity brings access to otherwise inaccessible possibilities has broad consequences for debates about the trajectory of Hegel's system as well as for his method of sublation (*Aufhebung*). Taken as a grand narrative, the developmental structure of the *Phenomenology* can be interpreted to provide a large-scale account of how necessity entails possibility and free contingency. The stages from consciousness to self-consciousness, from self-consciousness to reason, and from reason, spirit, and religion to absolute knowing, follow a necessary trajectory that is, at the same time, the demonstration of possibility. In absolute knowing, the complete coincidence of subjectivity and objectivity, what can be conceived of as the culmination of the *Phenomenology*, then prepares the way for the developmental stages of thought thinking itself in the *Logic*. Consciousness undergoes a series of developmental stages that lead to the possibility of philosophy.[34] This same motif—that the necessity of conceptual analysis generates further possibilities of conceptual analysis—describes the basic movements of the *Logic*. We can read the *Logic* as a complicated network of necessary deductions, where each concept becomes motivated by inherent restrictions and limitations of its determinate being, to generate itself as other concepts, and to become at its own end the contingency of others. Although the emergence of further concepts might seem to be the exhaustion and failure of former concepts, the emergence is also a transformation that realizes otherwise inaccessible ranges of possibilities from what seems to have been exhausted. In this way, earlier concepts, reduced to contradiction, become reintroduced at later stages of the *Logic*, with the enhanced capacity of free movement, since they are no longer beholden to the relative necessity that had made them determinate in the first place. This reading of the *Logic* as a whole is one of the broader consequences of Hegel's dialectical account of modality.

Part One

Possibility and Contradiction

1

Hegel on Totality:
From Being to Nothing

The aim of this chapter is to articulate Hegel's implicit conception of contradiction, as it occurs in the *Doctrine of Being*, through an analysis of his transition from being to nothing in the opening of the *Logic*. I outline a variety of interpretations of the being-to-nothing transition and I defend what I call the "Dialectical Totality Interpretation" as support for the conclusion that Hegel is committed to a version of totality that, at the same time, embraces genuine alterity. The Dialectical Totality Interpretation leads to a reassessment of totality as a preliminary formulation of what will become, for Hegel, the explicit contradiction of A and not A in the *Doctrine of Essence*.

Traditional connotations of totality as exclusionary exhaustion, pre-determination, and finitude have often been attributed to Hegel's thought, especially from critics such as Kierkegaard, Levinas, and more recently from William Desmond. But the Dialectical Totality Interpretation of the transition from being to nothing that I defend prepares the way for an alternative reading of totality in Hegel's work. In this chapter, I argue that Hegel's conception of totality should not be defined as the exhaustion of all positive content, but as the coincidence of being and nothing, as the contradiction A *is* not A, and as the completion of form and content by way of a dialectic with alterity.

The transition from being to nothing exposes a unique kind of totality that is particular to Hegel. To recognize that something *is* and *is not* is to exhaust all of the permutations of what that thing can be. The ontological ground for this is established in the being-to-nothing transition. While we normally think of totality in terms of finitude and identity, where to totalize means to exhaust and to comprehensively know, because the opening of the *Logic* combines being and nothing together, it offers a significantly different conception of totality.

Being and nothing form a totality through negation, where the exhaustion and completion of all determinate possibilities is at the same time the result of alterity. At later stages of the *Logic*, Hegel will develop this alternative conception of totality by privileging contradiction over identity (see my analysis in Chapter 2). Just as there is no position beyond the all-inclusive unity of being that is at the same time nothing, likewise, the formulation of A as not A completely captures the identity and all of the permutations of A. Hegel will eventually refer to this unique kind of totality as the concept (*Begriff*), which he develops extensively in the third doctrine of the *Logic*. Dialectical totality is also one of the crucial elements of the relationship between actuality and possibility. By recognizing how Hegel presents this type of totality in terms of the transition from being to nothing, we will be in a position to understand why Hegel claims that possibility is the "totality of form" (SL 479 and 485, WLII 204 and 212) and why absolute contingency turns out to be the same as absolute necessity. This conception of Dialectical Totality prepares the way for Hegel's further conception of "expanded actuality" and for his one-world system, which includes the totality of every possibility whatsoever.

The transition from being to nothing at the start of Hegel's *Logic* marks one of the most controversial but rewarding moments of the book. The transition is controversial because of the abstract nature of the indeterminate concepts being and nothing and because of the sheer immediacy of the conversion. It is rewarding, nonetheless, because it establishes the first movement and the whole trajectory of the book. This transition is, in effect, the second of four arguments that constitute the opening of the *Logic*. That being transitions to nothing comes directly after the question of how to begin a presuppositionless science at all (first argument), which Hegel addresses in "With What Must the Science Begin?" It also precedes two subsequent arguments: the argument for why being and nothing together transition into becoming (third argument), and why this prepares the way for determinate being (fourth argument). While not everyone will agree that there are four arguments to the opening, nor that each transition can be clearly distinguished from the others, nor even that Hegel's thinking can be organized as a series of arguments at all, I would like to focus, nevertheless, on the specific question of the motivation for the transition from being to nothing (second argument). I will start by explicating the being, nothing, becoming passages of the opening of the *Logic*. I will then catalog some of the most prominent commentaries on Hegel's transition into the various branches of Source and Non-source Interpretations, before defending the Dialectical Totality Interpretation. This chapter concludes with a discussion of how contradiction operates in the *Doctrine of Being* specifically.

Being, nothing, becoming

While it takes up less than a page of the *Logic*, the seemingly innocuous little transition from being to nothing has captivated many noteworthy commentators of Hegel. The British Hegel scholar G.R.G. Mure puts it quite well when he says that for readers of the *Logic*, it must come as a real shock to common sense to see Hegel claim that being *is* nothing.[1] Why does being transition into nothing? What exactly is the motivation for the movement? Let us start by explicating the official passage of the opening:

> *Being, pure being*—without any further determination. It is in its indeterminate immediacy equal only to itself, and yet it is not unequal in contrast to others. It has no inner difference but also no outer difference. If it were able to posit a determination or interior, from which a distinction could be drawn, or through which a distinction could be posited against another, it would not hold fast to its purity. Being is pure indeterminateness and emptiness. There is *nothing* in it to be intuited, even if one could here speak of intuiting. Or it is simply this pure, empty intuiting itself. There is not anything to be thought in it, or, what is the same, it is empty thinking. Because being is indeterminate immediacy, it is in fact *nothing*, and not more nor less than nothing. (WL 82–83)

Hegel's description begins from the fragment "being, pure being." Being is so simple that it does not even warrant a full sentence, as if the image associated with being were prior to the associations of the syntax of a full sentence (i.e., prior to the format subject-verb-object).[2] "Without further determination" suggests that the positing of "being, pure being" is itself the first mark of determinateness. And yet if being is otherwise truly indeterminate, as Hegel describes, then it cannot at the same time be one-sidedly indeterminate, since if it were, it would have determinate being over against it, and this would make indeterminacy determinate. When Hegel writes "[being is] equal only to itself, and yet it is not unequal in contrast to others," he complicates what we might normally think of as the "indeterminate." Being is at first indeterminate, but not yet even in the one-sided, exclusionary sense of not being determinate, as if what is determinate were something other than being. Being is, instead, an "indeterminate immediacy" that also has to include determinate being as well. This makes indeterminacy prior and completely inclusive, and makes being all comprehensive and presuppositionless.

Hegel therefore establishes being as comprehensive in the sense that everything and anything has being. If it were equal to itself *but not also equal to others*, something other than being would stand against being, as its opposite and determination. But since being has no further determination, there is nothing other than being. Since everything has being, being contains everything within it. There is no outside or external reflection for the concept of being. It simply *is*. Since everything has being, everything simply *is*, without further qualification and without further need of support.

Hegel arguably overemphasizes the total comprehensiveness of being when he then states that being has no difference within it. If being were really that which has no difference within it, then that which has difference within it would likewise determine indeterminate being. Instead, the point to recognize is that being is prior to the distinction between identity and difference. Being is indifferent in the sense that it indiscriminately fills all things. Each thing simply *is*, and insofar as each *is*, there is no difference between one thing and another. Being is the great leveler of difference. But Hegel should have also explained that just as it is not unequal to another, being is also not unequal to differences. Differences themselves *are*. Otherwise, being would merely be one side of a relation that has difference over against it. Hegel often criticizes this type of one-sided thinking as the folly of "external reflection," and so we should be careful to qualify in what sense being has no difference within it. If being is truly presuppositionless, positing "being, pure being" would have to precede the question of whether being has difference within it. We might clarify Hegel's point by explaining that, on the one hand, being contains no difference, since to contain difference would mean to generate determinateness and exclusion. Yet, on the other hand, being cannot be differentiated from that which does contain difference within it, since only through this ambiguity does being obtain the genuine status of indeterminateness.

And yet by visualizing that which is indeterminate in this way, we can only thereby visualize the concept of *nothing*, because to visualize being as anything at all would be to visualize it as determinate being against another determinate being. This is why in his initial description of being, Hegel describes the concept of nothing by writing: "There is *nothing* in it to be intuited … it is simply this pure, empty intuiting itself … " (my emphasis). The thought of being is an empty thought, without further determination. That Hegel's description of being reverts to a description of nothing suggests, on the one hand, that there is nothing that can be grasped from being, that, in other words, being fails to express anything meaningful at all. But this also suggests, on the other hand, that the only determination of being is nothing, in other words, that the positive meaning of being is as nothing. Hegel, again, overemphasizes the point when he describes being as "pure emptiness." Being is empty but not as something different from absolute fullness. In this sense, we can equally describe being as that which all things indiscriminately are as their most obvious, basic qualification. Being is synonymous with reality itself. But from this total immersion, because it is utter fullness, being is at the same time sheer emptiness. And yet, the only reason why being is an empty concept is because it is so full that nothing at all can exceed it. Since meaning requires distinction and difference, being fails to be meaningful and therefore concedes to the self-same concept of nothing. As interpreters of Hegel's description of being, we should not assume that when he attributes "empty thinking" to the concept of being, he presupposes that being is without meaning or value. To the contrary, being is so full of meaning, so comprehensive and fundamental, that only a concept of nothing can maintain it.

In the second paragraph of the opening of the *Logic*, Hegel repeats the parallel structure of "being, pure being"—not even a complete thought, prior to a syntax that would allow for more, just the flashes of indeterminate being, which transition into nothing:

> *Nothing, pure nothing*; it is simple equality with itself, complete emptiness, determination-less and content-less; indistinct in itself. If one can here say anything about intuiting or thinking, one would say that it makes a difference whether something or *nothing* can be intuited or thought. To intuit or think nothing also has a meaning. Being and nothing are distinct, and so nothing *is* (exists) in our intuiting or thinking; or, rather, it is empty

intuiting or thinking itself, and is therefore empty intuiting or thinking as pure being. Nothing is, therefore, the same determination, or, rather, lack of determination, and is, therefore, the same as *being*. (WL 83)

Hegel's descriptions of being and nothing are, at first glance, almost identical. It would seem that the term "nothing" could be substituted for the term "being" without any real change in the meaning of the description. As with his description of being, Hegel begins with a sentence fragment, this time, "nothing, pure nothing." And yet nothing is also the polar opposite of being. It is non-being rather than being, emptiness rather than fullness, absence rather than presence.

Hegel therefore establishes nothing as the opposite of, but also as the same as, pure being. It is the opposite of being in the sense that being *is* and nothing *is not*. However, nothing is also the same as being in the sense that the absolute fullness and total comprehensiveness of being can only be maintained, and can only be conceived of, if being *is* nothing. In other words, to describe being as indeterminate is to describe being as nothing. The semantic ambiguity of "being has *nothing* over against it" reveals the double meaning of being's relation to nothing. The pun expresses that, on the one hand, the concept "nothing" is the opposite, exterior, external contrast of being. But on the other hand, there is literally nothing that stands over against being. That which is the opposite of being is at the same time proof that there is no opposite of being, that even nothing *is*. In this sense, nothing at all can escape being or be otherwise than being. Either nothing *is*, in which case, it is not opposite to being, or it *is not*, but then it has no concrete position against being, and can only produce from this the conclusion that there is nothing other than being, or that this nothing over against being is nothing at all. This makes nothing different from, but at the same time, the same as being.

The concept of nothing is posited, then, as the final test of whether anything at all exceeds being. Nothing demonstrates, as the ultimate proof, that being is the presuppositionless starting point of the *Logic*. Even nothing, the sheer opposite of being, is contained in being. The conclusion that being *is* nothing is the only conclusion that secures being as first philosophy. This is a similar test to the one that Socrates uses in conversation with the citizens of Athens who claim to "know" something. This is a similar test as well to the one that Descartes uses in the *Meditations* when he asks whether anything is beyond all doubt.

To submit being to such a radical test, which Hegel proposes to do when he claims that being is without presupposition, is to significantly alter the concept of being. Being was supposed to be the full comprehension of indubitable reality. But because it can only achieve this status through the proof that being *is* nothing, the *Logic* guarantees indubitable being at the cost of conceding that being is, at the same time, the opposite of itself.

The transition from being to nothing is then further explored in Hegel's concluding description of becoming:

> *Pure being and pure nothing are therefore the same.* What is true is neither being nor nothing, but that being is nothing and that nothing is being—not as passing over, but as having already passed over into each other. What is more, the truth does not lie in their indistinctness, but rather in that *they are not the same*, that they are absolutely distinct, and yet that they are at the same time unseparated and inseparable, and that they immediately vanish into each other as into their opposites. Their truth is, therefore, this movement in which being and nothing immediately vanish into each other. This movement is *becoming*, through which both are distinguished, but by a distinction which has immediately dissolved into itself. (WL 83)

Hegel defines "becoming" as the conclusion that being and nothing are the same. Being turns out to be the same as nothing because only insofar as being *is* nothing is being all comprehensive as everything whatsoever. Hegel's description of becoming does not really add anything further to his descriptions of being and nothing. Or, the only addition is that with the concept of becoming, Hegel changes the emphasis from the positive concepts "being" and "nothing" to the process of the transition between these two concepts. One might say that if there is an addition at all, it is the recognition that neither being nor nothing as a singular concept is the true starting point—as if the question were, being *or* nothing?—but only insofar as being *is* nothing is the *Logic* able to commence.

We might interpret Hegel here as prioritizing becoming. If the truth of being and nothing lies in their transition, doesn't becoming turn out to be the real starting point of the *Logic*? But to agree to this is only half right. Hegel does propose that neither the fixity of the concept of being nor the fixity of the concept of nothing is enough to maintain the presuppositionless starting point. However, this also means that becoming is a compound concept, which cannot be thought apart from its presupposition in being and nothing. Becoming is, therefore, the real starting point, in the sense that it is the truth of being and nothing, but is also derivative, in the sense that it is not more than the summation of being and nothing together.

By defining this transition as becoming, Hegel establishes an unusual type of movement between being and nothing. More than a motion in which one side dissolves, mutates, manifests itself, moves upon, or otherwise passes over into its other, Hegel describes the transition of becoming as "having already passed over" into its other [*nicht übergeht, sondern übergegangen ist*] and as a "vanishing" [*verschwindet*] of one into its opposite. More than being capable of passing over into, or even of being in the process of passing over into, Hegel claims that to think being, and thereby to think nothing, is to have already witnessed their having passed over into each other. This is the significance of Hegel's use of the past tense that being "has already passed over" into nothing. The transition is so immediate that to think being at all is to have already thought being's transition into nothing. Invoking the past tense allows Hegel to describe the transition as so immediate that we are left to wonder whether being and nothing are really distinct at all. Hegel's choice of the word "vanishing" [*verschwindet*] is particularly appropriate in this regard. The distinction between being and nothing is a distinction of opposites, but becoming shows that each is really the same as the other. This self-sameness, which is also ambiguously the first mark of determinateness, can only be articulated as a transition that is so sudden and immediate that the two concepts literally vanish into each other. From this, we can define "vanishing" as that type of transition where the distinctness between terms is at the same time completely undermined in their identity. The ambiguity of whether being and nothing are distinct allows for the closest of transitions. In Hegel's vocabulary, the closest type of transition comes when two concepts vanish into each other.

We might assume from Hegel's initial descriptions that the transition from being to nothing, articulated as being *is* nothing, moves in only one direction, that is, only *from* being *to* nothing. To assume this is to assume that being has priority over nothing. Being is, after all, the first term of the triad. Nothing is second and can only be identified derivatively as what being turns out to be. However, Hegel complicates this path of interpretation by proposing that, because each "vanishes" into the other, the transition is not only absolutely immediate, having always already happened, but equally bi-directional. In a remark that comes after the official passages of the opening, Hegel calls the transition from being to nothing "ceasing-to-be." He calls the transition from nothing to being, in contrast, "coming-to-be." To describe becoming as both of these transitions together is to undermine what we would normally conceive of as a significant difference between something that is in the process of coming into being and something that is falling out of being. At this indeterminate first stage of the *Logic*, becoming does not yet discriminate between rising and falling.

Controversies surrounding Hegel's transition from being to nothing

The claim that being *is* nothing is controversial for a number of reasons. First of all, since nothing is normally conceived of in everyday thought as the opposite of being, it should look strange to a casual reader of Hegel to see directly from the outset of the book the conclusion that being *is* nothing. Even a reader who interprets Hegel's description conservatively as only a mediated and partial transition, rather than as the vanishing identity of each concept as the other, is still left with the difficult project of having to make sense of the broadest ontological unity that one could possibly conceptualize.

A second, equally difficult controversy comes up when we try to explain how the *Logic* moves from being to nothing in the first place. While the *Logic* is filled with movement, the question of the motivation for the movement from being to nothing is an especially important and problematic question, different from all other transitions in the book. The transition from being to nothing is the momentous first revolution of the *Logic*. While other transitions have to do with the inner tensions of various stages of the *Logic*, which can already be conceived of as in flux through various presuppositions, the transition from being to nothing is a special kind of transition because it exposes the risk of whether and by what means the *Logic* will begin to move at all. This risk is exasperated by the presuppositionless nature of the starting point of the *Logic*. Whatever the motivation is for the movement from being to nothing, our explanation will have to address Hegel's commitment to a presuppositionlessness starting point. The Hegel scholar Michael Rosen articulates this problem when he writes: "The forward movement of the *Logic*, if it is to be in keeping with Hegel's own understanding of his philosophy, must be rigorous and perspicuous *ex ante*. Any account which needs to supplement the forward movement with a retrospective justification must violate Hegel's self-understanding."[3]

On my account, the reason why Hegel begins from being as the only genuine presuppositionless starting point is because being is all-inclusive. Being must always already be presupposed whenever we recognize anything determinate at all. This makes it first philosophy. And yet being can only achieve this status of first philosophy if it is as inclusive as nothing is, to the extent that being is the same as, or at any rate vanishes into, nothing. There is no position beyond the ontological unity of being and nothing together. Being captures everything only insofar as it cannot be understood apart from nothing. This leads to a reconception of totality. Totality is the self-contradictory unity of being and nothing together. This reading of Hegel's starting point opens pathways for his subsequent conceptions of contradiction and possibility in the *Doctrine of Essence*.

Various interpretations of the being-to-nothing transition

Commentaries on the transition from being to nothing can be divided into two trunks, with a number of branches connected to each trunk. Source Interpretations make up one trunk of the commentaries, while Non-source Interpretations make up the other trunk. Source Interpretations include commentaries that view Hegel's motivation for the transition as hinging on a presupposition that dictates the movement from being to nothing, while Non-source Interpretations rely on arguments that the design of being itself causes the transformation to occur. Source interpretations can be divided into internal and external branches. Internal Source Interpretations include commentaries that view the transition as being motivated by a source located within the *Logic*. Some readers of this branch claim that the whole of the *Logic* is circular and self-referencing and that, because of this, later doctrines (the *Doctrine of Essence* and the *Doctrine of the Concept*) act as the source for the initial transition of the book. Other readers propose a more local version of internal source, claiming, instead, that the transition from being to nothing presupposes a robust conception of *becoming*.

In contrast to the Internal Branch of Source Interpretations, readers who defend External Source Interpretations claim that the transition requires an external assumption outside of the trajectory of the *Logic*. Some readers of this branch claim that Hegel assumes the act of *thinking* from the outset. Others say that Hegel is already committed to *dialectics*, and that being transitions to nothing only because *Aufhebung* dictates this movement. Both Internal and External Branches of Source Interpretations share the commonality of being critical of Hegel's claim that the *Logic* begins without presuppositions. External source interpreters hold the stronger version of this objection, claiming that although Hegel proposes to begin without presuppositions, being only has the ability to transition if Hegel tacitly, or even unintentionally, relies on an external source for this movement, which is, in effect, a presupposition. Internal source interpreters, in contrast, hold the weaker version of this objection, claiming that the *Logic* presupposes its own endpoint, or a point along the way, in order to commence.

The other main trunk of commentary consists of Non-source Interpretations. Readers who fall under this category embrace Hegel's claim that the *Logic* truly does begin from a presuppositionless starting point, and argue instead that the motivation for the transition from being to nothing has to do with the nature of being itself. One branch of this consists of Design Interpretations, that is, of readers who claim that the transition comes either from *teleological* design, or, alternatively, from specific *characteristics* embedded in the nature of being, and that this is what causes being to change into nothing. Another branch of Non-Source Interpretations proposes that there is an *apophatic* origin to the transition, that the reason being is nothing is because it fails to fulfil the very concept that it purports to be. The Apophatic Branch is closest to the Dialectic Totality Interpretation that I defend. I will briefly analyze these various Source and Non-source Interpretations and then explore the ramifications of the transition for a reconception of totality.

Source Interpretations

Source Interpretations have a distinct advantage and a distinct disadvantage over Non-source Interpretations. They have the advantage that they are able to consistently explain, by exposing a presupposition in Hegel's opening, why being transitions into nothing. Without being able to cite a presupposition, the initial movement of the *Logic* appears to move paradoxically as if from nowhere. Source Interpretations resolve this paradox—that there seems to be no rationale for the movement without begging the question, in other words, no way to propel being—by turning to a conventional and rational source for the movement. They have the disadvantage, however, of not being able to fully make sense of Hegel's thesis that the *Logic* begins without supposition. External Source Interpreters simply disregard Hegel's thesis, arguing that, despite Hegel's intentions, the *Logic* cannot be both presuppositionless and also generate movement. Proponents of the External Branch simply conclude that Hegel is misguided to think that the *Logic* is presuppositionless. All movement whatsoever requires an external source or cause. Proponents of the Internal Branch make a similar objection, although they are subtler than their External Branch counterparts, claiming that since the presupposition Hegel admits to is an internal, self-referencing presupposition, the opening of the *Logic* is at least partially presupposed.

One variation of the Internal Branch comes from Dieter Henrich's "*Anfang und Methode der Logik*." Henrich argues that the opening cannot be completely presuppositionless because this would leave Hegel without the resources to animate the movement from being to nothing, and from this to becoming. What the *Logic* requires is a premonition of its own content and endpoint. The transition from being to nothing, on Henrich's account, can only happen if the doctrine of being presupposes its difference from the doctrine of essence, as well as its integration with the doctrine of the concept. This effectively explains the transition. But Henrich's self-referencing interpretation can also be viewed as problematic because it diminishes the importance of Hegel's opening. Because the transition appears only as an indeterminate moment of Hegel's subsequent analysis of determinate being, essence, and the concept, Hegel's opening loses some of its significance and comes to be viewed, based on this interpretation, as a necessary but flawed preamble, which does not hold much weight on its own.

William Maker offers a variation of this interpretation in his book *Philosophy without Foundations*. Maker argues that the negative work the *Phenomenology* does of clearing away the assumptions of consciousness and subject–object dualism can be viewed as the motivation for the transition from being to nothing.[4] Much as Henrich would have the source of this motivation come from the presupposition of later doctrines of the *Logic*, Maker claims that what Henrich attributes to the role of "essence" Hegel has already attributed to the role of the *Phenomenology*, with the additional effect that the *Phenomenology* is not a presupposition for the opening in the same way that the later doctrines of the *Logic* would be since it only does the negative work of clearing away the assumptions of consciousness so that a logic can commence. However, we still face a problem when applying Maker's analysis of the relationship between the *Phenomenology* and the *Logic* to the transition from being to nothing. Either the *Phenomenology* is a presupposition of the *Logic* or it is not. If it is a presupposition, then one might conclude that the dissolving of subject and object through mutual recognition and absolute knowing prepares the way for the subsequent dissolving of being into nothing. But to present the relationship between the books in this way is to undermine the claim that the *Logic* is presuppositionless. The *Logic* would then have to appear as a sequel to the *Phenomenology*. The being-to-nothing transition would then have to appear as a continuation of absolute knowing. Maker clearly does not endorse this reading, claiming, instead, that the *Phenomenology* merely removes the assumptions of subject–object dualism without acting as an explicit presupposition of the *Logic*. But if the *Phenomenology* is not a presupposition in any significant way, then it does not make sense to point to the conclusion of the *Phenomenology* as the source of the motivation for the transition from being to nothing.

Another popular theory is that Hegel relies on a pre-established conception of becoming as the motivator for the transition. I think of this variation as a local version of the Internal Source Interpretation. Much as Henrich would have the reasoning for the transition lie in conceptions of *Essence* and the *Concept*, proponents of this local version see becoming as the real motivator for why being *is* nothing. There is a lot of merit to this version of the interpretation. Hegel does explicitly describe becoming as what results from the dual transformations of being-into-nothing (ceasing-to-be) and of nothing-into-being (coming-to-be). Becoming is, in effect, the key term in the triad. And, really, it is the key term of the *Logic* as a whole. The *Logic* is a book about becoming and transformation. Determinate being, the next step in the development, is an examination of what it means to become, and one can see how the rest of the book follows from this crucial concept. Nevertheless, without diminishing the importance of Hegel's conception of becoming in the least, I want to point out that becoming only appears sequentially *after* the transition from being to nothing. Hegel states quite clearly that becoming is a compound concept built from the simple concepts being and nothing, and that, for this reason, becoming is derivative. To argue that becoming is the motivating source for the transition is to ignore the order and primacy of being. As much as he values Heraclitus as the philosopher who nearly articulated the opening of the *Logic* through his Greek conception of "fire" as first philosophy, Hegel admits that the opening cannot truly begin with the concept of becoming. The consequence of this is that the transition from being to nothing cannot rely on becoming as its source, since it is, conversely, becoming that relies on being and nothing as its source. Readers who are sympathetic to this local Internal Source Interpretation might still acknowledge that once Hegel establishes becoming, one sees how the earlier transition already has the elements of becoming in it, and in a retroactive backward-looking way already presupposes becoming. But to argue for this interpretation is to miss the point of the problem, which is that being has to be able to transition into nothing *prior* to its subsequent transition into becoming, and that this cannot be fully accounted for retroactively without undermining Hegel's claims about presuppositionless science.

These are the main two variations of the Internal Source Branch. Let's now look at the External Branch, that is, the branch of arguments that claim that the transition from being to nothing requires an external source beyond the dynamic, internal movements of the *Logic*. One of the most prominent External Source Interpretations comes from critics who claim that the only way Hegel can transition between concepts is if he presupposes a philosopher who animates the developmental process through the act of thinking. In *The Opening of Hegel's Logic*, Stephen Houlgate associates this interpretation with Schelling, Trendelenburg, and Kierkegaard, who each object that the movement from being to nothing is artificial because it requires the presupposition of a thinking subject who does the work of moving the concepts along since the *Logic* cannot do this for itself.[5] The conceptual development of the *Logic* is only possible, on their accounts, if a philosopher stands hidden behind the narrative of the book and traces the movement of being and nothing through an act of pure, rational thinking. Textual evidence for this interpretation can be found in Hegel's initial descriptions of being, nothing, and becoming. These descriptions lead to the general suspicion that Hegel has artificially built into the opening a subject who attempts to think being, who finds only empty thoughts from this intuition, and who ultimately does the work of synthesizing being and nothing into the higher concept of becoming. In contrast to Henrich, who sees the motivation from being to nothing as coming from a presupposition internal to the *Logic*, proponents of this External Source Interpretation claim that Hegel is wrong to assert that the opening is presuppositionless since it necessarily posits the external reflection of a thinking subject.

The disadvantage of this external interpretation is, however, even more pronounced than the disadvantage of the internal interpretation. Since the reason for the transition comes from a source outside of being and nothing, this interpretation ignores one of the most important insights of the *Logic*, which is that the concepts must be able to unfold from themselves. "[Concepts] must be understood," Houlgate writes in his analysis of this topic, "to develop or 'move' because of their own *logical* character, not because of the way we think of them or experience them."[6] This insight is really at the heart of Hegel's claim that the *Logic* must be presuppositionless. Since he is so often critical of the standpoint of external subjective reflection, it is bizarre to accuse Hegel of incorporating a completely external act of subjective thinking into the foundational movement of the *Logic*. Even if the external interpretation can be viewed as a coherent explanation for the movement from being to nothing, since this reading rejects Hegel's starting point outright, it is more of a criticism of Hegel than an interpretation of the opening from the terms that Hegel establishes.

Incidentally, Houlgate cites Henrich's "*Anfang und Methode der Logik*" as a defense of the thesis that the concepts of the *Logic* move themselves, even if this movement happens through the presupposing of later stages of the *Logic*. This makes Henrich's position quite nuanced, and also shows that there is a big difference between the Internal and External Branches of Source Interpretations. Since the presupposition of later stages of the *Logic* is internal to the *Logic*, the concepts of the *Logic* still move themselves, even though they also presuppose themselves and only move because of this presupposition. This view leads to the conclusion that the *Logic* as a book is the enactment of one grand performance of the *concept* (*der Begriff*). It presupposes itself, references itself, others itself, moves itself, all as the seamless identity of thought thinking itself and reality realizing itself.

Another version of the External Source Interpretation comes from privileging *Aufhebung* over the opening of the *Logic*. This is one of the most common and tenacious interpretations of the transition. In this interpretation, readers claim that the primary reason why being transitions into nothing (and eventually why becoming comes out of the fusion of being and nothing together) is because Hegel is committed to dialectical reasoning, which has at its core, if not the express formula of thesis-antithesis-synthesis, as some commentators believe,[7] then at any rate the double-movement of lifting up and destroying. It is true that Hegel famously uncovers this double-edged meaning from the German term *Aufhebung*, which is, as he writes, both *Aufheben* as *to lift, to rise up* and *Aufheben* as *to cancel, to abolish*. And it is arguably true that this double-movement is the essence of Hegel's thinking. But what is also worth noticing is that Hegel's remark on "Sublation" (SL 81–82, WL 113–15) comes *after*, not before, the opening of the *Logic*. This remark on sublation is only one of the rare moments in his corpus where Hegel expounds on a general method of dialectical thinking. Since this gesture to his method comes only as the result of the starting point, and only as an aside, we should recognize the starting point of being, nothing, and becoming as an argument that supports *Aufhebung* as one of its conclusions, but not the other way around. Dialectical thinking, one could say, is a significant consequence of the opening of the *Logic*. The opening shows that without presupposing anything at all, being must transition of its own accord into nothing and that this transition generates dialectical thinking generally. Certainly, most local arguments in the *Logic* and the *Phenomenology* can be explained through the formula of *Aufhebung*. But to apply *Aufhebung* formally in this way is to miss much of what is important in Hegel's reasoning, especially since the being-to-nothing transition precedes the remark on "sublation." Interpreters who cite *Aufhebung* as the rationale behind the transition have mixed up the order of the argument. They have inadvertently made him into a dogmatic thinker and have also undermined his goal to begin without assumptions.[8]

Non-source Interpretations

The interpretations I have outlined so far are all either Internal or External Source Interpretations, in the sense that each interpretation of the transition explains the movement from a source other than the design of being itself, either internally from other divisions of the *Logic* or externally from tacit, unannounced presuppositions. But there are also branches of interpretation that explain the movement from being to nothing as coming explicitly from the logical character of being and nothing, rather than from a rejection of the claim that the *Logic* is truly presuppositionless. The advantage of Non-source Interpretations is that they remain a lot more faithful to Hegel's thesis that the *Logic* is presuppositionless. Some of the Non-source Interpretations are also able to offer closer textual evidence for their conclusions, since they work directly from Hegel's description of the transition. The main disadvantage of this trunk is that since interpreters only have being itself to work with in explaining the transition, these interpretations run into the danger of not being able to adequately show the rationale behind the motivation. The three main branches of Non-source Interpretations that I will discuss are called "Design Interpretations" and "Apophatic Interpretations," as well as my own "Dialectical Totality Interpretation."

Readers who stand behind the Teleological Approach to the Design Interpretation propose that there is a teleological impulse embedded within Hegel's conception of being that drives being on a path to transform into becoming. Songsuk Susan Hahn defends this interpretation in her book *Contradiction in Motion*. Just as we see the foreshadowing of the oak tree in the seed, we see the foreshadowing of the concept of nothing in being. Hahn explains the movement thus as teleologically designed: "Like the seed that necessarily carries within its internal structure its entire evolving history, the rational kernel of the concept Being necessarily—not in the sense of logical necessity but in the sense of teleological necessity already guaranteed by nature—carries within its structure an already completed series of concepts."[9] She sees the transition as being motivated by "the indivisible motion of living organism."[10] There are certainly merits to this interpretation. By incorporating one of Hegel's favorite examples—the seed growing into an oak tree—Hahn makes a compelling case for why being *is* nothing, without, however, drawing on presuppositions that lie outside of Hegel's description of being. But this explanation nevertheless misses the significance of question, *why is being nothing?* Hahn simply assumes that the transformation happens because it is foreshadowed. She offers an answer for *how the transition occurs*, but to answer in this way does not fully address *why it occurs*. What is it about being that makes it teleologically necessary for it to become nothing? The Teleological Approach has trouble addressing this question and therefore misses the point of the analysis.

A second version of the Design Interpretation comes from the Characteristics Approach. Proponents of the Characteristics Approach claim that Hegel endows being with specific qualities, and that it is these qualities that make being transition into nothing. I attribute this branch of Non-source Interpretations to Heidegger, who in the opening pages of *Being and Time* criticizes Hegel's conception of being for having the specific characteristics of "universality," "indeterminateness," and "self-evidence."[11] Heidegger sees Hegel as the culmination of a tradition of philosophers from the history of Western thought who cover over the primordial question of being. Plato and Aristotle "wrestled" with the primordial question of being, but from then on, heirs of the Greek tradition such as Descartes, Kant, and Hegel forgot the true nature of the question, since it, seemingly, had already been answered.[12] According to this interpretation, the reason why Hegel is able to animate the *Logic* in the first place is because he has already deemed the question of Being to be superfluous. Based on answers to the question of being that are already assumed from the outset, the *Logic* generates the movement from being to nothing. Because it is obscure and unworthy of investigation, being has the character of being empty, hollow, and indeterminate. And yet also because everyone already knows what being is about, it simultaneously has the character of universality, self-evidence, and obviousness. These characteristics of being necessarily infer that being *is* nothing, but that we should assume being has these characteristics from the outset is quite problematic, according to Heidegger.

To do a detailed analysis of Hegel's and Heidegger's respective approaches to the question of being would extend us beyond the scope of the present discussion, but suffice it to say that readers of Hegel who take seriously his claim that being is the presuppositionless starting point view Hegel not to be assuming an answer to the question of being, but rather to be asking the question of being in as genuine and radical a way as Heidegger proposes to do in *Being and Time*. Heidegger misunderstands the nature of Hegel's inquiry when he charges Hegel's conception of being with the prejudice of universality, indeterminateness, and self-evidence. While Hegel does describe the initial being (*Sein*) of the opening as indeterminate, once it stands in contrast to the first stage of "quality" as determinate being (*Seiende*), and while Hegel's recognition that being is the first and primary concept of the *Logic* suggests that it is also universal and self-evident to everyone, we should nevertheless view these characteristics to be a result of Hegel's inquiry into the question of fundamental reality, rather than as prejudices from which he begins. The whole notion of a presuppositionless starting point is a radical questioning into the nature of fundamental reality. Certainly, Heidegger's destructive technique of dismantling the history of Western ontological assumptions differs in significant ways from Hegel's presuppositionless starting point in being, which supports dialectical and in a way critically constructive, rather than destructive, approaches to the history of Western thought. I am not arguing that Hegel shared Heidegger's agenda in *Being and Time*. But I do think that Heidegger's criticism of Hegel's conception of being loses some of its force when we realize that Heidegger misses the connection between presuppositionlessness and radical questioning. One might say that Hegel's opening in the *Logic* is a precursor to Heidegger's opening in *Being and Time*, rather than, as Heidegger himself proposes, the swan song of Western metaphysics.

In contrast to these two approaches to the Design Interpretation, there is also an Apophatic Branch of Non-source Interpretations. This branch is reserved for commentaries that claim the rationale for the transition lies in the failure of being. "Apophasis" refers to the Greek term for negation. It has often been used in combination with the term "negative theology" to refer to theological debates about whether God can be named or expressed in positive terms, or whether we inevitably fail to articulate the infinite magnitude of God in any real way. I borrow the term apophatic from this tradition in order to emphasize the severity of the negative in the transition from being to nothing. Commentaries associated with the Apophatic Branch claim that the reason why being *is* nothing is because there is no way to express being in adequate terms. Because being (*Sein*) is indeterminate, there is no way to describe it in positive terms, without reducing it to determinate being (*Seiende*). Apophatic Interpretations are linguistic if the failure of being is primarily a problem of expression, that is, if the failure really lies in the articulation of being. Apophatic Interpretations are ontological if the failure of being is not only a failure of expression, but a failure *qua* being.

The Hegel scholar Michael Rosen outlines one variation of the Apophatic Branch, which he attributes to Ernst Tugendhat, through what he calls "being as intuition" in his book *Hegel's Dialectic and Its Criticism*.[13] Proponents of this interpretation claim that the transition from being to nothing finds its motivation through the "contentless intuition" of pure being. To approach being is to remove all content from the determinate images of reality. If we gain access to pure being only by muting all determinateness from being, "what we are left with," Rosen writes, "[is] being but, equally, nothing."[14] Rosen then says that Tugendhat has misunderstood certain key sentences in Hegel's description of being and nothing. Even though Hegel mentions intuition when he writes "there is *nothing* to be intuited in it, if one can speak here of intuiting" (SL 59, WL 82–83), Rosen objects that the modality of image-thinking (*Vorstellung*) is inappropriate to the opening of the *Logic*. Because of the proximity between *Vorstellung* and *Denken*, Rosen's objection is in a way similar to the objection to the External Source Interpretation, where Hegel is accused of inserting a thinking subject behind the scenes of the *Logic*. Rosen says that if Tugendhat were talking about the opening of the *Phenomenology*, which begins from the standpoint of consciousness, then *Vorstellung* would be an appropriate term to use, but not for the starting point of the *Logic*.[15] For Rosen, Hegel does not mean to derive nothing from being by way of a contentless image, but rather, as Rosen puts forward in what he calls the "Direct Approach," Hegel operates by way of "co-reference" such that the difference between being and nothing is a difference of the reference of words.[16]

Rosen also outlines a "Linguistic Approach," which he contrasts with his own "Direct Approach." Followers of the Linguistic Approach propose that the failure to express the meaning of being in language causes the transition from being to nothing. The reason why being *is* nothing is because the word "being" fails to express anything determinate, because language itself does not have the capacity to capture the meaning of pure being. The Linguistic Approach is apophatic in the sense that being, much like the word "God" in the Judeo–

Christian tradition of negative theology, fails to express the infinity of what is meant in positive terms. By contrast, the Ontological Approach makes an even larger claim about the failure of being, not only at the linguistic level that words cannot represent what being in fact *is*. Followers of the Ontological Approach claim that being itself fails *to be*. This is not only a failure of language and expression, but more deeply, the failure of being itself. It is the nature of reality itself, not only of a subject who perceives it or of words that express it, to be indeterminate and ungraspable. Beyond this difference, the linguistic and ontological versions of the interpretation offer a similar insight: the reason why being *is* nothing is because of a fundamental and explicit failure of being.

One advantage of this branch, generally, is that one is able to explain the rationale not only for the transition from being to nothing, but also for why the opening gives way to determinate being. Determinate being is the result of our inherent failure to grasp being itself. The *Logic* turns to determinate being as a product of its failure to grasp being itself. Nothing is the initial shape of this failure, and then determinate being is the more advanced continuation of the ineffable nature of being itself, a stage in which being is reduced to something determinate and graspable, but also to something less than itself, with an "other" over against it. Such a reading presents the *Logic* in a pessimistic light. The *Logic* ascends through developmental stages of conceptual analysis from the *Doctrine of Being* to *Essence* and from the *Doctrine of the Concept* to the absolute idea, but at the same time, it begins from a dark initial descent into the divisive tensions between indeterminate and determinate being. Proponents of the Apophatic Branch see the initial challenge of a presuppositionless starting point as giving way to the failure and indeterminacy of meaning. Being is, in effect, fallen. Through its descent, it arrives at nothing, becoming, and determinate being, and from this begins to ascend again slowly and systematically to the concept, where it finally succeeds as substance to be both foundationless and yet determinate and meaningful. The end of the *Logic* eventually returns to the height from which it began. The *Doctrine of the Concept* is, in this sense, the resolution to the apophatic problematic that Hegel's presuppositionless starting point announces at the beginning. The *Logic* as a book is, from this standpoint, a book about the fallenness of being, that is, of being's descent; but it is also a book about the recovery of being and its return to the concept. Being falls through division and limitation into something less than the presuppositionless totality, and yet it methodically recovers from this division and limitation to appear ultimately as both meaningfully determinate and total through the self-othering movement of the concept.

The main objection to the Apophatic Interpretation comes from the concern that to cite the failure of being as the primary rationale behind the transition is to over-emphasize the role that the concept of nothing plays in Hegel's theory. Hegel's explanation in the remarks that follow directly after his description of being, nothing, and becoming is definitive and clear: being precedes nothing and the two together mark the transition into becoming only from this specific order. As a thought experiment, Hegel actually does entertain three alternative, counterfactual openings to the *Logic*, which he attributes respectively to Parmenides, Buddhism, and Heraclitus. Let's go over all three of these counterfactual openings, as a brief digression. The point to keep in mind is that Hegel's rejection of the Buddhism starting point can also be construed as a rejection to the Apophatic Interpretation as well.

The first counterfactual opening, which Hegel attributes to Parmenides, starts from the position that "*only being is, and nothing is absolutely not*" (SL 60, WL 84).[17] But Hegel rejects this opening, which can be referred to as the "being-only-is" opening, because he claims that no movement could come from a conception of being as absolutely separate from nothing. Hegel argues, to the contrary, that being *is* nothing, that there is really no separation, or only the faintest separation, between the terms. The second counterfactual opening, which Hegel attributes, fairly or unfairly, to Buddhism, and which is the one that can be viewed to make trouble for the Apophatic Interpretation, begins directly from the concept of nothing, rather than from the concept of being: "In the oriental systems, essentially Buddhism," Hegel writes, "it is well known that nothing, the void, is the absolute principle" (SL 60, WL 84). Hegel argues that not only is this starting point one-sided and empty, but also that it reverts, in spite of its own commitments, back to being: "That *nothing* is the result of the argument, and that the beginning would then have to be made with nothing (as in Chinese philosophy) need not cause us to lift a finger. For even before we had lifted it, this nothing would have turned into being just as much" (SL 75, WL 105). Hegel is more generous to the third counterfactual opening, which he attributes to Heraclitus, and which he claims begins directly from the concept of becoming: "Against that simple and one-sided abstraction [of Buddhism], the profound Heraclitus proposed the loftier, total concept of becoming and said: *being is no more than nothing*; or also, all *flows*, that is, all is *becoming*" (SL 60, WL 84). Yet even Heraclitus misses the mark slightly, as we have already discussed, since Heraclitus, with his first principle of fire, does not seem to recognize that becoming merely makes the transition from being to nothing explicit. By rejecting each of these three counterfactual openings to the *Logic*, Hegel supports his own version of the opening, where nothing follows from being and becoming follows from both.

The reason why both the Linguistic and the Ontological Branches of the Apophatic Interpretation lose some credibility, then, is because they privilege nothing over being in a similar way to how Buddhism, according to Hegel, privileges nothing over being. This is more pronounced in the ontological version of the transition than in the linguistic version. That being fails *qua* being can only make sense from the terms of nothing as the primary concept, where being is merely the mark of the copula of nothing, a platform for the unthinkable, uncharacterizable trace beyond being. If we put aside the question of whether Hegel is fair or unfair to the tradition of Buddhism in the East when he associates it with the second counterfactual opening, Hegel's point about the one-sided emptiness of any opening that privileges nothing over being is persuasive enough, I think, especially when we work through the details of his reasoning: that any nothing-over-being opening necessarily witnesses nothingness revert to being as the more originary position. This is not to say that in Hegel's own version of the starting point, being is more primary or privileged than nothing, but merely that the starting point requires that being stand in the first position, even if the transition from being to nothing is recognized as seamless and immediate. This is the case because to say that "nothing *is*" requires the presupposition of the "is." While there are a number of advantages to the linguistic and ontological variations of the Apophatic Interpretation—foremost, this kind of explanation preserves Hegel's intention to maintain a presuppositionless starting point, while initiating enough developmental movement to propel the *Logic* into motion—the disadvantage is also significant: apophaticism threatens to over-emphasize the concept of nothing. Hegel suggests that such a mistake would throw the mechanics of the opening out of balance, or at least obscure the true combination of being, nothing, and becoming.

The Dialectical Totality Interpretation

In contrast to these versions of the Apophatic Interpretation, the Dialectical Totality Interpretation that I defend proposes that the transition from being to nothing commits Hegel to a weaker and more ambiguous form of apophaticism. Proponents of this interpretation attempt to retain some of the advantages from apophaticism, without prioritizing nothing over being. By using a more limited version of the thesis that the reason why being *is* nothing is because being fails, this interpretation retains the advantage of preserving Hegel's intention to maintain a presuppositionless starting point, while at the same time propelling the *Logic* into motion.

The key term of this interpretation is "total inclusiveness." The reason why being transitions into nothing is because being contains everything in the most complete way. The South African Hegel scholar Errol E. Harris interprets Hegel in this sense when he says that "being, as being, is all inclusive."[18] The primary theses of the Dialectical Totality Interpretation are that by establishing a presuppositionless starting point, Hegel means the most complete form of inclusion possible, and that such a radical form of inclusion can only be met if being is the same as nothing.

What Hegel is really looking for when he proposes to begin the *Logic* from a stance outside of all presuppositions is a concept that captures everything whatsoever, that leaves nothing outside of it, and that claims no dependency, prelude, or prior reference to an other. Being is precisely this concept. It captures everything. Each thing, one could say, depends upon being as its foundation and source. But this dependency is not reciprocal. Being does not depend upon any other thing. It simply "is" prior to another source. However, being is only successful at capturing everything if it is *equally itself and nothing*. Being can only maintain its status as the independent foundation for all things if it remains open to the total inclusiveness of everything and anything whatsoever. Total inclusion can only be established from the concept of nothing. That being *is* nothing is, in effect, the condition required of being if it is to succeed at capturing everything whatsoever within it and thereby of maintaining its status as the presuppositionless starting point upon which everything else depends. What the Dialectical Totality Interpretation shows, then, is that the rationale behind the transition from being to nothing has to do with being's own status as first philosophy.

A number of potential criticisms follow from this interpretation. One such criticism comes from the claim that the unity of being and nothing does not really lead to total inclusion, on Hegel's account, since "becoming" follows directly from this unity and can be conceived of as transcending the inclusivity of being and nothing together. Critics who hold this view see becoming as a significantly new and different term. However, while becoming is clearly the third term of the opening, there is no reason to conclude from this that becoming exceeds the domain of being and nothing. Hegel describes becoming, not as an excess or transcendence of this domain, but as the truth of the transition. Becoming describes two opposite but equal movements: "'ceasing-to-be' is the movement from being to nothing and 'coming-to-be' is the movement from nothing to being" (SL 80–81, WL 111–12). And yet in neither of these movements does becoming show itself to be anything other than the unity of being and nothing. Becoming is, instead, the result of the total inclusion of being and nothing. Everything is already contained within being and nothing. Becoming is simply the transition from one to the other. What becoming ultimately shows is that the bi-directional transitions from being to nothing and from nothing to being are already contained in each single concept "being" and "nothing."

Another similar objection comes from the claim that the transition from being to nothing does not adequately capture everything whatsoever because it is vague, abstract, and therefore cannot grasp determinate being. But once again, there is no reason to conclude that this further stage of determinate being offers a significantly new domain exceeding the parameters of being and nothing. Because being turns into nothing, being does fail, in a certain respect, to express itself as both totality and determinate being. But this is, more accurately, the failure of determinate being, since what is determinate, *the something*, has over against it another something, *the other*, which forms a limit (*Grenze*) and marks being as less than the totality (SL 95–101, WL 131–39). And yet insofar as determinate being (*Dasein*)[19] is also the pure indeterminate being of the opening (*Sein*), the limit that separates being from its other equally produces the determinateness of each as the other. Whereas determinate being comes from the limitation (*Grenze*) of something and its other, indeterminate being underlies all determinateness as an open totality that contains both sides of the limitation. This is why the limitation is both the separation of being from itself as well as the transgression and return to the self as if from an other. Insofar as determinate being is determinate, something is not its other; but since determinate being is still being (*Sein*), the being of "this" is the same being as "another." What this shows is that while the immediate being of the starting point lacks determinateness, that it lacks this does not make the unity of being and nothing any less totalizing and inclusive. That Hegel ultimately turns from indeterminate being to determinate being (the fourth argument of the opening) helps to support the theory that the being-to-nothing transition is utterly comprehensive and that determinate being depends upon the opening.

Critics might also conceivably object that the Dialectical Totality Interpretation begs the question. Since this interpretation points to the total inclusiveness of the starting point as the reason why being transitions into nothing, critics might worry that this key term, *total inclusion*, turns out to be both the conclusion and the support for the conclusion. But this is an objection to any interpretation that does not rely on a source outside of Hegel's description of being and nothing. After all, the reason why internal and external sources are compelling for us in the first place is because they explain the transition in a traditionally rational and linear way. But the philosophical problem of how to begin requires an unusual explanation. The rationale behind the transition will not be able to rely on a position prior to the beginning. This, inevitably, exposes the transition from being to nothing as one of the most difficult transitions to analyze in the whole of the *Logic*. From the position of the opening, we do not yet have the resources to set up normal accounts of inference. While this issue of begging the question certainly complicates any interpretation that attempts to work directly from Hegel's description of being and nothing, we should acknowledge that the project of the opening requires a different way of showing evidence and we should therefore suspend our suspicions that the argument from being to nothing is circular or self-referencing, or, at any rate, that circularity and self-reference are in this way problematic.

There is also the objection that the Dialectical Totality Interpretation makes Hegel appear to be a foundationalist philosopher. Richard Dien Winfield argues, convincingly I think, that because Hegel's opening is presuppositionless, it is therefore radically *foundationless*. Hegel breaks from a long tradition of Western philosophers who debate over what characteristics of determinate being are the source for the origination of all things. While I do think that Hegel's opening is his version of first philosophy, and that all determinate being originates from this opening, I do not think that the total inclusivity principle conflicts with Winfield's reading of the *Logic* as foundationless. Much like Thales claims that everything originates from water, or like Heraclitus proposes that everything originates from fire, or like Descartes deduces the *Cogito, ergo sum* as the indubitable principle of reality, or like Fichte begins from the certainty of "I am I," Hegel upholds his compound dialectical account of being, nothing, and becoming to be the ultimate origin of all things. But, in a different sense, Hegel's opening marks a radical break from the long tradition of inquiry into the exact character of first philosophy, since the opening Hegel has in mind starts without presuppositions and is therefore *indeterminate*, whereas all other philosophers who purport to have uncovered the origin of all things offer one or another specific concept of *determinate being* from which all things arise. Because his being-nothing-becoming opening is the starting point of the *Logic*, and is independent of a prior source, but has determinate being as its dependent, Hegel is, in a certain respect, a foundationalist. However, because the opening is presuppositionless, Hegel is really also a foundationless thinker. In other words, Hegel has the same goal as the foundationalists who preceded him of discovering the origin for all things, of establishing something that is certain beyond all doubt, and which is totally inclusive. However, his "foundation" is strikingly different from all other foundations insofar as it is presuppositionless and therefore indeterminate, whereas all other foundations begin idiosyncratically from some aspect of determinate being, as an arbitrary, and, in Hegel's view, false or dogmatic starting point.

I think that the advantages of this interpretation outweigh these criticisms. Since it explains the transition as integral to the requirements of a presuppositionless starting point, it avoids the problems associated with Internal and External Source Interpretations. All source interpretations undermine the very nature of a starting point, as Hegel conceives of it. To claim that other sources stand in as prior to the opening makes the concept of a "beginning" ineffectual. But the Dialectical Totality Interpretation explains the transition explicitly from the concepts of being and nothing, without undermining the point of a beginning by inserting artificially internal or external sources. Even the Teleological Interpretation, which purports to begin directly from being itself, explains the transition without fully addressing the question of the rationale behind the movement. Even though Teleological Interpretations claim to begin from being itself, because they view being as having a designed shape that propels it into nothing and becoming, these interpretations are similar to Pre-Socratic theses about first philosophy, such as Thales's thesis that everything is water, or Heraclitus's thesis that everything is fire. Likewise, both the Design Branch and the Characteristics Branch infuse too much content into the concept of being. The Dialectical Totality Interpretation has the advantage over these branches of explaining this movement without having to rely on pre-established content.

The Dialectical Totality Interpretation offers the best support for what Hegel articulates as the goal of the opening, namely to begin from the rigor of an indubitable first mover. How to begin without presuppositions is one of the great quests of philosophy. This problem preoccupied the ancient Greek world from Thales to Socrates, but also marked the emergence of the Modern world from Descartes's method of doubt to its continuation in German Idealism.[20] Since the Dialectical Totality Interpretation proposes that being's status as first philosophy is also what requires its transition into nothing, this reading has the advantage of supporting Hegel's argument that being is the beginning. Being's transition into nothing is, in effect, the explanation behind why being must stand in the first position as the principle foundation for the *Logic*. Detractors aside, this interpretation is successful at showing that the motivation for the transition lies in the immanent goal of first philosophy as absolutely independent of any precondition.

Desmond's objection to Dialectical Totality

In his book *Hegel's God: A Counterfeit Double?*, the Hegel scholar William Desmond outlines one of the most interesting objections to Dialectical

Totality through what he calls "holistic immanence." According to Desmond, Hegel aims to radicalize totality by establishing the "absolute whole" of reality through the immanence of God. In contrast to conventional accounts of the absolute transcendence and overpowering infinity of God, Hegel presents a vision of God who, embodied through the life of Jesus, is both finite and infinite at the same time, both everything and yet also concrete and graspable. According to Desmond, Hegel's philosophy breaks from dualistic accounts of a two-world order, where God stands above or beyond the world as an unrealizable infinity. Hegel makes God immanent and realizable. Because of this, there is only one world. Because of this, the finite is in the infinite, and the infinite is in the finite.

According to Desmond, the consequences of Hegel's "holistic immanence" are twofold. On the one hand, by uniting the finite and the infinite, Hegel seemingly leaves no exterior position beyond God, or, from the terms of the opening of the *Logic*, no position beyond the unity of being and nothing. On the other hand, by uniting the finite and the infinite, Hegel changes the constitution of what it means to be infinite and, by analog, what it means to be other or outside. If the infinite can only be established in relation to the finite, it cannot exist *qua infinity*, but always only in terms of the finite, that is, only as what can be grasped by the understanding. Based on these two consequences, Desmond concludes that although Hegel promises a conception of absolute totality from which there is no exterior, there is nevertheless a remainder.

Desmond's criticism of Dialectical Totality has to do with recognizing that there is a position beyond Hegel. This position beyond Hegel is the position of the infinite insofar as it transcends all relation to the finite. Desmond argues that the position beyond Hegel is an impossible position of sheer transcendence, what Levinas refers to in *Totality and Infinity* as the absolute Other, what Derrida refers to in *Speech and Phenomena* as *différance*, an impossible beyond which is nevertheless beyond. This position beyond is the other that exceeds its entanglement with the subject, an excess that comes not from the perfect dissolving of subject and object in absolute knowing, as Hegel proposes at the end of the *Phenomenology*, but rather from the withholding of dialectical relations, as the absolute other of alterity, or, in Desmond's words, the God beyond.

Desmond articulates this problem quite clearly in terms of self consciousness and absolute knowing in the *Phenomenology*. The dialectical journey of the *Phenomenology* begins from the initial shapes of consciousness (sense certainty, force and understanding, etc.) and the uneven shapes of self consciousness (the death struggle, the master–slave dialectic, the unhappy consciousness, etc.) but eventually develops a robust account of mutual recognition and reason, where, ultimately, subject and object dissolve in absolute knowing. Desmond symbolizes the basic dyadic relation between subject and object as S-O (S = subject; O = object; - = relation). He then symbolizes the advanced stages of the *Phenomenology* with the speculative relation S(S-O): "not the dyadic subject-object relation (S-O); but the triadic self-relation which includes in itself the dyadic subject-object relation: S(S-O)."[21] According to Desmond, this additional S of subjectivity brings the otherwise open relationship back to identity and totality for Hegel. In this way, the subject grasps the object, and grasps it as other, but as an other that is framed from within the terms of the subject and is therefore recognizable and knowable. Certainly, the additional S equally transforms the constitution of subjectivity as much as it reconfigures the object so that it can be understood and grasped. Desmond is not merely claiming that in absolute knowing the other has been subsumed under the control of subjectivity alone; the subject has also become the communal *we* of spirit and reason, even refashioning itself and making itself other to itself in order to grasp the complete unity of reality.

What the force of Desmond's criticism of Hegel's totality aspirations amounts to is that in this relation of S(S-O) both subject and object conform into a unity, and that because this unity is understood through self-reflection, that is, the additional S, the other as object is not wholly other, but has become instead the other of relation. It is this other outside of all relation that has been lost. According to Desmond: "In its self-relation, that other is not a radically alien other, but *its* other … It is the absolute self that, in relating itself to an other, relates itself to itself as including that other within itself."[22] All that is missing from Hegel's totalizing account is the other *qua* other, the other that falls completely outside of dialectical relation. This is what Hegel cannot account for, says Desmond. His system grasps everything. And yet there exists an inexplicable remainder beyond Hegel.

Dialectical Totality is the good infinite

According to Desmond, the one position that Hegel is unable to approach with his "holistic immanence" is the absolute Other of a transcendent God who has no association with the finite whatsoever. This remainder takes the form of an infinity that breaks off from and cannot be made common with its finite counterpart. In this sense, although it is fair to interpret Desmond as being cognizant of the argument Hegel outlines in the "Infinity" passages of the *Logic* between the "bad" and the "good" infinite, Desmond's recognition of a God beyond, and of an inexplicable remainder beyond Hegel, nevertheless tacitly relies on a categorical separation between the infinite and the finite, much like Hegel's conception of the bad infinite relies on an opposition to the finite. By arguing that there is an absolute transcendent God and that this God is a remainder beyond Hegel, Desmond aligns himself with an extreme version of the bad infinite, where the infinite is completely separated from the finite.

I will briefly outline Hegel's distinction between the bad and the good infinite and I will argue that Hegel does not claim that the two types stand in direct opposition, but, instead, that the bad infinite is a necessary moment of the good infinite. Desmond does not recognize that for the good infinite to be genuinely infinite, as Hegel claims, the good infinite will also have to make use of the bad infinite as one of its pathways. The remainder that Desmond views as standing beyond Hegel is a reminder that the good infinite has to be able to anticipate, if it is truly infinite. Desmond's objection undermines how completely inclusive the good infinite has to be. I argue, instead, that the good infinite is a further conceptual advancement on Hegel's initial vision of Dialectical Totality as it appears through the unity of being and nothing.

Hegel describes the bad infinite as a conception of the infinite that stands in stark opposition to the finite. He writes:

> Because it is posited against the finite, the infinite is called the *bad infinite*, the infinite of the understanding, evaluated as the highest, absolute truth. The understanding is satisfied that it has truly reconciled the finite and the infinite, but what is true is that the understanding has become entangled in unreconciled, unresolved, absolute contradiction … The reason why this contradiction is directly apparent is because [in this relation of the bad infinite] the infinite remains over against the finite, thereby positing

> *two* determinations, *two* worlds, one infinite and one finite. In the relation between these worlds, the infinite is merely the limit of the finite and is therefore merely a determinate infinite, *an infinite which is itself the finite.* (WL 152)

The infinite and the finite are, from this conception, both one side of the other. Neither is the whole. Each is one-sidedness. In this way, each is dependent on the other and each limits the other. The infinite is the "non-finite" (SL 122, WL 170). The paradox here—or, as Hegel describes it in the passage, the "unreconciled, unresolved, absolute contradiction"—comes from a conflict in the definition of the infinite. The infinite is supposed to be beyond all limits as the "limitless." But if it stands in opposition to the finite, it gains this determination through the limitation that it is not the finite. But to have such a limitation goes against the very definition of infinity that led to its separation from the finite in the first place. The infinite is, therefore, not truly infinite if it has over and against it the finite as a realm that is other than it. Hegel goes so far as to claim that if the infinite is separated from the finite, such as when we conceive of the separation of two or many possible worlds, the infinite turns out to be the same as the finite.

Hegel claims that in separating the infinite from the finite, we reduce the infinite to the finite. His argument for this is not simply that the infinite and the finite are interconnected by mutual determination, as when we say that because darkness is the opposite of light, darkness and light are incorporated into each other by negative contrast. Hegel's argument for why the infinite turns out to be the finite is a lot more sophisticated than this. To separate the infinite from the finite is to limit the infinite to only that which is infinite and to present the finite as a separate, exterior world, which the infinite is not. Therefore, the infinite is limited. Therefore, the infinite is finite.

Hegel then turns to the "good infinite." The good infinite emerges from our reflection that to separate the infinite from the finite reduces the infinite to the finite. The good infinite is simply the affirmation of this unity. The infinite can only be conceived of as genuinely infinite if it is not limited by its opposition to the finite. It has to include the finite as part of what it is. Only from the stance of such radical inclusion, where the infinite is so limitless that it is not even limited by the finite, can we come to terms with an infinity that is truly infinite.

The infinite is not truly infinite if it has over against it the finite as a realm that is other than the finite. The only way to achieve true infinity is by including the finite in the infinite *from the terms of the finite*. However, this leads to a further paradox. The truly limitless is at the same time that which is limited. Hegel's true infinite is, therefore, not only the unity of the finite and the infinite, as Desmond suggests when he argues that there is an impossible remainder beyond the infinite–finite correlation insofar as Hegel cannot include an absolutely transcendent infinite that has no relation to the finite whatsoever. Hegel's true infinite equally embraces not only the unity of the infinite and the finite but also each severed side of the finite and the infinite, which constituted the initial conception of the bad infinite. In other words, the affirmative infinite celebrates not only the unity of the finite and the infinite but also the sheer transcendence of an infinite that stands beyond the finite as one of the principle moments of infinity. After all, if the infinite were unable to include a conception of infinity that completely transcends the finite, then the affirmative infinite would have a limit over and against it and would be as spurious as the bad infinite.

It would be a mistake to conclude that Hegel opposes the good infinite to the bad infinite. His conception of the good infinite should be understood as a higher, more developed and resolved comprehension of the contradiction inherent in the bad infinite. The only difference between the good and the bad is that, while in the bad infinite, the unity between the infinite and the finite is implicit and unresolved, in the good infinite, this same unity is upheld as the exhaustion of all limitation. The reason why the good infinite is truly limitless is not because it succeeds at divorcing itself from the finite, but because by including the genuinely finite, there is no other position that could possibly stand against it in exterior contrast. Similar to the unity of being and nothing, the reason why the good infinite is limitless is because it includes the finite as an exterior which is and is not an exterior. On the one hand, the finite that it includes has to remain in a respect exterior to the infinite. Otherwise, Desmond's criticism would hold. Otherwise, there would be something—a finite and an infinite that has no relation to the other—that remains exterior. However, paradoxically, on the other hand, this finite which is exterior to the infinite is also included and therefore makes up the interior of the infinite, which contains, as a Dialectical Totality, every possibility whatsoever.

The bad infinite is, paradoxically, one of the folds of the good infinite. It is not only included as a position that the good infinite ultimately overcomes. It is also included in its own terms, as an infinite that has no relation to the finite. The infinite is only genuinely limitless if this position is also, paradoxically, upheld. Such a unity is a Dialectical Totality much like the unity of being and nothing, with the conceptual development that the totality is now recognized as limitless *because it includes the limited* as part of what makes it truly limitless. This unity will become, as we will see in Chapter 3, the unity of actuality and possibility.

Dialectical Totality and contradiction

One of the consequences of the Dialectical Totality Interpretation is that we come to form an implicit recognition of a concept of contradiction that underlies the *Doctrine of Being*. This is not to say that the official concept of contradiction should have appeared earlier in the *Logic* than where it appears in the *Doctrine of Essence*.[23] I believe that Hegel was right to place it in the "Essentialities" chapter, and that this is the natural progression of the *Logic*, which has to generate the order of the concepts in precisely the way he laid them out, if form and content are to remain the same, as Hegel advocates in the "Introduction" that precedes his presuppositionless starting point. My point is only that, although the proper emergence of contradiction occurs in *Essence*, there are nevertheless earlier and later formulations of contradiction, which appear inadequately and prematurely as Dialectical Totality through the unity of being and nothing, and then again, one might say, over-maturely, in the *Concept* as the explicit relationship of self-othering and self-movement. Contradiction is, in a sense, an umbrella term like *Aufhebung*, and so it should be viewed as a motor for the developmental revolutions of new concepts in the *Logic* in general.

The conception of contradiction that appears in the opening movements of the *Logic* is a conception of contradiction as *totality*. Contradiction is the most inclusive relation possible. What is contradictory is contradictory precisely because it excludes nothing. There is no position for A other than that A is not A. Contradiction fills all sides and leaves no remainder. Likewise, the unity of being and nothing forms a contradictory relationship, from which no exterior is possible, not because some exterior which could have been is not, but because that which is exterior to being, namely "nothing," is already included in being. Contradiction is not just a unity of A and not A. Such a unity would subsume A and not A under the heading of identity. Contradiction is also the separation of each term, A on the one side, and not A on the other side. A and not A have to be seen as both apart and together to view them as a contradiction. Whether it takes the form of the finite and the infinite together, or of being and nothing, or of A and not A, proponents of Dialectical Totality argue that there is no way to go beyond a relationship that includes the positive and the negative together. One finds oneself always caught up somewhere within the relation. Since the other is included, to be other than this relation is already to be included within it. This also holds for the non-relation of Desmond's transcendent God. Proponents of Dialectical Totality conclude that even this position has to be inexplicably included even as it is excluded. The inexplicable impossibility of the inclusion is resolved as contradiction. In this way, contradiction is the most inclusive totality possible.

2

Hegel on Contradiction: From the Categories of Reflection to Ground

Hegel's treatment of contradiction in the *Doctrine of Essence* of the *Logic* is one of the most polarizing and yet most exciting aspects of his work. Readers have been drawn, in particular, to Hegel's polemic remarks about the primacy of contradiction over identity, such as the following:

> It is one of the biases of all previous logic and of ordinary thinking generally that contradiction is viewed to be less essential and less immanently determinate than identity. But if it were a question of ranking the two, and each had to be kept separate, then contradiction would be recognized as more profound and more essential than identity. (WLII 75)

This statement is controversial because it challenges us to call into question a law that seems, on the face of it, to be so basic that it is indisputable. The law of non-contradiction is so basic and fundamental that any engagement with rationality seems to presuppose it. Scientists and mathematicians appeal to it as the most obvious source of individuation and meaning. Even our everyday perception and common sense support the conclusion that contradictions should be avoided. Any philosopher who dares to question the supreme principle of non-contradiction threatens to throw logic and scientific reasoning into a quagmire of chaos and absurdity.

Nevertheless, Hegel is notorious for calling this law into question. And yet, readers of the *Logic* are often in disagreement about what the exact parameters are of Hegel's investigation into the nature of contradiction. Some readers claim that Hegel defiantly disregards the basic law of non-contradiction, proposing, instead, that for Hegel true contradictions really do exist, and not only in rational conception, but equally in the very fabric of reality. Other interpreters propose less direct readings of Hegel's thesis from productive contradiction, either by limiting Hegel's statements about contradiction to only certain forms, such as only in relation to essences, or by presenting Hegel as a thinker of *reductio ad absurdum*, who views the impossibility of real contradictions, rather than their positive existence, to be constitutive of reality.

In this chapter, I explicate Hegel's transition from contradiction to ground in the *Doctrine of Essence* and argue that this transition is crucial to understanding Hegel's controversial claims about the primacy of contradiction over identity. Hegel's conclusion that contradictions "fall to the ground" exposes his commitment to the productive nature and real existence of contradiction, on the one hand, but also to the impossibility of directly actualizing contradiction without a set of mediating concepts that buffer and soften contradictions before they can emerge into actuality. This reading of the transition from the contradiction passages to the ground chapter leads to what I call the "substitution interpretation," an interpretation that views the earlier forms of reflection (identity, difference, diversity, opposition) along with movement and vitality as substitutions that emerge in the place of and are grounded by contradiction.

In Chapter 1, I outlined a model of contradiction as *totality*. Even though Hegel does not discuss contradiction officially until around the midpoint of the *Logic*, one can find a powerful insight about the nature and role of contradiction in the opening lines of the book, based on the transition from being to nothing. The reason why Hegel points to the transition from being to nothing as evidence for why the *Logic* is presuppositionless, in the first place, is because a foundationless opening requires the broadest and most abstract combination of concepts (being *and* nothing together) with the result that literally nothing falls outside of it. Such a broad combination of concepts expresses a conception of totality that is at the same time a conception of contradiction. That being *is* nothing is the principal and most fundamental contradiction of the whole book.

Hegel officially discusses contradiction in the "Essentialities or Determinations of Reflection" chapter, as the culmination of his analysis of the related terms "identity," "difference," "diversity," and "opposition." I argue here in Chapter 2 that Hegel's official discussion leads to a second, interrelated conception of contradiction, not only of contradiction as *totality*, but also of contradiction as *productivity*. As a way to understand how contradiction can be productive, I offer fresh textual analysis of Hegel's "Essentialities or Determinations of Reflection" chapter and its seemingly strange transition to the "Ground" chapter, thereby exposing the nuanced points-of-transition from identity to difference and from difference to contradiction. The goal of this explication is to make sense of why Hegel would turn from contradiction to ground in the first place, and what exactly the motivation is for this transition, which Hegel describes as "essence determin[ing] itself as ground" (WLII 80) and as contradiction "sink[ing] to the ground [*zugrunde geht*]" (WLII 70). Proponents of the "substitution interpretation" propose that although contradictions really exist, they can only be expressed through substitutions such as contraries, essences, life, death, secrecy, movement, etc., which expose the vanishing point at the impasse where contradictions appear through their disappearance. Hegel's theory of possibility relies on the interaction between these two conceptions of contradiction. Possibility is a *totality* because it contains the form A is -A, but since it is reduced in actuality to only a moment of itself (i.e., to either A or -A), actualization *produces* possibilities that would not otherwise be there as a way to express the suppressed form of contradiction inherent in the actualization of possibility.

Before explicating the "Essentialities or Determinations of Reflection" chapter, let's briefly list some of the most important interpretations of what Hegel means by the primacy of contradiction over identity.

Qualifying Hegel's treatment of contradiction

Readers of the *Logic* have adopted a number of strategies to make sense of Hegel's controversial claims about the primacy of contradiction over identity. One strategy is simply to ignore the theme altogether or to visualize Hegel as a philosopher who is only marginally involved with the question of contradiction. Some interpreters think that Hegel's statements about the primacy of contradiction are really only statements about opposition. Such interpreters claim that dialectics is really, at its core, about the strife and opposition that come from integrating conflicting viewpoints, but that it falls short of anything as radical as the denial of the law of non-contradiction.[1] Another strategy is to use Hegel's statements about the positive nature of contradiction as evidence for why we should reject his work. Karl Popper takes up this approach when he claims that Hegel's poor use of logic is "dangerously misleading" and that it threatens the basis of scientific reasoning.[2] Bertrand Russell also takes up this approach. Russell claims that by disregarding the law of non-contradiction, Hegel has built "vast and imposing systems of philosophy ... upon stupid and trivial confusions."[3] The implication here is that Hegel has made a series of blatant logical mistakes (e.g., disregarding the law of non-contradiction, confusing identity in the subject with identity in the predicate, conflating contraries with contradiction, etc.), which doom his project from the outset. The implication is also that these logical confusions are what enable Hegel to unveil his hugely complicated grand system in the first place. Russell probably has Hegel in mind in his *History of Western Philosophy* when he states as a general maxim: "the worse your logic, the more interesting the consequences to which it gives rise."[4] While Popper and Russell dispute Hegel on logical and rational grounds, the nineteenth-century philosopher Eduard von Hartmann rejects Hegel's ideas about contradiction because he thinks such a position can only lead to meaningless open-endedness and indeterminacy. Hartmann claims that because Hegelians ignore the law of non-contradiction, there is no way to enter into a dialogue with them—those who desert the law of non-contradiction can derive anything from anything.[5]

Readers who are more generous to Hegel take up the strategy of qualifying his statements about contradiction, either by showing that he does not actually mean to disregard the law of non-contradiction at all, or by claiming that he only means to disregard the law of non-contradiction in one specific way. Generally, the point of these qualifications is to ease critics who would otherwise object that Hegel's treatment of contradiction is flagrant and dangerous. By qualifying Hegel, readers are able to distance his position from the purely formal version of contradiction, which many readers find objectionable. I will outline six different ways to qualify Hegel's claims about contradiction: by way of radical non-contradiction, essence, organic life, self-identity, as well as the non-qualification interpretation, and my own substitution interpretation.

One of the most effective ways to qualify Hegel is to show that his commitments to contradiction are really commitments to a more radical form of the law of non-contradiction. This view, of which Robert Brandom can be seen as a proponent in his book *Tales of the Mighty Dead*, interprets Hegel's claims about the productive force of contradiction to be an extension of *reductio ad absurdum* (179).[6] *Reductio ad absurdum* ("reduced to absurdity"), which is often cited along with the law of non-contradiction, contains within it a principle of movement in the sense that false conclusions necessitate the truth of their opposites. *Reductio ad absurdum* is often used as a proof in argumentation. Because the opposite of p contains contradictory reasoning, therefore p. The law of non-contradiction also supports the individuation of things and entities in the world. It is used as proof for the separation and individuation of things from things. Proponents of this view retain the notion that contradiction must be avoided, but nevertheless recognize the significance of contradiction insofar as all things move away from it and become determinate and individuated because of it. The reason why this is a more radical stance on the law of non-contradiction is because non-contradiction becomes recognized as an *active* principle of argumentation and individuation, rather than as a merely passive and obvious axiom of basic reality. There is textual evidence for this interpretation, as we will see later, in the transition from the contradiction passages of the *Logic* to the chapter on "Ground." Once identity passes all the way to contradiction, "essence determines itself as ground" (SL 386, WLII 80). Hegel's phrase *zugrunde geht*, literally "gone to ground," suggests that the upholding of contradiction is untenable, cannot be maintained, and that ground is what emerges instead. But this view also fails to explain Hegel's direct statements about the real existence of contradiction, such as that "something is alive … only to the extent that it contains contradiction within itself: indeed, force is this, to hold and endure contradiction within" (SL 382, WL 76).

In "Hegel's Metaphysics and the Problem of Contradiction," Robert Pippin proposes another method for qualifying Hegel's treatment of contradiction: contradictions only exist in terms of essences. Pippin defends Hegel against Russell's criticism that Hegel seems to conflate predication by disregarding the distinction between identity in the subject and identity in the predicate.[7] That A is both A and not A is not a contradiction as long as *not A* is a predication of *A*. However, Pippin rejects this criticism by arguing that since the subject and the predicate share the same copula, Hegel is right to complicate the assumption that subject-identity and predicate-identity are truly separate.

Common sense wants to uphold the laws of identity and non-contradiction as obvious and self-evident for everybody. Otherwise, we might be led to seemingly absurd conclusions such as that, in terms of formal propositional logic, p is both p and not p, or that, in terms of determinate reality, real things (books, umbrellas, people, countries) turn out to be the opposite of what they are. This prompts Pippin to clarify that Hegel is only committed to a productive theory of contradiction in one specific way, in terms of universality as the coincidence of essence and accidents. Some contradictions are absurd and cannot occur in actuality, such as that 2 plus 2 equals 5. But there are also reasonable explanations for why contradictions exist. Pippin emphasizes that since no one particular can encompass all of universality, predication is contradictory in the sense that it is both one instance of the universal and the totality of the universal.

Another branch of scholarship, developed in part by Songsuk Susan Hahn's book *Contradiction in Motion*, takes Hegel's claims about the primacy of contradiction to reveal its positive existence in reality and actuality. Hahn qualifies Hegel's account of contradiction by limiting it primarily to organic life and to the process of teleological development. She offers a broad interpretive reading of the *Logic* as a whole in her chapter "Organic Holism and Living Concepts" by arguing that, for Hegel, the concepts of the *Logic* are living and ensouled, in the sense that they move themselves through teleological design. Much of Hahn's book focuses on the role that contradiction plays in Hegel's local arguments about the organic life of organisms as these appear in the *Doctrine of the Concept* of the *Logic* and in the *Philosophy of Nature*. In terms of these local arguments, Hahn claims that Hegel's enthusiasm for contradiction is not for formal or determinate contradiction, but for only a special kind of contradiction that is inherent to organic life. Determinate negation has to do with how things refer to their opposites through exclusion. Referencing Brandom's analysis of Hegel as a radical proponent of the law of non-contradiction,[8] Hahn says that, because of determinate negation, for example, the color red refers to the color blue by way of not being blue. But this formal version of inclusion through exclusion differs significantly from real teleological development, where a seed incorporates its opposite as a process of growth to become a plant. "It is true that Hegel sensibly acknowledges that the law of contradiction is indispensable for analyzing a restricted domain of objects and situations, namely, inert, inanimate bodies at rest and 'finite situations'—by which I take him to mean inanimate objects that don't undergo change or development. But Life-forms, not inert bodies, represent the primary class of objects for Hegel."[9]

Hahn's analysis could have driven deeper into the very difficult task of making sense of the interaction between determinate negation and teleological development. How exactly does the exclusion of not A from A, which Brandom sees as Hegel's radicalizing of the law of non-contradiction, expose the resources of developmental teleology, wherein one's opposite becomes incorporated into what one is? Hahn proposes that formalizing determinate negation leads to the law of non-contradiction, where propositions function under bivalence, and where things are clearly what they are and are clearly not others. Yet developmental teleology operates from a significantly different conception of contradiction. Since the plant includes opposition as the motivating teleological force behind the process by which it grows into itself, its movements are produced from contradiction.

Karin de Boer also qualifies Hegel's theory of contradiction in her book *On Hegel: The Sway of the Negative*, which is largely about Hegel on tragedy, by claiming that contradiction becomes productive, for Hegel, when it is recognized as a condition for self-identity. De Boer underscores a distinction Hegel makes early on in the "Being-for-Itself" passages of the *Logic* between a "spurious" mode of being that repels contraries and a "true" mode of being that integrates contraries. Self-independence only comes about through the integration of contraries that at first appear in opposition.[10] There is a kind of speculative treatment of contradiction that is a necessary condition for being-one-self. In contrast to the process of dissolving a contradiction in the understanding, which de Boer attributes to Kant's "Antinomies," Hegel's speculative treatment of contradiction recognizes that the same act of dissolving contraries at the point of contradiction equally exposes the one-sided nature of being a contrary, and thereby generates a "true" mode of identity through the incorporation of differences, oppositions, and conflicts. Referencing the "Spirit" passages of the *Phenomenology*, de Boer claims that the reason why Antigone and Creon meet their fate is because they fail "to achieve … a mode of independence capable of incorporating its counterpart into itself."[11]

Graham Priest presents the most direct approach to Hegel's theory of contradiction, what I call the non-qualifier approach to Hegel on contradiction. Priest does not attempt to rescue Hegel from the formal version of the claim that A is not A. Nor does he revert to the law of non-contradiction. Nor does he limit Hegel's meaning to essences, organic life, or self-identity. Instead, Priest views Hegel as an important precursor to dialethism. Dialethism is the theory that "some contradictions are true (at least at some times)."[12] Priest proposes that with dialectics, Hegel gives a similar account of contradiction. Contradictory propositions make up an essential part of formal logic. Contradictions sometimes exist, and not merely in the sense of the law of non-contradiction. They exist in a positive sense as well, as part of the fabric of thought and reality. According to Priest, Hegel demonstrates this constantly by tracing the movements of dialectics. Hegel's commitment to *Aufhebung* is equally a commitment to the existence of contradiction.

On my estimation, the main issue with Priest's approach is that he treats Hegel's dialectic purely formally. "I give a formal model of dialectical progression," he writes in "The Logical Structure of Dialectic."[13] While this reading makes Hegel's method quite clear and accessible, it is also problematic for two reasons: (1) it disregards Hegel's argument in the Introduction of the *Logic* that form and content cannot be separated, that the form of dialectical reasoning is, at the same time, its content. (2) It reduces Hegel's complicated local arguments to a simple formula, and, because of this, covers over many of the subtleties and nuances of dialectical reasoning. Hegel does not assume dialectics from the outset. His local arguments show that dialectics is the case. Whenever Hegel's arguments are effective, this is because they show the reasons why sublations must occur.

These various qualifications (as well as Priest's non-qualification) of Hegel's treatment of contradiction do not have to be viewed as standing in conflict with each other. Each succeeds at showing why Hegel's position is not absurd. The reading that I endorse, the substitution interpretation, offers a compromise between the claim that Hegel avoids contradiction by radicalizing the law of non-contradiction and the claim that Hegel embraces the real existence of contradiction. On the one hand, proponents of the substitution interpretation think Hegel is committed to the primacy of contradiction over identity, and that because of this, contradictions literally exist. However, on the other hand, they also complicate the direct existence of contradictions by claiming that contradictions necessarily withdraw from actualization and cannot appear directly as existence. As they withdraw, they produce substitution concepts that stand in their place. In other words, proponents of the substitution interpretation hold both the real-existence-of-contradiction position and the avoidance-of-contradiction position as one coherent interpretation. Because of this compromise between avoiding and embracing contradiction, this theory is able to incorporate Pippin's insight that contradictions exist through the universality of particularity, by establishing the existence of essence as one of the primary modes by which contradictions exhibit themselves through other concepts. The theory also draws from Hahn's analysis of how living organisms express contradiction by being alive and by struggling against death, de Boer's analysis of how contradiction is inherent to self-identity, and Priest's claim that Hegel is a precursor to dialethiesm. The advantage of the substitution interpretation is that it allows for all of these insights. Let's look closely at Hegel's transitions from identity to difference, from difference to contradiction, and from contradiction to ground, before establishing the main principles of the substitution interpretation.

The categories of reflection

Hegel's "Essentialities or Determinations of Reflection" chapter comes after the chapter on "Show" [*der Schein*][14] and before the chapter on "Ground" [*der Grund*].[15] Hegel divides "Essentialities" into three further subchapters—"A. Identity," "B. Difference," and "C. Contradiction"—and separates each division with further sub-divisions and remarks. The most notable subchapter appears at "B. Difference," where Hegel further divides the text into "(1) Absolute Difference," "(2) Diversity," and "(3) Opposition." The most notable remarks appear in the third subchapter on "Contradiction," where Hegel discusses the law of the excluded middle and the law of contradiction. It is also worth noting that the chapter on "Ground" comes *directly* after the section on "Contradiction" and, as I will argue, helps to shed light on Hegel's conceptual movement from identity to contradiction.

The "Essentialities" chapter presents a series of premises that explore why difference [*der Unterschied*], diversity [*die Verschiedenheit*], opposition [*der Gegensatz*], and contradiction [*der Widerspruch*] are all contained within the seemingly simple formal axiom A is A. Hegel's account of the dialectical movement between identity and contradiction launches an attack on what would seem to be self-evident about the claim A is A. The chapter is motivated, in part, by Hegel's criticisms of old assumptions about the categories of reflection, which were often understood as static, universally valid propositions of the form that "'Everything is equal to itself; A= A,' or, negatively, 'A cannot be A and not-A at the same time'" (SL 354, WLII 36).

Against these old assumptions, Hegel argues for all of the following: (1) The categories of reflection are not pre-given axioms "incapable of proof" [*unbeweisbar seien*] (SL 354, WLII 36),[16] but should instead be submitted to rigorous critique; (2) the categories are not unrelated to each other, as a distinct set of numerable laws, but are rather dialectically intertwined in the sense that they emerge out of each other as each other; and (3) the categories do not only apply in the narrow sense to propositions, but should be considered in a more expanded sense as applying also to things and reality, and as including not only the traditional formula of identity (A is A) but also the earlier categories of being (i.e., quality, quantity, and measure) as well as difference (A and not A), and contradiction (A is not A). Let's look at all three of these points in more detail:

(1) That we do not need to give an argument for the validity of the laws of identity and non-contradiction is an assumption that is at least as old as Aristotle, who decisively articulated these laws as the most basic of axioms in *Book IV* of *the Metaphysics*, (sections 3–6). We tend to accept both the laws, that something can only be equal to itself and cannot be itself and the contrary of itself, as well as the equivalency between the laws, that non-contradiction is another way to articulate the law of identity, as irrefutably simple and evident to everybody, to the extent that the proposition A is A appears as tautological and without need of an argument. However, Hegel attacks this assumption in the "Essentialities" chapter, arguing instead that just as we must begin from a critical, presuppositionless starting point in the *Logic*, we must also be

thoroughly critical of even the most basic and seemingly self-evident laws of identity and non-contradiction. If it turns out that things simply are what they are and are not what they are not, then this is the result of the *Logic*'s own development. But if it turns out that the relationship between identity and contradiction is more complicated than common sense assumes, it is the task of the *Logic* to uncover these complications and articulate the form that these determinations of reflection actually take.

(2) What Hegel discovers from this critical standpoint is that the categories of reflection are not unrelated, but emerge out of each other and at the same time conflict with each other dialectically. Hegel's subsequent exposition from identity to difference, diversity, opposition, and contradiction should be viewed as detailed evidence for the conclusion that the categories are significantly relational. In contrast to Aristotle's definition of a "category" as what is definitively "said and asserted of every existent," Hegel claims that "a determinateness of being is essentially a transition into the opposite of it; the negative of every determinateness is just as necessary as that determinateness itself" (SL 355, WLII 36-7). That the laws are numerable on their own and yet codependent as well complicates the traditional assertion that the laws of identity and non-contradiction are simply equal to each other. On Hegel's account, the further categories of difference, diversity, opposition, and contradiction emerge along with the reflection of identity, rather than simply the equivalence of non-contradiction.

(3) This more complex articulation of the law of identity causes us to expand the domain of the categories from its traditionally narrow application as the function of the validity and invalidity of propositions, to include, instead, its application to things and reality in general. This expansion includes the earlier categories of being (quality, quantity, and measure), thereby exposing the continued relevancy of the *Doctrine of Being* for the *Doctrine of Essence*. But this expansion also undermines the assumption that the categories can only be understood from the terms of thought and rational conception, as if identity and contradiction and reflection in general could only be understood through the intellect and imagination of consciousness. What Hegel establishes, instead, is that the categories of

reflection are equally categories of *being* as much as they are of *thought*. This opens the way for the exciting conclusion that if contradictions exist, they do not only exist in terms of rational conception, as if they were only held together in the fantasies of one's mind, but also exist in the very fabric of reality as the clots and folds of being itself.

From identity to difference

Against the background of his critique of these assumptions, Hegel's exposition of the argument from identity to contradiction nevertheless begins from a premise about identity. The *Logic* generates the concept of identity from the recognition that the negativity of essence is at the same time the being of essence. "[Essence's] negativity," Hegel writes, "is its being" (SL 356, WLII 38). One might assume that essence is otherwise than being, but since it is the reflection of being, it is a negativity that is at the same time the self-reference of being. Hegel calls this "identity" because essence, as that which being is not, reveals what being is. Such a movement against being, which is at the same time an explanation of being, takes the form of A is A.[17] The immediacy of being is reflected into itself. The copula between the subject and the predicate projects the negativity of A. But this A is still the same A throughout. Its reflection shows that it is both different from itself and the same as itself.

The clue to a dialectic between identity and difference starts from the realization that the identity must contain difference in the process of confirming that the subject and the predicate are the same. "Difference is the negativity that reflection possesses in itself, the nothing which is said in identity discourse" (SL 361, WLII 46). The act of confirming identity posits difference through the iteration of a second A in the position of the predicate. Difference comes in the anticipation brought about by the copula that the predicate will be something other than the subject. In this way, the simple form that A is equal to itself exposes identity to its opposite. Furthermore, the role of difference is more than a simple moment of hesitation in the reflection of the copula. The subject is only understood to be identical with itself if it posits difference alongside the identity of itself in the predicate position. Hegel explains this relationship in terms of self-subsistence and absolute difference. A is equal to itself because it does not require anything other than itself. And yet the form that A must take as the confirmation of its own identity requires reflection, which in turn requires absolute difference. The identity requires confirmation in the copula that it is equal to itself. This means that identity self-subsists but also depends on its own negativity. Identity, therefore, subsists through difference. Difference, therefore, emerges alongside identity.

Yet, this takes the further formulation that difference, emerging alongside identity, is both itself and identity. "Difference is ... itself and identity" (SL 361, WLII 47). Identity comes in the form of absolute difference, A and not A. The determinate negation of the identity, not A, is itself a form of identity. But difference comes from the comparison between A and not A (SL 361, WLII 46). Difference is supposed to be the opposite of identity. However, the reflection of identity reveals that its truth lies rather in the positing of itself as a difference from itself. Difference is therefore the more comprehensive term because it contains *both* the form of identity and the identity of the negation, both A and not A together (SL 362, WLII 47).

Hegel then proposes that difference is diversity. This further transition comes from exposing that if difference is both moments of identity and its negation together, then this state of affairs generates a plurality with members that are *indifferent* to each other. Indifference is the key term of this transition, as Hegel clarifies when he writes: "the different subsists as diverse, *indifferent* to any other, because it is identical with itself, because identity constitutes its base and element" (SL 362, WLII 48, my emphasis). The indifference of diversity generates plurality from the splitting up of identity in difference, where each difference is itself an identity but has over against it a multiplicity of others, which, in turn, are each identities as well. As Hegel writes, identity "*breaks apart* within itself into diversity" (SL 362, WLII 46).[18] These differences are, nevertheless, indifferent to each other because that which is different from the identity is nothing other than the self-same identity throughout. Hegel describes this relationship as a subsistence of differences. On the one hand, the terms of identity are distinguished from each other. On the other hand, the reason why the distinguished terms are indifferent to each other is because identity still dictates the parameters of this relationship. While identity falls apart and therefore produces diversity through its differences, the indifference of each side of the diversity allows for the subsistence of each as identical with itself and as different from all others.

From difference to contradiction

Diversity can only explain the coincidence of identity and difference in an implicit way. When this coincidence becomes explicit, opposition reveals itself to be the truth of diversity (SL 365, WLII 52). The barrier of indifference that held diversely different identities together breaks down because the relation A is A requires one self-coherent identity throughout, not a fragmented plurality of differences. Borrowing from terminology that appears later in the *Doctrine of Essence*, Hegel claims that the reason why opposition emerges from diversity is because diverse moments each claim to be the whole and yet only one can actually be the whole (SL 367-70, WLII 55-9).[19] Diversity presents the unity of identity and difference by way of an indifferent conjunction, but opposition presents this same unity as in conflict. The difference inherent in the identity turns from a structure of plurality, where each side is respectfully indifferent to the differences of others, to a situation in which the differences between each side form an explicit conflict, where each side claims to be the whole, even though all sides cannot equally subsist as the whole. "The positive and negative are such, therefore, not just *in themselves* [*an sich*], but in and for themselves [*an und für sich*]" (SL 370, WLII 59). This claim, that each side of an opposition is the absolute [*an und für sich*], marks the distinct character of its concept. Conflicts arise, however, because of mutual exclusivity: each side claims to be the absolute, but if one side is, then the other is not.

The reason why diversity turns into opposition is because the unity between identity and difference must be made *explicit*. Diversity comes from a respect for the differences, but this respect for differences can only be sustained for as long as the sides of reflection remain indifferent to each other. Diversity ultimately collapses into opposition because making the unity explicit is one of the conditions of the unity from the outset. This is the case because the difference inherent in the reflection of the identity *A is A* cannot be separated from the identity from which the reflection began.

This same reason also initiates the transition from opposition to contradiction. Contradiction emerges as the true, explicit unity of identity and difference when we recognize that the opposition is not an opposition that one has with another, but is rather a unity in conflict with itself. If the difference inherent in the identity cannot be separated from the identity, then the unity is not generated from an external contrast between two categorically different entities, but turns out to be a conflict inherent in the same identity throughout. Opposition cannot be sustained because each side that claims to be the whole *is the whole*. In opposition, each side *claims* to be the totality of identity. In contradiction, however, each side not only claims to be the whole. Each side *is* the whole (SL 374, WLII 64). Each moment of diversity *is* the totality of the identity.[20]

Contradiction turns out to be the primary concept of reflection because that which A reflects into is the opposite of itself *as itself*. That the reflection of A contains the opposition of A is the truth of the transition from diversity to opposition. That this opposition is at the same time the identity of A with itself exposes the transition to full-blown contradiction, where A turns out to be A and not A in the same time, manner, and place. Contradiction comes from the recognition that the sides of opposition are not really "sides" at all, as an external comparison would have us believe, but each is, in effect, the absolute *in and for itself*. Contradiction emerges because the relation that is shown to be oppositional is not many relations, but one and the same relation of A with A.

From contradiction to ground

Hegel makes his position about the existence and primacy of contradiction clear in the final remark of the chapter, on the Law of Contradiction (SL 381-5, WLII 74-80). Here, Hegel proposes that for as long as we continue to hold the law of identity, and the corresponding law of non-contradiction to be sacred, we should also come to recognize "the one determination into which they pass over as in their truth, namely *contradiction*, [which should] be grasped and enunciated as a principle: 'All things are in themselves contradictory'" (SL 381, WLII 74). This formulation of the law of *contradiction* is significantly different from the law of *non-contradiction*, which states that A cannot be both A and not A. Hegel proposes, instead, that movement and vitality are guided by contradiction, in the controversial sense that contradictions are built into the fabric of reality, and that all things are in their self-identity at the same time self-contradictory. Hegel goes so far as to claim that we are wrong to think that identity is more primary than contradiction. Let's look again at the quote in Hegel's remark:

> It is one of the biases of all previous logic and of ordinary thinking generally that contradiction is viewed to be less essential and less immanently determinate than identity. But if it were a question of ranking the two, and each had to be kept separate, then contradiction would be recognized as more profound and more essential than identity. In contrast to contradiction, identity is merely the determination of simple immediacy, that is, of dead being. But contradiction is the root of all movement and vitality. The only reason why things move, have a purpose, and are active is because they have a contradiction within them. (WLII 75)

The task of weighing the primacy of identity and contradiction is only a thought experiment for Hegel, since the two concepts cannot be divided from each other. Nevertheless, Hegel's point is that if we could separate them, contradiction would appear as the primary concept. Against a long tradition that reads identity and synthesis into an abstracted, non-contextualized version of dialectics, here Hegel establishes the primacy of contradiction over identity as the essence of living vitality over against "dead being."

What is less clear from the text is why Hegel would propose that contradiction passes over into ground. "Ground" is arguably one of the stranger, metaphorical concepts to appear in the *Logic*. The "Ground" chapter establishes essence as the ground, or reason, for all things, and then explores a dialectical relationship in the "Absolute Ground" and "Determinate Ground" subchapters between form and essence, form and matter, as well as form and content, concluding with Hegel's analysis of the conditional and the unconditioned. Hegel conspicuously refers with the term "ground" to Leibniz's famous principle of sufficient reason, which states that all things must have a reason or ground for why they are (SL 388, WLII 83). As if to mitigate the force of the claim "all things are in themselves contradictory," Hegel subsequently proposes, as the next major transition of the *Logic*, that contradiction "sinks to the ground":

> The contradiction is, therefore, resolved as ground, as essence, which is a unity of the positive and the negative ... Opposition and contradiction are, in ground, both removed and preserved. The contradictory, self-subsistent opposition was already disposed to be ground. All that was added was the determination of unity with self, a unity which emerged because the opposites sublated themselves and made themselves into the other, and from this they sink to the ground, and yet at the same time reunite together. Therefore, their going under, as positedness or negation, is, moreover, essence as self-reflection and identity-with-self. (WLII 69-70)

The term "ground" brings up a number of associations. It refers to reason as support, as when an argument supports its conclusion with premises or when a lawyer points to conflicting evidence as the ground for a dismissal. The term can also refer in a related way to the core or origination of something, as in the sense that the ground is the essence, substratum, or foundation for why something is what it is. And yet the term also has the added connotation of being in a literal sense a means of support, such as that the earth is the ground or the surface. Hegel emphasizes this literal usage through his equally strange phrase "sinking to ground" [*zugrunde geht*], which he mentions in a number of different ways in relation to opposition, contradiction, and essence. That contradiction "sinks to ground" indicates that the transition from contradiction to ground has two interrelated meanings:

(1) Although contradictions exist and are primary, they must nevertheless dissolve through mediation. Hegel describes the process of sinking into ground as a process of withdrawal. Contradictions withdraw into the ground, which stabilize and preserve what is too volatile to appear in its own immediacy. With the transition from contradiction to ground, Hegel therefore gives an indication of why ordinary thinking works so hard to separate the sides of contradiction so that real contradictions do not seem to exist, even to the extent that ordinary thinking replaces the law of *contradiction* with the law of *non-contradiction*, and then projects this as equivalent to the law of identity. Hegel goes so far as to claim that ordinary thinking abhors contradiction and that we consistently attempt to forget or degrade contradictions wherever they make their mark. Ordinary thinking constantly separates "'above and under,' 'right

and left,' 'father and son,' and so on *ad infinitum*" (SL 383, WLII 77), as if to find shelter from the abyss of contradiction by ignoring the truth of the relation, that each side of the terms is a reflection of its opposite to the point of contradiction. Just as we stave off contradiction by separating sides that cannot be separated from each other, we also have a tendency to describe movement through stasis, difference through identity, paradox through solution, and attempt to ground essences (such as the essence of a goat or a tree) with a conception of transcendence that goes beyond its appearance. Although Hegel prioritizes what he calls "speculative" or "intelligent" reflection because it "holds fast contradiction" and "does not allow itself to be dominated by it as in ordinary thinking,"[21] the transition from contradiction to ground nevertheless exposes that withdrawing from appearance by dissolving into ground is a fundamental characteristic of the concept of contradiction. Essentially, the reason why contradiction sinks to ground is because it can appear only through its disappearance.

(2) And yet, that contradiction turns into ground reveals contradiction to be the foundation for all things. What appears through the disappearance of contradiction, when it withdraws into the shelter of static, identity thinking, is at the same time conditioned by contradiction and claims contradiction as its ultimate reason for existence.

The substitution interpretation

The aim of this textual explication from identity to contradiction and from contradiction to ground is to describe how the transition helps us to rethink Hegel's insights about contradiction as primary for the other categories of reflection. What the "Ground" chapter reveals is that the earlier formulations of diversity and opposition already contain the agent of contradiction within them. Ground shows that "difference as such is already *implicitly* contradiction; for it is the *unity* of beings which are, only in so far as they are *not one*—and it is the *same reference connecting them*" (SL 374-5, WLII 65). Diversity and opposition (as the two sub-concepts of difference) are already implicitly contradiction. In other words, they are only posited as concepts of reflection insofar as they are implicitly contradictory. Each appears as a distinct concept only through the obscurity of the truth of their contradictory nature. Diversity is contradiction when it is dressed up with sides that seem to be indifferent to each other. The world then appears as a plurality of identities that are indifferently different from one another. Diversity is therefore one of the ways that contradiction appears through explanatory concepts, which substitute for it, cover it up in obscurity, and thus also mitigate the contradiction and let it emerge through the veil of concepts that seem less than contradictory. And yet the worldview of a diverse collection of self-substituting identities refers back to contradiction as the reason, or "ground," of its meaning.

Likewise, the transition from contradiction to ground shows that opposition is also an expression of contradiction when it is dressed up as a relation of contraries, as if what stands in conflict is something other than the self-same identity throughout. Just as reality is filled with diversely indifferent entities, opposition is likewise a common type of relationship. Ordinary thinking strains to undermine contradiction by substituting it for contraries and sub-contraries, which in effect hide the contradictory nature of oppositions. And yet what the appearance of an opposition also shows is that contradictions both exist and also that they cannot appear directly in the light. Contradictions reveal themselves, instead, through the appearance of diversity and opposition, and reveal themselves only partially through these "gentler" formulations.

Because of the transition from contradiction to ground, the main tenets of the substitution interpretation are recognized as:

(1) Thought fails to think contradiction, but nevertheless produces a litany of mediating concepts as a by-product of the collapsing of contradiction into ground. These mediating concepts are produced from the impossibility of grasping contradiction directly. These concepts are nevertheless produced from the necessary attempt that thought think contradiction directly, that reality must realize contradiction. Because being is fundamentally self-contradictory, it is necessary for thought to think contradiction, even though this task is impossible.

(2) And yet thought nevertheless succeeds at thinking contradiction indirectly through the mediation of other seemingly non-contradictory concepts. Per (1), a set of mediating concepts emerge from the

inability to think contradiction in any real sense. The failure to think contradiction produces shapes of reality through the collapse of contradictory sides. But as a second principle, per (2), we realize that these mediating concepts do actually allow us to think contradiction, even though only in an indirect way. The existence of contradiction appears through concepts which seem to compartmentalize the juxtaposition of positive and negative elements, such as difference, opposition, and contrariety, where both the positive (A) and the negative (-A) seem to be at least partially separated. In spite of the separation, these concepts express contradiction. Contradiction exists, because it exists through them. Contradiction is thinkable, because it is thought through the mediation of concepts which pretend to be less than contradictory.

Contradiction as contrariety

Aristotle's articulation of the law of non-contradiction can be reinterpreted as a statement about substitution. A cannot be both A and not A in the same *time, manner, and place*. Proponents of the substitution interpretation view the qualifications "time," "manner," and "place" to be ways of dressing up contradiction so that it does not appear to be contradictory. The contradiction of being A and not A no longer appears contradictory when divided by time. We say that the same person throughout is both young and old, but because the person's life is divided by time, the same person exhibits contrary qualities (young and old) and yet this is not a contradiction. Likewise, contrary qualities occur simultaneously as long as there is a difference of manner, as when a pun simultaneously gives off two ambiguous meanings but this is not viewed to be completely contradictory. The qualification *manner* compartmentalizes contraries that would otherwise appear as contradictory. Yet again, we qualify the contradiction of being both A and not A by interjecting spatial and place designations, which mediate A and not A and let contradictions exist. Aristotle is certainly right when he lists these primary qualifications to the law of non-contradiction. The only addition that proponents of the substitution interpretation make is to point out that it is the primordial existence of contradiction, not the law of non-contradiction, which causes the qualifications of time, manner, and place. It is contradiction itself that gives these qualifications their role of mitigating, softening, and explaining away the otherwise inadmissible revelation that A is both A and not A.

This reinterpretation of the law of non-contradiction comes down to a detail about the difference between contraries and contradictories. Ordinary thinking assumes that a pair of contraries is categorically different from a pair of contradictories. Contrary properties can adhere to the same substance—hot and cold, for example, can be attributed to the same source. Because hot and cold are merely properties, it would seem to be a basic category mistake to conflate contrary properties with outright contradiction. Aristotle articulates the difference between these categories with his square of opposition, which establishes the distinct separation between contraries, subcontraries, subalternations, and contradictions.

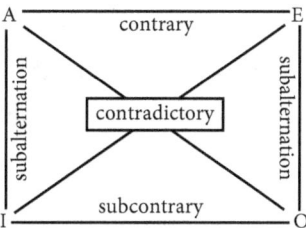

According to the diagram,[22] the pair A and O is contradictory, which means that A and O have opposite truth values (i.e., if A is true, then O must be false, and vice versa). However, the pair A and E is merely contrary, but not contradictory, which shows only a degree of opposition: If either A or E is true, then the other must be false (in other words, both cannot be true). But if A is false, then E can be either true or false (in other words, both can be false). The case is similar with subcontraries: because propositions I and O are subcontraries, both cannot be false; either one or the other must be true, or both must be true. Based on Aristotle's square of oppositions, we are led to the same conclusion that our common sense also leads us to: contraries and subcontraries are categorically different from contradictory relations. The reason why contraries can exist in thought and reality, while purely contradictory relations cannot, is because contraries are only partially oppositional, while contradictions are blatantly oppositional. Partial opposition is a way to explain propositions or events as non-contradictory. Fire exhibits the contrary qualities of being both hot and not hot as long as a qualification holds between time, manner, or place. Fire is hot if we stand too close to it, not hot if we stand at a good distance from it. The fire is not hot when we begin to light it, hot when it is fully burning, not hot, again, when it has died down. In this way, the opposition of the pair hot and not hot is only a partial opposition, mediated by qualifications. In this way, we explain how something that might otherwise appear to be contradictory is merely contrary.

The only addition that the substitutionist makes is to frame the difference between contraries and contradictories as a relationship of mediation. Proponents of the substitution theory claim that contraries and contradictories are not completely separate but, instead, that contraries express contradictions in a non-contradictory way. The fire is both hot and not hot. This is a result of the fundamental characteristic, according to Hegel, that being is self-contradictory, that contradiction is more fundamental than identity, and that contradiction is the ground or reason why things are what they are. The substitutionist merely points out that concepts which qualify contradiction are really generated by contradiction. The result is that what is contrary *is* contradictory both because it appeals to contradiction as its source and ground, and because it is the impossibility of grasping contradiction directly that makes the structure of the merely contrary possible in the first place.

Contradiction as essence

The *Doctrine of Essence* is a doctrine about the coincidence of existence and essence. In our everyday thinking, we tend to make light of this coincidence. We say that things are in one way particular and in another way universal. We tend to ignore the strange, double quality that things are both expressions of universal concepts and also purely singular existents. All things have this double quality. When I look around my office, I see all sorts of objects: the chair, the table, the laptop, the window, etc. These things appear in their immediacy as particular things. They claim factual existence and, in doing so, reference only themselves. However, on the other hand, when I look around my office, I see things which are, at the same time, instantiations of essences. *This* chair that I sit on is unique in itself, and yet it is also an instance of *a* chair. In Hegel's account, the particular and the universal constantly appear together as a unity. Each side appears as a unity in the sense that we can only think of particular things insofar as each is bound up with universal conception. And yet, Hegel claims that "essence must appear" (SL 418, WLII 124), which adds the further nuance that the unity of the particular and the universal is not only a unity of instances referring to essences, but also the real, determinate appearance of essence. *The* chair that I sit on is really *a* chair. The universal must exist and make itself known in the particular instances of everyday, factual reality. What I see when I look around my office is, literally, the universal. The universal exists as the coincidence of itself and the particular.

Proponents of the substitution interpretation recognize Hegel's claim about the coincidence of existence and essence to be a claim about the primacy of contradiction. But they also recognize that in our everyday explanation of the particular as being a mere instance of a universal, thought attempts to withdraw from the underlying contradiction that existence and essence are one. We tend to think of the particular as merely an instance of a universal, which in turn is located somewhere else, in the Platonic heavens, in the things themselves, or simply in our ideal definitions. Proponents of the substitution interpretation view the artificial division of the particular from the universal to be a necessary by-product of the impossibility of grasping contradiction directly. Because thought cannot fully approach contradiction, thought makes sense of the unity by compartmentalizing the particular and the universal. But by dividing and explaining the contradiction, the further consequence, according to the substitutionist, is that the existence of the contradiction appears indirectly through the cracks of the division. It is a necessary but artificial explanation. The compartmentalizing is, in this way, both a product of real contradiction and also a product of its withdrawal.

The grammatical distinction in English between the definite and the indefinite article can be viewed as an expression of the contradictory unity of existence and essence, but also of its necessary division into seemingly non-contradictory elements. While the definite article "the" indicates that a thing is determinate and particular, as in the case of "*the* chair that I sit on," the indefinite article "a" refers to the same thing from the disposition of the universal. *The* same chair that I sit on is also *a* chair. Hegel's point is that since the thing in question has the same identity throughout, its existential and universal modes cannot be thought of as categorically separate from each other. There is a profound way in which the mundane particularity of this everyday world we experience is at the same time, and in a contradictory sense, the universal world of ideality. The chair is both the site of its particularity and its universality. When thought attempts to divide this site, and compartmentalize the particular from the universal, thought thereby attempts to conceal from itself one of the most fundamental contradictions of basic reality. The prevalent conception of a higher, separate religious reality comes from this desire to deepen the separation between existence and essence. The notion of multiple possible worlds that exceed but do not fully combine with this world is also a product of an overly artificial separation between what is particularly here and now and its universal expression.

Since Pippin makes a similar point about contradiction and essence in "Hegel's Metaphysics and the Problem of Contradiction," let's look back at his essay from the stance of substitution. Pippin qualifies one of the most controversial statements Hegel makes in the *Logic*—"everything is inherently contradictory"—by claiming that this statement should be understood from the context of the local argument Hegel outlines in the *Doctrine of Essence* about the contradictory nature of the particular and the universal. However, even while limiting Hegel's meaning in this way, Pippin acknowledges that Hegel's conclusion still might seem to be absurd to many readers, especially if we invoke Russell's difficult objection that Hegel seems to have conflated identity in the subject with identity in the predicate. For there to be a contradictory unity between the particular and the universal, we would have to accept both the statements (as per Pippin's example):

(i) "Socrates is male."

And

(ii) "Socrates is not male."[23]

Pippin argues that because existence and essence are a unity, both (i) and (ii) have to be true. On the one hand, this person, "Socrates," is male. However, on the other hand, "Plato, Alcibiades, and others are also male but are not

Socrates."[24] This leads to the paradoxical result that the particular person "Socrates" is both the universal and not the universal since other people are also male but are not Socrates. The obvious way around this conclusion, as Pippin points out, is to follow Russell's distinction between identity in the subject and identity in the predicate: "Has [Hegel] not obviously confused here, as Russell complained, the 'is' of predication with the 'is' of identity, a distinction he should be well aware of if he has read Plato, especially the *Sophist*, as carefully as is sometimes claimed?"[25] Traditional thinking has us avoid this problem by recognizing that although Socrates is male, he is only one instance of the universal category "male." He shares part of the universal category without completely exhausting this category.

Pippin nevertheless defends Hegel's position against Russell when he writes:

> The problem with such criticisms, however, is that, far from having overlooked this issue, Hegel considers it as the heart of what he is interested in claiming. His whole point is that the 'is' in question for an *essential* determination must always be the 'is' of identity, and in that sense the contradiction does arise in just the way described. That is, in investigating some essence, Hegel insists that we can never be satisfied with simply predicating a universal of some particular.[26]

According to Pippin, the reason why Hegel finds the division unsatisfactory is because it covers over the otherwise contradictory status of "Socrates," who both exhausts and does not exhaust the category "male." That Socrates shares this category with Plato and others needs to be understood as significantly paradoxical. Traditional thinking—upheld by Russell, for example—does the disservice of repackaging the contradiction as something less than contradictory.

The only amendment the substitutionist would make to Pippin's analysis is to establish the division of identity in the subject and identity in the predicate as a necessary substitution for the otherwise unthinkable conclusion that the unity of existence and essence leads to contradiction. What Pippin does not fully explain is that this contradiction cannot be thought except through mediation. To recognize a distinction between existence and essence is to have already conceded to this mediation. The distinction itself appears because we cannot fully think the contradiction that *essence exists*.

Contradiction is the source of the division, before and after the copula, into subject and predicate. Thought can only partially approach this coincidence. This partial approach, partial withdrawal, is expressed in the divorce of the particular from the universal, in the partitioning of identity into subject and predicate, and in the appearance of superiority and transcendent distance of the universal, which claims mastery over the particular. Thought allows itself to think the contradiction through the division of existence and essence. But Hegel's point is that we make this division artificial if we lose track of the underlying motor of the contradiction as source of this division. Russell's categorical separation of identity into subject and predicate obviates the underlying unity of the copula. Likewise, to divide reality into transcendent realms of earthly and ideal forms, without recognizing the underlying unity of these realms, is to misunderstand the source and severity of this division. Possible world theorists who categorically separate worlds from worlds, and thereby recognize a deep division between the actual and the possible, misinterpret the fundamental unity of modal reality.

Contradiction as life and vitality

Hegel says that "contradiction is the root of all movement and vitality." Proponents of the substitution interpretation take him to mean that the self-movement of organic life is an expression of contradiction, both in the sense that contradiction underlies self-movement as its motor, but also in the sense that ordinary thinking suppresses the full actualization of contradiction by covering over the unity of self and other inherent in the process of life and death. Organic life expresses contradiction in a number of ways. It expresses contradiction through its movements, in the sense that a body pushes off itself and thereby moves itself as if it were other to itself. It expresses contradiction through teleology, in the sense that life grows into itself from an inchoate state that is nothing other than itself, but is also the other of itself. It expresses contradiction in the sense that each part of an organism gives an account of the whole organism, in the sense, following Goethe's philosophy of organic life, that *each part is the whole*. Hahn has already discussed these various expressions of lived contradiction in her book *Contradiction in Motion*, by exposing the contradictions inherent in the teleology and self-movement of living organisms. Instead of focusing further on Hahn's analysis, I will briefly articulate how the substitution interpretation supports Jay Lampert's excellent analysis of the superfluity of digestion and ingestion in his article "Speed, Impact and Fluidity at the Barrier between Life and Death: Hegel's Philosophy of Nature."

Lampert emphasizes that for Hegel it is self-movement that distinguishes organic life from inorganic life. Hegel's claim that contradiction is the root of all movement is a lot more apparent when we think of a self-moving substance as opposed to when we think of movement that is dependent on another. When something moves something else, for example when I push the coffee mug across the table, the passive and active agencies remain separate and seemingly non-contradictory. The mug follows a passive course based on the active movement of my hand. But self-movement works quite differently. Since, with self-movement, the source of the movement is at the same time the object of the movement, one finds oneself divided within oneself to the point of contradiction. To move oneself requires that one treat oneself as an other to oneself, by pushing off oneself. Since the self cannot fully be an other to itself, but only acts as other to gain momentum and to put itself in motion, contradiction underlies the division.

Even dependent movement, where something moves something else, gives some indication of contradiction in the sense that what moves is both here and there, both this and not this, both at rest and in motion. But self-movement offers a much more apparent expression of this contradiction because the same source is both self and other to itself, both alive and dying, both active and passive, both dependent and independent. As Lampert explains in his essay, a living body is both alive and dead. It moves itself by pressing bones against bones. "If the bone is a dead piece that the living body relies on for shape, it follows that a live body has to have some of its own death inside it."[27] Bones are an indication of the contradiction that the lived body is both alive and dead. But bones are also an indication of the contradiction inherent in self-movement. We use dead bones to move ourselves. Bones are like an other to us. But they are also assimilated into our bodies. Bones are a dead division within us which simulate the process of one thing moving *another*; however, since bones are part of our lived bodies, this process of moving oneself as if by use of another turns out to be the movement of self against self. The bones are dead organism but are what allow for self-movement because they allow the other to be divided in itself. Just as self-movement requires that the self be an other to itself, living organisms need to be partially dead in order to be alive and have self-volition.

Organic life expresses contradiction through *digestion* in the sense that by eating the other, one digests the other as oneself. When we eat, we consume the alterity of the other and make it part of us. We live through the death of others. The independence of living organisms is sustained through their dependence on the constant digestion of the other. We eat the other and make it us, but when the body overheats, or when there is nothing to consume, the body is even in danger of digesting itself as if it were an other to be eaten.[28] Ordinary thinking makes light of this profound aspect of vitality by presenting digestion as a normal, everyday occurrence, where an organism sustains itself simply by consuming something that is only external and not implicated in the interiority of the animal. However, the substitutionist recognizes that there is a subdued, underlying contradiction inherent in the process of sustaining one's life through nutrients, by taking in the other and converting it to material that fuels the self.

Lampert claims that, for Hegel, it is "superfluity," or an overflow of digestion, that separates higher forms of life from lower forms of life. "Hegel says that lower animals use up all the nutrients they eat in self-transformation, but higher animals produce 'superfluity' or 'overflow' (*Überfluss*) in the form of excrement and bile."[29] The higher forms of animals generate self-movement by storing up a surplus of energy produced from the digestion of the other. The blood and organs of the body help to "burn up the body's otherness"[30] and much of the surplus is expelled as excrement and bile from the body. However, what is produced from the superfluity of digestion is not only excrement and bile and the waste extracted from the constant circulation of blood and sweat. What is produced is also the possibility of determining one's own movements, rather than being determined by another. Self-movement requires free agency that can only come about in the higher animals from such an overflow of digestion. More than this, it is the soul that originates from superfluity. It takes the buildup and redirection of surplus alterity to transform the physical self-movements of an animal's body into the mental life of an ensouled substance.

The story Lampert uncovers here in these passages of Hegel's *Philosophy of Nature* is an alternative version of the story of how spirit emerges from consciousness in the *Phenomenology*. Spirit emerges from an overflow of digestion, as the implicit contradictory process that comes from merging the other as oneself. It is also this same superfluity that allows the higher animals to reflect on death and reshape it.

Ingestion is the other side of digestion. While digestion describes how life consumes life in order to live, through the process of making the other oneself, ingestion describes the opposite direction of this same process, where an alien agent—disease—throws the organization of a living organism into the chaos of a merged exterior. Whereas in digestion the self assimilates the other, turning it from the "flesh" of the other into the nutrients that sustain life, ingestion assimilates the self into the alien character of the other, forcing the self to break down in a chaos of alterity. "Disease arises," Lampert writes, "when one organ brings the rest of the organism crashing down around its particular overactivity."[31] Ingested with an advanced stage of disease, the body ends up living a "double life."[32] It hosts the exterior agent of the disease as itself. It is taken over by the other but it is taken over by the other as its own process of sickness, not simply as a battle between two separate agencies, but as the struggle of a divided body that is in one sense doubled but in another sense still unified.

Lampert claims that the medicine one takes to cure disease is also a form of ingestion. The fever one endures as part of the process of removing the disease from the body is also a process of assimilating the body and uniting it with the alterity of the other. "Something foreign to life [is] used to restore life."[33] To stop the disease, the body must find a way to ingest the other in a different way from how the disease had ingested the body in the first place. Medicine requires submitting to the exterior and making oneself other to oneself as a means of counteracting the disease that involves us in the same process of dissolution.

Vitality and movement are substitutions, in other words, representatives, of contradiction in the sense that sustaining life comes from digesting one's other and movement happens from self-opposition, from lifting and pushing against oneself, by making an other of oneself. Organic life expresses contradiction through *digestion* in the sense that by eating the other, one digests the other as oneself. And, likewise, it expresses contradiction through *ingestion*, as when a disease takes over and the body is thrown into the chaos of the exterior. Just as substance expresses contradiction through movement that has nothing other than itself as its source, the movement is, at the same time, a mark of the impossibility of grasping contradiction completely. The inability to be both self and other to oneself throws things into motion and animates life. The concept of movement is, in effect, a consequence of a deeply layered contradiction about the nature of becoming, which is both being and nothing, both self and other, both actuality and possibility, at once. Ordinary thinking flees in the face of the task of thinking this fundamental contradiction by reducing the significance of the contradiction underlying self-movement to a mundane conception of independent substance, where things simply move, and move themselves, without further reflection.

Hegel does not mention death as part of the reason why contradiction is more primary than identity, but we can view this also to be as prominent as life at translating otherwise inexpressible contradictions. Just as life maintains the impossible actualization of A as not A for as long as this can be sustained, through the constant digestion of the other as oneself, death acts as a substitution concept for the utter and complete exhaustion of a body that has become itself and its other and can no longer sustain this in life. Each of these concepts gives meaning to what stubbornly remains under the surface and refuses to appear in actuality or thought. But just because contradictions cannot appear directly in the light of reality does not mean that contradictions do not exist. What this means, instead, is that contradictions appear combined with mediating concepts, which stand in their place to represent them. One might say that the reason why contradictions do not appear directly and cannot be thought adequately is because life and death are there in their stead. Or, one might say that the reason why life and death have determinate meaning at all is because being desires to realize itself as explicitly contradictory, but since it fails to express this directly, life and death and other concepts of this sort approximate the revelation of contradiction as much as possible in the place of it directly.

Contradiction is productive

The reason why contradiction reverts to "ground" is because to make a contradiction explicit by unveiling it completely in actuality would commit oneself to the most violent, radical transformations of being as becoming. The reason why contradiction must constantly be covered over and explained away by concepts that are only implicitly contradictory is because identity would otherwise be torn apart in the most violent way by the negativity of itself as itself. Hegel recognizes in the transitions of difference as diversity and opposition, as well as through explanatory concepts such as contrariety, essence, life, death, vitality, and movement, that although contradiction is the most primary category of reflection, it can only appear through the more peaceful exteriors of these other categories. Contradiction is, as Hegel writes in terms of contradiction and actuality, "averse to light" [*Lichtscheue*] (SL 488, WLII 216). It exists through the mediation of other concepts, which help to ground it, because it is too powerful and too radical to appear directly in the light of thought and being. Contradiction is, therefore, the "root of all movement and vitality" in the sense that all things are self-contradictory insofar as they move and live, but also in the sense that the movement and vitality are themselves the expression of contradiction as it withdraws into ground.

It is not just that contradictions withdraw. The contradictory sides of a speculative contradiction destroy each other, and mutually dissolve in this destruction. But the destruction is also production. Substitution concepts rise up at the same time as contradictory sides dissolve. What is really happening when substitution concepts explain contradictions as non-contradictory is that the sides dissolve in destruction. Contradiction then withdraws at the moment of this dissolution. And something further is then produced from the ashes of the destruction. The substitution concepts still trace the movement of the contradiction, but without harnessing the force of the contradiction any longer, even while they are nevertheless seared by the contradiction that produced them. Far from being a concept for the meaningless absurdity of the indeterminate, the tension that forms from the partial emergence and partial withdrawal of contradictions helps to produce the determinate meaning of thought and reality through shapes that are at once born from their flight from contradiction but also from their secret allegiance to contradiction.

3

Hegel on Possibility: From Actuality to Absolute Contingency

Hegel's relentless investigation into the nature of negativity has been well documented in countless commentaries about Hegelian logic and Hegelian thinking in general. Jean-Luc Nancy's *The Restlessness of the Negative*, Slavoj Žižek's *Tarrying with the Negative*, and Karin de Boer's *The Sway of the Negative* name some of the most prominent book-length studies of Hegel's preoccupation with negation and dialectics. One of Hegel's most important insights about the nature of modal reality also begins from a preoccupation with negativity. As the basis of the "Actuality" chapter of the *Logic*, Hegel claims that if something is possible, this means that it can become actual, but that it also can *not* become actual. There are, in effect, two sides of possibility in Hegel's account. There is the positive side, that something possible can become actual. But there is also the negative side, that something can remain merely possible as the possibility *not to be*. In this chapter, I argue that the negative side of possibility—that what is possible can also *not be*—plays a significant role in Hegel's modal argument, that the actualization of possibility leads to a productive contradiction, but that, because this contradiction cannot be sustained, modal reality takes on a developmental structure in which actuality expands to include the concrete existence of the totality of possibility. Hegel's argument that actuality expands to include the totality of possibility is the basis of his one-world vision of modal reality.

Possibility has been traditionally conceived of non-dialectically as the possibility *to be*. We typically define possibility in terms of "truth verification" as the minimum condition for the validity of a proposition, as when we say that if p is possible, there would be nothing contradictory about p becoming actual.

This definition of the possibility *to be* can also be applied to things and events, and not only to propositions. To have the possibility to do something—e.g., to be able to play an instrument or to travel the world—is usually recognized as a clear indication that, putting aside the question of whether the possibility is probable or not, its actualization *can* in any event come about, since there is nothing inherently contradictory about it. Possibility serves the function of truth verification in this way. To recognize that something is possible is to recognize that its *actualization* is possible. But what is missing from this traditional, non-dialectical conception of modality is that when we recognize something as possible, we imply, at the same time, that what can become actual can also *not become actual*. Hegel's dialectical account of possibility exposes this conception not only of possibility's positive side—to be able to play the piano—to be able to travel the world—but also of possibility's negative side—that in being able to play the piano, we can also *not* play it—that in being able to travel the world, we can also *not* travel it.[1]

If the negative side of possibility were not also present in this category, possibility would be the same as necessity in the sense that whatever is deemed to be possible would have no other recourse than to become actual. But to uphold this most basic distinction between possibility, as what *can* be, and necessity, as what *must* be, is to acknowledge a conception of the negative side of possibility. The difference between the *can* and the *must* is that the *can* includes the *can not*. Essential to the basic conceptual terrain of the possibility *not to be* is the difference between "being able not to be" and "not being able to be." That something can *not* happen is conceptually quite different from the notion that something *cannot* happen.[2]

Hegel's treatment of the possibility *not to be* can be traced back to the *Metaphysics* 9.3, to Aristotle's claim, against the Megarian's, that even when a builder is not in the act of building, the builder does not lose the capacity to build but retains this as proof of the existence of unactualized potentiality (CWA 1046b29–1047b2). Hegel's emphasis on the negative side of possibility, along with Aristotle's pioneering work on this theme, comes to be a significant precursor for many contemporary continental discussions of modality that attempt in one way or another to make use of the possibility *not to be*, from Martin Heidegger's prioritizing of possibility over actuality in *Being and Time*[3] to phenomenological accounts of possibility that place existence ahead of essence, from Agamben's work on the political ramifications of the potentiality *not to be* in *Homo Sacer*[4] to Bernard Stiegler's premonition in the *Technics and Time* series that our contemporary technological age suffers from the malaise of over-abundant possibilities.[5]

This legacy of possibility and negativity from Aristotle and Hegel to the contemporary continental tradition is an alternative to mainstream theories of modal reality, which begin primarily from a definition of possibility *as truth verification*, as with modal logic and possible world semantics, which marginalize the negative side of possibility by emphasizing the role that possibility plays for the sake of actualization. Even Aristotle's acknowledgment of the ontological status of the potential *not to be* in his defense against the Megarians can be interpreted as an aberration to his more influential arguments in the *Metaphysics* 9.8, where he states that actuality is prior and more primary than potentiality. Similarly, Hegel's preoccupation with negativity and his conclusions about "absolute possibility" (SL 486, WLII 213) and "absolute contingency" (SL 488, WLII 216–7) have, more often than not, been covered over by the entrenched myth that Hegel's investigations into the nature of negativity serve his ulterior motive to subsume difference under the dominance of identity and to subsume possibility under the hegemony of actuality.

The aim of this chapter is to make sense of Hegel's commitments to the ontological status of the possibility *not to be*, to expose the relationship between possibility and contradiction, and, from this, to explicate Hegel's "Actuality" chapter as a foundational source text for the principles of modal optimism, which act as the focal point for the rest of this book. Hegel's commitments in the "Actuality" chapter begin from his celebration of the thesis that possibility is as much about non-actuality as it is about actuality. Based on these commitments, Hegel explores the category of the possibility *not to be* by drawing on strategies for how to actualize both sides of possibility as one actuality. This leads straight away, for Hegel, to a modal iteration of contradiction. What is fundamentally impossible, and therefore contradictory, would be to actualize the possible *itself*. However, from this impasse, as a result of the productive nature of contradiction, Hegel deduces the rest of the modal categories of reality as an expansion of actuality that comes to include the negative side of possibility as part of the process of actualization.

A classic treatise on the nature of possibility, the "Actuality" chapter offers an original and comprehensive vision of modal reality.[6] In it, Hegel presents the developmental progression of four dialectically interrelated modal concepts (actuality, possibility, contingency, and necessity) multiplied by three types of modality (formal, real, and absolute), for a total of twelve modal categories. One can also find various other implicit modal categories through the application of modality to formal and real contradiction, multiplicity and limitation, dispersion and condition, reflection and freedom, as well as substance and accident. Hegel's chapter works through Aristotelian distinctions such as the difference between activity (*energia*) and actuality (*entelecheia*), between passive and active possibility, between privation and impotentiality, between necessary and sufficient conditions, between inchoate matter and complete form, as well as many others. Hegel's chapter investigates Aristotelian questions such as the debate about whether actuality is more primary than possibility, whether unactualized possibilities exist in a significant ontological sense, and whether some facts of existence are contingent while others are necessary.

On my reading, Hegel outlines three models by which thought attempts to realize the actuality of the possible *itself*. Each model runs parallel with the three part division of the "Actuality" chapter into formal, real, and absolute modality. Hegel calls the first "formal contingency." In this model, actuality includes its opposite through the strategy of indifference. Hegel calls the second "real" or "conditional actualization." In this model, actuality is at first dispersed in other actuals but eventually comes to realize itself teleologically in and as others. The dispersion strategy makes use of conditions, which are both actuality and possibility at the same time, and thereby attempts to actualize the possible *itself*. Hegel also discusses a third model of actuality in the "absolute" subchapter. The absolute model explores the modal ramifications of substance, which is both actuality and possibility at once. All three models can be viewed as substitution explanations, as an application of the interpretation from Chapter 2 of this book, since all three models fail, in one sense, to completely present an actuality of the possible *itself*, but succeed, in another sense, to partially express the inherent contradiction of modal reality.

I have divided this chapter into seven sections. The first section, "The two sides of possibility," discusses Hegel's acknowledgment of the traditional conception of possibility as *truth verification* and as the possibility *to be*. In contradistinction, this section also examines Hegel's statements about the possibility *not to be* in formal terms. I then explore in the second section, "Modality and contradiction," what I think is Hegel's groundbreaking and controversial conclusion about modality: that actuality must be able to express *both sides* of possibility at once. While the actuality of both sides of possibility leads, at first glance, to an unresolvable modal paradox, that is, to the contradiction of conjoining A and -A, the third section, "The actuality of the possible *itself*," anticipates why Hegel is nevertheless committed to the seemingly untenable actualization of both sides of possibility. The fourth section, "Formal contingency: The indifference strategy," explores Hegel's formal resolution of this paradox, which accounts for the strategy of indifference, where the conflicting sides of possibility stand together through the division of *what is* and *what could have been*. "Conditional actualization: The dispersion strategy," the title of section five, outlines a second, more advanced approach to the problem of how to actualize contrary possibilities through an explication of real modality, dispersed actuality, conditions, and relative necessity. The final two sections of this chapter focus on a third type of actuality expansion. Section six, "Absolute modality: The substance strategy," presents Hegel's concepts of absolute actuality and possibility in terms of his related theory of substance. Finally, section seven, "Absolute necessity is contingency," analyzes Hegel's controversial statements about the necessity of absolute contingency, which serve as the conclusion to Hegel's modal theory.

The two sides of possibility

Hegel's modal argument begins from the concept of formal actuality. "[Formal actuality]," Hegel writes, "is nothing more than a *being* or *existence* in general" (WLII 202). Formal actuality is the modal version of "being" [*Sein*] from the opening of the *Logic*. It is also the modal version of Hegel's term "existence" [*Existenz*] from the beginning of the "Appearance" [*Erscheinung*] section of the *Doctrine of Essence*, which precedes the "Actuality" section of the *Logic*. This initial actuality refers to the fact of being and the fact of existence as the mere givenness of reality. Formal actuality is the starting point of modal reality in a similar way to how being is the presuppositionless and yet indeterminate foundation for the development of the *Logic*. Whatever is immediately actual has the indubitable and indisputable authority of having already been posited as being. Actuality simply "is." When I look around at my everyday surroundings, I witness the fact of actuality as the being of immediate reality. I see the chair, desk, and window of my office as simply there, as obviously and definitively actual. Transformations and fluctuations of the content of actuality cannot alter the fact that whatever is actual "is." This makes actuality formal and immediate, but also empty and indeterminate.

But whereas existence is distinct from pure indeterminate being in the sense that its correlate is essence, actuality is distinct in the further sense that its correlate is possibility.[7] In other words, the concept of actuality is the same as the concepts of being and existence, with the one noteworthy difference that while indeterminate being implies nothing (*Nichts*) and existence implies essence (*Wesen*), actuality contains the further implication that it has possibility (*Möglichkeit*) over against it. While the chair, desk, and window are merely given as part of the environment of my room, these features have equally emerged into actuality from possibility.

With the claim that "what is actual is possible" (WLII 202), Hegel thereby defines "formal possibility" as the in-itself (*Ansichsein*) of actuality. We make a simple inference from the immediate, self-evidence of actuality, that whatever is actual must have been possible. If I am jogging in the park, then jogging in the park must have been possible and cannot have been impossible. Immediate actuality has this authority. Its possibility is obvious and cannot be contested. This is why we attribute a high level of truth to the immediate presence of what is already there. By recognizing that whatever is actual is possible, we therefore recognize possibility as *truth verification*. What is actual is a fact of existence, but it is nevertheless the role of possibility to verify this. In this way, Hegel anticipates the traditionally analytic definition of possibility as the minimum condition for the validity of a proposition. He also thereby anticipates the traditional conception of possibility as the possibility *to be actual*, in the sense that if something is already actual, it must have also been possible. We can interpret Hegel to be, at this stage of the argument, in dialogue with Aristotle, who claims, in book *Theta* of the *Metaphysics*, that possibility is always for the sake of actuality and that actuality is conceptually prior and more primary than the possible. By beginning his modal analysis from actuality, and by calling possibility the "in-itself" and the reflection of actuality, Hegel places himself in dialogue with Aristotle over the various accounts of the logical, ontological, and teleological priority of actuality.

Hegel's modal argument, therefore, begins from the two seemingly innocuous claims (1) "actuality is ... being or existence" and (2) "what is actual is possible" (WLII 202). We make a simple inference from the immediate, self-evident existence of actuality to its status as possibility. If I am jogging in the park, then jogging must have been possible and cannot have been impossible. But it is equally apparent from the inference of these two claims that the possible is not necessarily actual. Actuality entails possibility, but possibility does not in the same manner entail actuality. Fitting and Mendelsohn explain this in *First-Order Modal Logic*: "Now, p ⊃ ◊p (i.e., *It's actual, so it's possible*) is usually considered to be valid ... but its converse, ◊p ⊃ p (i.e., It's possible, so it's actual) is not [valid]."[8] While the statement "it rains" necessitates "it possibly rains," the statement "it possibly rains" does not necessitate "it rains." This is the case not only for truth functional sentences, but for entities and things in the world as well. Although I might buy a house next week, the possibility of this does not necessitate its actuality. This is even more obvious when we think of examples of what is merely possible, where the possibility as such has never been demonstrated in actuality. Fantasy and science fiction stories offer countless examples of what is merely possible, of what has not yet and might not ever become actual. While we can speculate about these various possibilities, their mere projection in possibility does not necessitate their actuality.

In this positive sense, possibility is merely the reflection of actuality into itself. "To say that *A is possible*," Hegel writes, "is merely to say that *A is A*" (WLII 203). Because the sea battle is possible, it would not break the logical coherence of the event if it were to become actual. In this sense, the possible is already predisposed to become actual. There is no difference added to the content of the possible when it becomes actual. But to say that the sea battle is possible is only to say that if it were to become actual, this would not be impossible—which is to say nothing at all. To say that "A is possible" is to express only the most empty of determinations that what is possible can be, because if it were to become actual, this would be no different than this content as possibility.[9]

However, Hegel acknowledges not only the positive side of possibility as the tautological validity of actuality when it is reflected into itself, but equally the negative side of possibility. The possibility of actuality turns out also to posit the opposite of the actuality. Hegel writes:

> *A is A*; equally, *-A is -A*. Each of these statements expresses the possibility of … content determination. But, because they are identical statements, each is indifferent to the other. That the other is also added is not *posited* in either. Possibility is the comparing relation of both statements; as a reflection of the totality, it implies by its definition that the opposite also is possible. Possibility is therefore the relating *ground* that, *because* A equals A, -A also equals -A; entailed in the possible A there is also the possible not -A. (WLII 204)

This further claim about formal possibility significantly changes the course of Hegel's analysis. Hegel claims that if A is possible, this means not only that A is identical with itself (that A is A), in the truth-functional sense of the possibility *to be actual*, but also that the opposite of its identity (-A) is equally possible, in the sense of the possibility *not to be*, as a projection of the negation of the actual. As the most general domain of content, possibility is the relating ground between these two equally true yet empty articulations of the law of identity that A is A but equally that -A is -A. All possibilities of content are contained within these two articulations of the law of identity. Possibility is the totality of form. It contains both A and -A together. Possibility is, therefore, the modal version of Dialectical Totality, which we outlined in the first chapter of this book. It contains all of the permutations of actuality because it contains the opposite of the actual as one unity. Since possibility is both the possibility to be actual and the possibility to not be actual, it is the indeterminate but also the total form of actuality.

This leads, on Hegel's account, to a modal contradiction that drives the rest of his deduction of the modal categories.

Modality and contradiction

Possibility is the relationless, indeterminate container for everything generally. In terms of formal possibility, *everything is possible that does not contradict itself*. The realm of possibility is a limitless multiplicity. But every

> multiplicity is *determinate in itself and as against another* and has negation in it. In general indifferent diversity passes over into opposition; but then opposition is contradiction. Therefore everything is just as much something contradictory and, because of this, *impossible*. (WLII 203)

Because the possible contains both the actual and the opposite of the actual, Hegel refines his definition of "formal possibility" by characterizing it as a "limitless multiplicity" (*die grenzenlose Mannigfaltigkeit*). As the unity of being and non-being, possibility is a relationless, indeterminate receptacle, open to the being, nothing, and becoming of anything and everything, of any content whatsoever. Hegel continues to refine this definition by pointing out that formal possibility is bounded only by the law of non-contradiction.

However, Hegel then finds from this same initial definition of possibility as indeterminate receptacle the seemingly strange conclusion that whatever is formally possible is just as much something impossible and self-contradictory. Since possibility contains both the identity of the existent-actual and the contrary of the existent-actual, and contains both equally as one unity, everything is possible that does not contradict itself; however, the totality of everything is just as much something impossible and self-contradictory. This is the case because possibility harbors self-contradiction within the function that it serves as actuality's identity-with-self. This is why Hegel claims provocatively that "possibility is self contradiction … in other words, it is the impossible" (WLII 204).

Commentators have offered a great deal of explanation to justify Hegel's seemingly paradoxical claim that "everything is possible" and "everything is just as much something contradictory and therefore impossible." The main branch of this comes from Burbidge, who suggests that Hegel means everything together is impossible, stressing the universality of everything, while at the same time "everything" is possible, stressing the mere possibility of each determinate thing.[10] Although both walking and not walking are equally possible—everything is possible in this way—to both walk and not walk in the same time and manner would be impossible. While I think this branch of commentary is plausible, I also think that Hegel actively intends the passage to be paradoxical. The modal contradiction that he discovers at this point in his argument acts as the motor for the subsequent modal categories, from "formal contingency" to "real" and "absolute necessity." If we explain why the passage is not paradoxical, we lose much of what is important about Hegel's modal argument. In this respect, Lampert really interprets Hegel well when he emphasizes how "polemical" the passage is, arguing that "the function of a possibility is to express the totality, but that no one possibility can express everything the totality expresses without generating contradictions. Each possibility thus fails to express all that it *itself* expresses."[11]

When we refer to something as possible, we refer to both its positive and its negative side. But to actualize both sides of possibility at once would be to actualize contradiction. To have the possibility to play the piano means both to be able to play it and to be able not to play it. However, to actualize both playing it and not playing it as one activity would be to actualize contradiction. Likewise, I can move to Paris or not move to Paris. These are two possible directions my life could take. However, to actually move to Paris *and* not move there in the same time and manner would be impossible.

Since possibility contains both the identity of the existent-actual (A) and the contrary of the existent-actual (-A), everything is possible that does not contradict itself; however, this makes possibility just as much something impossible and self-contradictory. This is the case because possibility harbors self-contradiction (A and -A) within the function that it serves as actuality's identity-with-self. Hegel emphasizes in this passage that possibility is, at first, only the reflection of actuality *into itself*, which means that as the minimum condition for the validity of propositions and things, possibility merely affirms the identity of actuality (that if A is possible, then A is A). However, because this simple function of reflection includes the negation of actuality (that what is possible can also *not be*), possibility therefore also contains the moment of contradiction. When we recall what had seemed to be the innocuous claim from the first lines of Hegel's chapter, "what is actual is possible," we are now faced with the paradoxical task of visualizing an actuality of both A and -A. We are now faced with the seemingly contradictory concept of an actuality of the possible *itself*.[12]

> Now, since its determination is reflection, as we have seen, a reflection that sublates itself, possibility is therefore also the immediate and, as such, becomes *actuality*. (WLII 204)

Possibility has both a positive and a negative side, but to actualize both sides would be to actualize contradiction. Try to think of A and -A as one unity. This is impossible. Even the pure conjecture of the imagination cannot visualize A and -A together without transposition. Certainly, I can transpose A and -A. But transposition requires a distinction of time, manner, or place. It requires a disjunction of the actual in the possible. To attempt to render in actuality the immediate status of the possible *qua* the possible is to present only the indeterminateness, incompleteness, and vagueness of the possible. This is why we fail to grasp the actuality of the possible *itself* at the formal level. While the possible A contains the possible -A, actuality cannot present this with any determinateness. Or, in other words, its only determinateness is this indeterminacy. Possibility as both the actual and the opposite of the actual turns out to be the first sign of determinateness, according to Hegel. This is why in the "Actuality" chapter Hegel transitions from formal to real modality, from the purely logical stage of possibility as indeterminate receptacle to content-related possibility (i.e., potentiality). Hegel's rationale for the transition from formal to real modality mirrors his rationale at the beginning of the *Logic* from the indeterminate starting point in being, nothing, and becoming to determinate being. That being transitions into nothing is proof of its indeterminacy, and yet this is also the first mark of its determinateness as becoming (SL 59-60, WL 82-3). Similarly, the actuality of possibility turns out, at first, to be the total absence and indeterminacy of the possible that has no further relation to the actual. And yet this is also the first mark of its determinateness, from which Hegel deduces formal contingency.

The actuality of the possible *itself*

The essential question we face when we explore this textual analysis of Hegel's passages about possibility is why, after setting up this conventional modal argument, which amounts to the bi-furcation of the possible in the actual and amounts to a multiplicity of alternative possibilities, which are merely possible, Hegel would then claim, in what must appear to be a quite controversial step of his argument, that the actual must be able to express both sides of possibility as one actuality. From the perspective of possibility as alternatives, we normally think of actuality as one of many possibilities but not as the totality of possibility, that is, not as both sides together. This is our intuitive everyday sense of modal reality. That whole variety of other possible outcomes cannot also come from this decision. The actual is, in this sense, only one of many determinate possibilities. And the possible is that which can be actual but it is also that which can remain unactualized. Why does Hegel set up this traditional argument only to break from it by claiming that thought must also be able to form an actuality of the possible *itself*, not only an actuality of one side or the other of the possible, with the other side removed?

The primary reason Hegel offers for why thought must actualize both sides of possibility at once is that reality requires the existence of unactualized possibilities as part of the constitution of what makes it true, and that this truth is actuality in the greatest sense of the term. His reasoning lies in the analog between possibility and Dialectical Totality from the start of the *Logic*. To be all inclusive and presuppositionless, being must be the same as nothing. Likewise, to maintain the authority of actuality as being and the mere fact of existence, actuality cannot be one side or another of modal reality, but must rather be the totality of itself as the possible.

His technical argument for this comes from his initial definition of possibility as the reflection of actuality into itself. Possibility functions as both the affirmation of actuality (that if A is possible, then A is A) but also as the opposite of actuality (that if A is possible, then -A is equally possible). "What is actual is," as Hegel says, "possible." This seemingly innocuous process of reflection opens a pathway for the contradiction of actuality as both itself and the opposite of itself. When we think about what the seemingly simple statement, "what is actual is possible," really means, we are forced to admit that actuality ought to express not only the existent actual that it itself is (e.g., playing the piano), at the expense of its opposite (e.g., not playing it), but also the full expanse of the possible *itself*, including the possibility *not to be*. This leads to different types of examples, such as the teleological examples Hegel mentions in the real modality passages, where possibilities are at first dispersed in others and are actualized through conditions. This leads, in effect, to his second conception of possibility as *a degree of quantity*, to a model of actualization that strives to include as much of possibility as can be included in one actuality. Ultimately, Hegel challenges us to be critical of common-sense assumptions about the nature of modal reality, such as that actualization must always form a disjunction, rather than a conjunction, of the sides of possibility.

Hegel argues that actualization must be able to take up the contrary sides of possibility as the self-same actuality. In this way, Hegel's conception departs from most traditional conceptions of modal reality, which prioritize the ontological status of actualized possibility over unactualized possibility. While most traditional conceptions of modal reality describe actuality as one strand or another of the possible with the other side of the possible removed at the point of actualization (e.g., either playing the piano or not playing it, but not both), Hegel's theory is unique because he requires actuality to express the totality of possibility. Hegel's deduction of the modal categories—which continues along from the moment of formal contradiction to formal contingency and necessity, and from this to his teleological account of possibility in the "Real" subchapter, and from this to the absolute modality of substance in the "Absolute" subchapter—depends upon his initial assertion that thought must attempt to actualize both sides of possibility as one actuality.

Hegel's conclusion that there are two sides of possibility and that actuality must be able to express both sides together exposes, on the one hand, Hegel's recognition of actuality-primacy, in the sense that Hegel does not let the possible remain completely unactualized. The contradiction of actualizing both sides of possibility arises because thought attempts to actualize not only the positive side, which is usually conceived to be the normal side to actualize, but also the negative side together with the positive. It is Hegel's recognition of actuality-primacy, one could say, that leads to the paradox in the first place, where thought tries to form an actuality of the possible *qua* the possible. But this same conclusion also reveals, on the other hand, Hegel's recognition of possibility-primacy. For what is actualized is not the divided possible, the actual A at the expense of -A, or vice versa. What is actualized is the totality of possibility (both A and -A together). To the extent that Hegel can be viewed as being involved with the theme of modal priority at all, he turns out to argue for a dialectical co-primacy between actuality and possibility, where both concepts are, in different respects, prior to the other. By claiming that thought must think the actuality of the possible *itself*, Hegel thereby lifts the ontological status of unactualized possibility to the status of actuality. Traditional, non-dialectical accounts of modality, in contrast, avoid this contradiction by lowering the ontological status of unactualized possibility to non-actuality, and by categorically separating actuality and possibility from each other.

On my reading, Hegel expands actuality in three different ways. He calls the first expansion of actuality "formal contingency." This type of actuality includes the negative side of possibility as *what could have been*. Hegel then calls the second expansion of actuality "real" or "conditional" actualization. An actuality that is a condition holds both sides of possibility together in the sense that a condition contains the possibilities of other actuals (e.g., the stone is a condition for the statue). Hegel calls the third type of expanded actuality "absolute actuality." In the absolute modality passages of the chapter, Hegel anticipates how to conceive of substance as an actuality that is explicitly both sides of possibility together (i.e., both *this* particular goat and the universal instantiation of *a* goat). These three expansions of actuality mitigate the contradiction and do not let it fully emerge in its pure, unmediated format. In effect, they dress up the contradiction so that it does not appear as unsustainable. And yet, just as each type of expanded actuality offers an explanation for the possible *qua* the possible, each likewise posits the possibility *not to be* as existing alongside, in unity, and synthesis with the actual.

That actuality expands to include the possible *itself* is a consequence, therefore, of a substitution for the initial modal contradiction. The actual expands because it cannot fully and directly account for the possible. But its expansion is equally an expression of this contradiction. In effect, the contradiction acts as a "motor" for the development of further modal categories. The further categories of real and absolute modality, as well as formal contingency, and its relation to necessity, are in one way failed attempts to comprehend possibility, but are in another way the successful emergence of the possible in the actual.

Formal contingency: The indifference strategy

> This unity of possibility and actuality is *contingency*. The contingent is an actuality that is, at the same time, determined only as possibility, whose other or opposite equally is. This actuality is merely being or existence, but is posited in its truth as having the value of positedness or as having the value of possibility. On the other hand, possibility is *self-reflectedness*, in other words, the *in-itself* posited as positedness. What is possible is an actual in

the sense of actuality. It has the same value as contingent actuality. It is itself something contingent. (WLII 205)

Hegel claims that the unmediated actualization of the possible *itself* leads to an unsustainable contradiction, in which, it turns out, the possible becomes impossible. But this does not stop thought from attempting to conceive of both sides of possibility as one actuality. The immediate, unsustainable contradiction of actualizing both sides of possibility at once generates a series of developmental stages of the modal categories. Each stage of Hegel's developmental modality "softens" the contradiction of actualizing the possible *qua* the possible by expanding our conception of actuality to include the negative side of possibility as part of its constitution. Formally, something cannot be both itself and the opposite of itself since this would lead directly to contradiction. But if the actualization of the opposition inherent in possibility were to become "softened" to the point at which the two sides of possibility were no longer to lead to contradiction explicitly, this would affirm the differences that the opposition had contained without causing the erasure of these differences from existence.

Essentially, Hegel expands the category of actuality to include the positive and negative sides of possibility as one actuality. The first model of expansion is "formal contingency." In contingency, the negativity of the possible—that what is possible *can* and *can not* be—becomes contingent actuality. What is immediately actual is a fact of existence. But this fact is contingent, which means that it *is* but its other *could have been*. The negative side of possibility appears through whatever happens immediately to exist in actuality, and in this way, possibility *itself* is also posited, however indirectly. Because A is a contingent actuality, A posits -A as what equally exists. Contingency thus presents, in a certain respect, the actual A as containing the existence of -A within its own concept. The reason why this is not a contradiction is because A and -A contain each other in a relationship of indifference. The indifference strategy explains as non-contradictory what would otherwise be the explicit contradiction of A and -A together. To recognize actuality as contingent actuality is to insert enough mediation between the positive and negative sides of possibility so that the actualization of the possible *itself* can appear in existence. However, it appears this way only partially and insufficiently through the division of *what is* from *what could have been*.

Let's visualize what Hegel has in mind. The actual world appears in its immediate givenness. This is the simple actuality of concrete existence. The horse, for example, is there in the barn. The other swimmer is there in the lane. If I look at a map of the earth, I see the mountains and the lakes as already there, as what is simply given to their region. Yet, since this that just appears before me is itself possibility, I recognize in what is already there something more than what is already there.

This leads to two further points. I recognize alongside the actual-existent that the possibility of its opposite has of itself an existence, and that this existence could have been what is actual. But I also recognize not only that possibility exists, but also that the immediately existing actual only happens to be. While what immediately appears has the authority of truth, it appears at the same time as finite, since it appears with its other alongside it.

Hegel is not only saying that in the contingent actual, the other appears too, and that these sides together express the possible itself. He is also saying that actuality depends upon the equal existence of the possibility *not to be*. The swimmer passes me in the lane; yet, the quality of this simple event is formed in the contingency and instability that what happens could not have happened. I see in the body movement of the other swimmer not only the appearance of what could have been but the literal texture of the possibility *not to be* as it exists in the actuality of what is.

Formal contingency shows us that even though what emerges in actualization is only some limited actuality of content, the negative of this actuality equally could have been actual. Formal contingency is itself the immediacy of actuality, yet what is posited in contingency is at the same time the existence of non-actual possibility. In this way, formal contingency initiates a revision of the relationship between existence and possibility because it posits the negative side of possibility alongside the actual.

However, contingency is equally grounded in the impossibility of actualizing the possible *itself*. In other words, the only reason why *this* actual is and its opposite is not is because contradiction cannot directly emerge into actuality without mediation. Formal contingency is the first of many modal substitution categories that mitigate the otherwise untenable contradiction of actualizing the possible *itself*. Just as contradiction reverts to ground in the "Essentialities of Reflection" passages of the *Doctrine of Essence*, formal possibility reverts to formal contingency as an initial explanatory concept. Possibility projects both sides of the actual at once. But since to actualize both sides at once would result in contradiction, formal contingency emerges instead of contradiction as an actuality whose opposite could have been. Contingency is, in this way, a replacement for the possible *qua* the possible, which cannot otherwise emerge into actuality. Contingency is, therefore, produced by contradiction in the sense that it stands in the place of impossible actualization. But this also means that it is grounded by the law of non-contradiction in the sense that contingency emerges *because* contradiction cannot emerge otherwise. Hegel repeats the transition from contradiction to ground in the modal transition from formal possibility to contingency.

"Formal necessity" is Hegel's term for the formal division of the possible into "actualized" and "unactualized" possibility. He defines formal necessity as what results from the impossibility of actualizing the possible *itself*. Since actualization cannot sustain both contraries of possibility, one side or the other of the possible emerges at the expense of its negation. Contingency is grounded by the impossibility of actualizing the possible *itself*. This impossibility is the force of necessity. Since both sides of possibility *cannot* emerge together, possibility simultaneously emerges and withdraws. Hegel defines formal necessity as the necessity of this division. Whatever is actual comes at the expense of the actuality of its opposite. This actuality is, on the one hand, contingent because its actualization equally points to its other as what could have been. But this actuality is also necessary because there is no way to actualize the possible itself. Possibility *must* always come divided into the compartments "actualized" and "unactualized." Contradiction would otherwise occur directly in actuality. Although contingency comes close to expanding actuality to include the possible *itself*, its failure to hold these sides together comprehensively and without the division of indifference is expressed in the term "formal necessity." Formal necessity is, for Hegel, the modal version of the law of non-contradiction.

Conditional actualization: The dispersion strategy

> This necessity is *actuality*, but of a kind which—because its unity now is *determined to be indifferent* with reference to the *difference of* the formal determinations (that is, of itself and possibility)—has a *content*. As an

> indifferent identity, this content also contains the form as indifferent—as merely diverse determinations—and is in general a *multifarious* content. This actuality is *real actuality*. (WLII 207-8)

Formal contingency is for Hegel the first development of an expanded conception of actuality that includes both sides of possibility at once. Contingency initiates a progressive series of modal deductions that witness more and more adequate expansions of actuality. Contingency is only the first stage of this development, however, because it can only hold the sides of possibility together through the indifferent mode of an actual-existent, which could have been otherwise but is not otherwise than it is. It fails to express the possible adequately because it fixates on only one side of the possible while tracing the other side only hypothetically and derivatively. That contingency reverts to formal necessity as the law of non-contradiction reveals that this first attempt at expressing the possible *itself* is an inadequate substitution of modal contradiction. Hegel then turns from "formal" to "real" modality, generally, in order to investigate more adequate expressions of actualizing possibility.

The second model of expansion is "conditional actualization," which begins from real actuality. Hegel defines "real actuality" as an actuality that takes into account the content, rather than the form, of actualization. Whereas formal actuality is indifferent to content determinations, real actuality is indifferent to the form determinations instead. Formal necessity revealed the limitations of formal modality. Actualization failed to express the possible *itself* through anything but division. But Hegel then circumvents the conclusions of formal modality by exploring a significantly different type of modality, a modality that is indifferent to the determinations of form. Whereas formal actuality is indifferent to content differences—it is just the simple coincidence of something as identical-with-itself—real actuality is indifferent to the form determinations, and this in turn opens actuality to the differences of content. The product of this is a teleological view of modality, where the immediate givenness of actuality becomes the conditions for the possibility of further actualizations.

> Likewise, real actuality also has *possibility* immediately present within it ... This real possibility is itself *immediate existence*, but no longer because the possibility as such, in its formal moment, is immediately its opposite, an unreflected actuality. Instead, because it is *real* possibility, it has this determination directly within itself. (WLII 208)

Just as formal possibility presents the positive identity of actuality (that if A is possible, then A is A), likewise it presents actuality with the opposite of itself. This same process now happens to real possibility; however, it happens not only between the actuality and its abstract opposite (A and -A), but between determinate actuality and other determinate actuals (A and B). -A is the immediate other of A in the formal sense that something possible can and can not be. But B also signifies the other of A, only not in the abstract terms of self-identity. B is rather the mediated other of A, in the sense that if what is really actual is possible, this is established only from within an interlocking community of determinate others.

Hegel defines "real possibility" as possibility when it is recognized in the context of its determinations with others. While formal possibility projects the abstract opposite of the actual (A and -A), real possibility contains the possibility *not to be* in the much more determinate sense of real contrasts (A and B). Formally, I can move to Paris or not move to Paris. The possibility contains the abstract opposite of the actual as sheer identity and negation. But real possibility contains a spectrum of existing determinations which relate to one another in an intertwining context of oppositions. In terms of real possibility, I can move to Paris or Seoul or anywhere else in the world, depending on the circumstances involved. The negation that is implicit in real possibility is as concrete as the positive affirmation of the possibility in actuality. This makes real modality relational, in the sense of negative contrast.[13]

This shift from formal possibility to real possibility prepares the way for a more effective strategy of expanding the actual to include the possible itself. Because the positive and negative sides of real possibility become determinate sides (A and B), the possibilities of something appear dispersed in the immediate actuality of others. This leads to a concrete, visible integration of the oppositional sides of possibility in actuality. The partial contradiction unfolds through the determinate actions of the determinate context, and especially through teleological development, as when the seed becomes the oak tree, or when animals digest each other. Because the possibility of A first appears in the actuality of B, this prepares the way for further actualization through what Hegel calls "conditions," which reincorporate A's possibilities as one's own.

> Real possibility constitutes the totality of conditions, a dispersed actuality, which is not self-reflected, but is determined, instead, to be the in-itself, but of another, and is supposed to have returned to itself. (WLII 209)

Hegel describes the relationship between real actuality and real possibility as a process of dispersion. The possibilities of something are not simply its own but are rather the possibilities of other actuals. In this respect, dispersed actuality offers a significant advancement upon the earlier disposition of formal contingency. Formal contingency had presented the sides of possibility *indifferently*, by positing the equal existence of the non-actual other. This expressed the possible *itself*, but in an inadequate way, because contingency still held the contrary sides of possibility apart from itself. In contrast, the dispersion strategy does a better job of integrating the negative side of possibility by dispersing the negation within the existing actuality of others and then gathering up the negation through the development of further actualizations.

Hegel turns to conditions to explain how actuality expands to include possibilities that are at first dispersed in the actualities of others. A condition is Hegel's term for an actuality that is at the same time the possibility of further actuality. A condition is actual in the sense that it is immediately given as the fact of existence. For example, insofar as the stone is a condition for something, it is immediately actual and first appears as the earth itself. But a condition is also possibility in the sense that it has latent within it the result of further actuality. The stone is given as prior, but it carries in its immediate content the further possibilities of the statue, the house, the street, and so on. A condition is an actuality that is not just itself. Hegel claims that a condition gets used up (*verbraucht werden*) or sacrificed (*aufopfern*) in the process of actualization (EL 220). It is immediate actuality but also the material for what can become actual if it completes itself in the process of actualization.

In this way, one's own possibilities, which are at first dispersed in the actuality of others, become reintegrated into a further, new actualization, which is also nothing other than the same actuality throughout. A becomes itself through possibilities dispersed in B. We could conclude from this that B is merely a vessel for the emergence of A as something that it already implicitly was. But Hegel argues that if one's own possibilities are dispersed in another, and if further actualization integrates something (A) with its determinate opposite (B), this makes B not only a vessel for A, but the genuine occurrence of A and B together. The implication is, nevertheless, that such an occurrence of A and B is not fully, explicitly contradictory, since the actualization is mediated by conditions. We end up with a second version of substitution. On the one hand, there is a contradiction inherent in the integration, and yet, on the other hand, the conditional element of the integration softens the contradiction enough so that it can come into existence. Take, for instance, the example that Hegel was so fond of using, most notably in the "Preface" to the *Phenomenology* and in the plant passages of the *Philosophy of Nature*: the acorn that becomes an oak tree (PH 7). The acorn grows into the oak tree by realizing itself in the dispersed conditions of the water, sunlight, and nutrients in the soil. Yet even though the seed is at first only potentially an oak tree, and even though it only comes to be itself through the alien character of "exterior" conditions, which pass into it, we do not think of this teleological life process as an outright contradiction. The effect of the dispersion softens the contradiction and lets the seed emerge as the oak tree. We thereby cover over the underlying contradiction by compartmentalizing the actualization process, by separating the seed as potential from its result as the oak tree, and by viewing the conditions as in one way immediate actualities (i.e., water, sunlight, and soil) and in another way as the possibilities of the further actualization (i.e., the necessary sustenance that allows the seed to become the oak tree).

We can still see why the term conditions carries for Hegel only that implicit actualization of contrary possibilities and not the explicit inclusion of all possible outcomes in one actuality. There are good reasons for this. Since they begin as immediate actualities whose content contains the further possibilities of other actuals, conditions come to access greater concentrations of possibility through the mediation of sacrifice and result. As the conditions go under and the resulting actuality rises up, the possible itself appears in the realization of this entire circuit. However, since this process requires sacrifices (*Aufopferung*), transitions (*Übergang*), and distributions (*zerstreuen*) in order to soften the contraries and to let them stand momentarily together, conditions include the negativity of the possible in only a fleeting, indirect, and unsustainable way. We might conclude from this that although actualizing conditions grants access to the real existence of alternative possibilities in the one sense that they become included within a greater notion of reality, this model of actualization can only actualize them to a limited extent. The possible *qua* the possible appears in its totality as the necessity of being, but it can only appear through the mediation of sacrifices, transitions, and distributions, and only in a volatile and unsustainable way as the holding together of contraries before they become contradictory.

When we talk about the process of suspending contradiction by softening contraries, this describes how something can become both itself and the opposite of itself, even if only as a momentary trace of what appears in its divergence from actualization. Formally, something cannot become both itself and the opposite of itself since this would lead directly to contradiction. But if the contrariety in this opposition were to become softened to the point at which an actualization of these contraries were no longer to lead to contradiction, this would affirm the differences that the opposition had contained without causing the erasure of these differences from existence. This is why Hegel outlines in his theory of real modality how through sacrifices, transitions, and distributions, something can become both itself and the opposite of itself. We can define sacrifice as the loss or destruction of what is initially actual, as the going under that is also a rising up, a kind of *Aufhebung* which happens simply because what is immediately actual contains the possibilities of other actuals. Since the deer contains a possibility for the wolf's vitality, that the deer is sacrificed in this process is one of the results of the hunt. A transfer describes a slightly different process for how to soften the contraries. The form of what is immediately actual sometimes remains intact even while it is at the same time the possibility of other actuals. Bank transfers are an example of this since the monetary value remains intact even though the money changes hands. In contrast, a distribution describes the process in which an actual is literally in the possibility of another actual through relative contrast. For example, the cat's claws are dispersed in the actuality of others, in the mouse who finds the claws to be a fierce possibility, and in the bear who finds the claws to be a mild annoyance. Each of these processes shows that to soften the contraries is to mitigate the opposition to such an extent that an actualization of something as the opposite of itself is no longer self-contradictory.

Although softening contraries undermines contradiction, it also preserves moments of opposition before they become contradictory. This preservation is, in effect, the preservation of moments that would otherwise be contradictory. To actualize across conditions is to overcome the initial impasse that formally an actuality is only actual if it excludes the equal possibility of itself as its opposite. To actualize across conditions is to set aside, or bracket out, the law of non-contradiction, and thereby to gain access to otherwise inaccessible possibilities. Sacrifices, transitions, and distributions are the price that one pays to undermine the law of non-contradiction, to preserve contraries, and to concentrate more of the possible in the actual.

> The negation of real possibility is, therefore, its identity with itself. Because it sublates itself, it is thus within itself the recoiling of this sublating, it is real necessity. (WL 211)

Hegel's theory of conditions anticipates a model of actualization that includes contrary possibilities within the same actuality. Under the logic of this model, something is both itself and the opposite of itself, yet this is not impossible because the actualization has come to capture the conditional movement of what Hegel calls "real necessity." By real necessity, Hegel means the necessity that is embedded in conditional actualization.

We can read in the connotations of the term conditions the same compulsion that Hegel has already established in terms of formal necessity. Because what is actual is possible, actuality *cannot* only be one side or the other of the possible, but must come to form itself as the totality of possibility. The other, although it would seem to remain against the actual as what the actual is not, must become consumed in the process of actualization. This is why, although conditions are immediately actual, they are also the possibility of something initial coming to its end in actuality. Conditions "fall under" as actuality becomes itself. Although one's possibilities are dispersed in the externality of other actuals, since these "actuals" are only the conditions for the possibility of something initial coming to its end in actuality, the thing in question nevertheless remains self-coherent throughout this process. And yet, it remains itself only if it satisfies conditions that compel it to realize itself in and as others. Certainly, there is a difference between necessary and sufficient conditions in this regard. There may be many ways to satisfy the conditions that let something emerge into further actualizations. The seed might still become an oak tree through adverse conditions, or when it follows an alternative path to realize its potential. Nevertheless, the identity of the seed as a potential tree will be torn apart by the identity of others if conditions are not satisfied at a basic level. The implications of this entailment as real necessity are developed in a lot more detail in Chapter 4, where I discuss Hegel's argument that necessity produces possibilities.

> However, because it has a presupposition from which it begins, that is, because it has its starting point in contingency, this necessity is at the same time relative. (WL 211)

If something is really possible, this makes it necessary. But directly after saying this, Hegel claims that the necessity in this is at the same time relative because it has its starting point in "real contingency." Hegel probably has a traditional definition of hypothetical necessity in mind, such as Aristotle presents in the *Physics* 2.9 when he says that "in all … things which involve that for the sake of which: the product cannot come to be without things which have a necessary nature, but it is not due to these (except as its material); it comes to be for an end" (CWA 200a7-10). In terms of conditional propositions, real necessity appears in the relationship between the antecedent and the consequent, but this relationship nevertheless has contingency at its base because one does not need to take up the conditional in the first place. In other words, even if we assume that B must follow necessarily from A, it is still contingent whether one presupposes A or not. The engine burns gas and produces motion, but only if the conditions that make it function are already in place. Let us assume they are in place. Then the engine cannot not function. However, to assume this is to expose the relativity of real necessity. Because the conditions could have been otherwise, what follows of necessity is at the same time relative and therefore contingent. Relative necessity is, in effect, goal-oriented necessity.

Absolute modality: The substance strategy

> The unity of necessity and contingency is present here *in principle*. This unity is called *absolute actuality*. (WLII 213)
>
> This actuality, which is itself as such necessary, since it contains necessity as its *in-itself*, is *absolute actuality*—an actuality which can no longer be otherwise, for its *in-itself* is not possibility but necessity itself. (WLII 213)

Absolute actuality is the actuality that emerges from the conditions of possibility when all of the conditions are completely present, not only in the hypothetical sense of relative necessity beginning from contingent external actualities, but in the sense of total inclusiveness, where necessity and contingency are in principle the same. Real actuality took its possibilities to be equally determinate, external requirements, existing initially in other actuals, but one recognizes in absolute actuality that the possibilities are the self-movement of the same actuality throughout. In this sense, absolute actuality is the realization of real actuality. Real actuality only entertained the alien character of possibility so that this actuality could become itself. When real actuality overcame the conditions of its possibility, it included the other within itself. The conditions released themselves of externality, and what was initially possible became itself in the other. Absolute actuality is then the realization that real possibilities only seemed to be dispersed in other actuals, but that this process of satisfying external conditions is the self-same movement of actuality throughout. This only works if the actuality includes the other as the constitution of itself (and if the other includes the self as the constitution of the other).

This is why Hegel says that from the completion of the conditions, "the something is [...] determined as being equally actual as possible." The actual that results from the actualization of conditions is not a new distinct actuality emerging against the background of many contrary possibilities. Nor is it an actuality that entirely succeeds the initial actuality of its conditions.

What results is rather an actuality that is both itself and possibility. Hegel calls this substance. "This *identity of being with itself* in its negation is now *substance*. It is this unity as *in its negation*" (SL 553, WLII 216).

Substance requires us to think from the terms of a third model of actualization. From this model, what is actualized is the absolute conversion of actuality and possibility into each other, an actuality that completely sustains itself in possibility, one that turns its other into what it is, but only by becoming the other of itself.[14] Take, for example, a goat grazing on the hill, what Aristotle calls a primary substance.[15] What the absolute model of actualization shows is that the goat is at one and the same time both existence and essence. She is *this* individual goat who is at *this* particular moment drinking water at the pond. But she is also *a* goat. She is the embodiment not only of her immediate existing actuality, but also of all possibilities of her essence. Since she is *a* goat, she is both always determinate (always on the hill, or in the pasture, always here or there) and yet also free from the limitations of her determinateness (her being on the pasture does not exclude the possibilities of contraries in her essence). She is free determinateness because her individual existence as *this* goat is at the same time the totality of her possibilities as her essence.

Hegel claims that the relationship between absolute actuality and possibility is a relationship of absolute conversion. By this conversion, Hegel means even more than his formal and real claims that actuality and possibility are transitional concepts. Whereas in the conditional model, the conversion of actuality and possibility into each other is only implicit since the possibilities of one thing exist only dispersed in the actualities of others, Hegel's subsequent discussion of absolute modality and his subsequent chapter "the Absolute Relation" present the total, explicit conversion of actuality and possibility into each other, where the possibilities that seemed to be dispersed in others turn out to be one's own, and where the actualization turns out to be self-actualization. The absolute model of actualization goes further than the conditional model because it explains how to think the absolute conversion of actuality and possibility. Insofar as each individual substance is both existence and essence at the same time, each is the absolute conversion of actuality into possibility and of possibility into actuality.

> Absolute necessity is the truth in which actuality and possibility generally, as with formal and real necessity, withdraw. (WLII 215)

The substance strategy offers the most complete expression of the possible in the actual. The two sides of possibility, which appear as disjoined and separated formally by the law of non-contradiction, and appear as dispersed in terms of conditional actuality, become in absolute necessity the total inclusion of all possibilities whatsoever in existence.

To establish this radical modal notion of inclusion, Hegel has to revert to the concept of being from the opening of the *Logic*. Being is the "whatever" of the is. It includes anything and everything within it. In this sense, the actualization of being contains possibility in the most extensive sense. Absolute necessity is being because being is that which nothing could exceed. There is no way around being, no possible remainder or outside. In this sense, being is absolutely necessary and could not be otherwise. However, it would be misleading to say that Hegel has simply returned to the beginning of the *Logic*, since this concept of "being" would bring along with it the connotations of indeterminateness, emptiness, and stasis, which I doubt Hegel intends. When he says that absolute necessity is both pure being and pure essence (SL 487, WLII 215), he most likely already means the one substance, and means this in the most inclusive of ways. The consequence of absolute necessity is that this disposition must include in actuality the existence of unactualized possibilities as part of the constitution of what substance is, in the sense that whatever something becomes, it still is. This consequence is also becoming as self-movement, since Hegel also seems to be suggesting that, if something is a disposition of everything, it must become otherwise in order to be itself. This means that unactualized possibilities cannot simply retain their initial status as the unactual, but must also expand what it means to be actual, and come to include themselves in the actual.

Each differentiated actuality, if it follows the logic of absolute necessity, is the complete conversion of actuality and possibility. Of course, the individual goat grazing in the pasture cannot go in every possible direction, nor make all of her possibilities actual. If she is in the pasture, she cannot possibly be standing with the other goats in the barn. If she is a goat, she cannot in the same manner not be a goat. Hegel has already established these contradiction-limitations with his theories of formal and real modality. In this sense, actuality and possibility are only partially transitional concepts and are not yet in a relation of absolute conversion. But if we think about what this individual goat is, we establish her existence and her essence as one. In terms of her essence, the individually existing goat can go in every possible direction (relative to what a goat can be). She can graze in the pasture and stand with the other goats in the barn. Her individual existence is like a metaphysical gateway that directly corresponds to all of her possibilities as her essence. As the existence of her essence, she can receive all sorts of contrary determinations.

But by the absolute conversion of actuality and possibility, Hegel means even more than the metaphor of a gateway between existence and essence. In this way his theory is distinct from Aristotle's theory of first-order actuality as the many substances. Hegel literally means that existence and essence are the same. What is this individually existing goat? She is *a* goat. The indefinite article exposes the individual to the universality of possibility. It is true that without existence, essence would be empty of determinateness, and that without essence, existence would have no movement or possibility. But Hegel means absolute conversion. The modal concepts are the same, not merely mutually dependent.

The absolute conversion of actuality and possibility therefore causes the most intense agitation of movement in every possible direction. Since the individual goat is its genus-being, not just a member of its genus, but the living existence of essence, the individual goat must receive all contraries as the totality of its possibilities. But only the logic of affirmative multiplicity could allow for the reception of all contraries; otherwise, the difference of each contrary would cause contradiction. Goats move about because existence and essence are one. They grow and pass away because they must expose what they are. They are sometimes standing, sometimes sleeping, sometimes eating, sometimes playing. Goats must exhibit all of these possibilities to be what they are. If existence and essence are one, then each instance of existence is the totality of essence. It is, as Leibniz claims and I will further analyze in Chapter 5, "all of one piece, like an ocean" (TH 131).

Existence and essence are the same only if all contingency has been removed from the actualization. If any contingency were to remain, then the actuality would not produce free movement because the remainder of contingency would dictate the determinate order of things. This is why Hegel says that this field is absolute necessity:

> Necessity as *essence* is concealed in *being*. The contact these actualities have with each other seems like an empty externality. The actuality of one in the other is *only* possibility, contingency. For being is posited as absolutely necessary, and as the self-mediation which is the absolute negation of mediation-through-another, or being which is identical only with being. An other that has actuality in its being is, therefore, *only possibility* as such, and is in this way determined as empty positedness. (WLII 216)

At the same time, however, the field only removes all contingency if it includes all contingency whatsoever. Absolute necessity is thus the most powerful structure of contingency, in the sense that everything within this field both can be and is the other of itself.[16] By the free play of its determinateness, each actuality can give no reason but itself; its restrictions, self-imposed, come directly from being. Each actuality is only itself because each is the shape of all others. Although each actuality is inherently determinate, this determinateness is open to all contingencies because it is grounded only in being.

The field of total inclusion makes everything necessary, but is only this inclusive because it is at the same time the most fluid of all contingencies. Hegel thus concludes that contingency is absolute necessity. He says that if necessity is the essence of these free actualities, this is the case because necessity and contingency are the same. Free movement happens only because there is nowhere to move. Hegel writes:

> This contingency is absolute necessity. It is the *essence* of those free, necessary actualities. This essence is *light-shy*, because in these actualities nothing can shine through, because there is *no reflection*, because they are grounded purely in themselves, shape themselves, manifest themselves only to *themselves*—because they are only *being*. (WLII 216)

As the complete unity of actuality and possibility, being must go in every possible way. This is indeed the final stand. By absolute necessity, if being goes in every possible way, there is nowhere further left for it to go. All possibilities become necessary. But Hegel then finds the strange but exciting result that the ability to be otherwise is secured only from the complete foreclosure of otherness. The structure of absolute necessity, because there is no further otherness or contingency, yields the most fluid openness of movement, an absolute necessity that is just as certainly absolute contingency, a whole field of differences and determinations, the narrowness of which has become so complete that the restrictions this necessity had imposed upon actualization are no longer restrictive.

It is therefore necessity that generates the freedom to be otherwise. Each actuality is free to be other than itself because in the process of being other than itself, each is itself. More than this, these actualities are only what they are if they are also the totality of all others. Necessity is the force that compels the freedom of their movement. Each actuality must be the freedom of itself in all others. This is the imperative of their freedom. They are completely taken by this imperative. They have no chance to opt out or find another way. From the disposition of absolute necessity, each actuality can only be itself insofar as it is simultaneously the totality of everything whatsoever. If each is the totality of everything, then no matter what each becomes in terms of determinate content, each cannot be otherwise than this that it is. Yet, precisely because each is the totality, each is also free from this determinateness.

When we recognize the goat as *a* goat, we appeal to her essence, but we really appeal to her contingency. To be what she is, she must be other than this immediate facticity, other than this individual goat standing at the fence. But this being otherwise is at the same time the original position of her immediate facticity as an individual. When we recognize her as a goat, we let the contingency "shine through" her. But what shines through the individual goat is more than her genus as an animal. Being itself shines through. This goat *is*. A goat cannot be other than this. But at the same time this necessity is the goat's absolute freedom to be otherwise. Contingency shines through at the level of being. Being makes the goat inherently necessary and completely free to be otherwise. This is what Hegel means by free actuality (SL 487-8, WLII 216). The determinateness of being this is at the same time free otherness. All determinate things perish at the sign of this essence. The goat attempts to sustain herself against the sheer magnitude of her being. She follows the narrow path of her conditions. But just as she feels the force of her conditions, commanding her to eat and sleep and care for her own, she also feels the force of her ultimate necessity in being, and this is the force of her own destruction in contingency.

Absolute necessity is contingency

Hegel's conclusion is not only that possibilities necessarily exist as part of substance. His conclusion is also that because of the movement inherent to inclusive necessity, unactualized possibility is no longer a static category because actuality and possibility have become one unity. This leads to the consequence that contingency is inherently necessary to Hegel's system, in the sense that free movement can only happen from within a structure where nothing can be otherwise because everything is already in play. But this also leads to the consequence that thought can express the totality of possibility (both the positive and the negative side) in one actuality.

The traditional reading of Hegel's dialectic between absolute necessity and contingency is that Hegel ultimately recognizes the concept of contingency as a necessary element of his system. This is the most popular interpretation of Hegel's conclusion about modality, since it leads to a reassessment of the role of contingency in Hegelian thinking. Contingency turns out to be one of many necessary concepts. It is of absolute necessity in the sense that it must be included alongside the hundreds of other concepts that Hegel necessarily deduces from the presuppositionless opening of the *Logic*. This popular reading proposes that the system itself cannot be otherwise, that the concepts of the *Logic* are determined rationally by necessity, not by contingency, but that, in a paradoxical way, there also exists a place for the concept of contingency among the other concepts. This is paradoxical because, if contingency is one among many necessary concepts, the question then arises of whether the presence of contingency opens the way for new alterations of the otherwise seemingly rigid deduction of the concepts.

However, the textual analysis I have outlined in this book—which draws us along a path from the being-to-nothing transition to contradiction in the *Doctrine of Essence*, and from this to his modal argument—reveals another viable conclusion about the necessity of contingency. By absolute necessity, Hegel proposes that the reason why things cannot be otherwise is because everything has already been included to the extreme point of absolute contingency. This conclusion is apparent from the inclusive nature of contradiction, a modal version of which Hegel prioritizes in the "Actuality" chapter. There is no further position above and beyond the contradictory position of A is -A. To include the negative along with the positive side is of absolute necessity because A is -A anticipates every possible permutation in every which way of A. This type of necessity comes from the inclusion of the negation, rather than from some determinate limit, which would restrict what can and cannot be. Absolute necessity closes off the possible field of determinations, not by limiting this field to some determinate content at the expense of others, but rather by maintaining the utter and complete openness of negation. Absolute necessity is contingency. The inclusion of the negative makes things unable to be otherwise because they are in every which way already otherwise than they are.

My analysis of Hegel's modal argument attempts to defend this alternative reading of the dialectic between absolute necessity and contingency and to show that this interpretation is as viable as the traditional reading that contingency is one of many necessary concepts in Hegel's system. While there is certainly textual evidence to support the traditional reading of Hegel's conclusion, and while this reading does lead to the exciting revision of Hegel as a thinker who includes contingency in his work, there are also issues with this traditional reading. If Hegel means that contingency is only one of many necessary concepts, necessity turns out to be more primary than contingency, in the sense that all concepts are of necessity and come from necessary developments. In contrast to necessity, contingency plays only a marginal role as merely one of these necessary concepts. But the reading I propose is more robustly dialectical. Absolute necessity turns out to be, in the most genuine sense, absolute contingency. This reading is also more obviously applicable to Hegel's conception of substance, which follows after the "Actuality" chapter as the culmination of the *Doctrine of Essence*. This reading is also much more applicable to the thematic of the *Doctrine of Essence* generally because it explains the modality behind how something is both universal and individual at the same time. It also leads to the thesis from modal optimism, which takes up the second half of this book.

Part Two

The Thesis from Modal Optimism

Hegel's argument from modality offers a complex and subtle conclusion about the nature of actuality, possibility, necessity, and contingency. His developmental methodology uncovers some of the most profound debates about modal reality, such as the question of the ontological status of unactualized possibilities, the critique of the primacy of actuality over possibility, the relationship between contradiction and modal reality, the thesis that necessity leads to otherwise inaccessible possibility, and the groundbreaking but controversial conclusion that contingency and absolute necessity are dialectically intertwined.

The primary aim of Part II is to explore one particular inference from Hegel's modal argument, the thesis from modal optimism, the claim that infinite sets of infinite possible series exist in this actual world. Proponents of modal optimism subscribe to the theory that although the surface of this actual world expands and contracts by degrees of possibility, there is an underlying ontological commitment to the immanent yet infinite totality of the possible. What is exciting and controversial about Hegel's dialectic between absolute necessity and absolute contingency is that, if we extend its ramifications, we arrive at an optimistic thesis that secures the richest, most abundant, most complex varieties of possibility as constitutive of the actual world we live in. Modal optimism reveals that this actual world, whether it appears to be or not, contains within it, in absolute not relative terms, the most perfect variety and the best quality of possibility in actuality, because that which it contains is nothing less than the possible *qua* the possible.

Since the thesis from modal optimism is a thesis that Hegel himself has only partially alluded to in the "Actuality" chapter, the task ahead of us is to reconstruct what Hegel would most likely have endorsed if he had explicitly articulated this thesis in the *Logic*. To this end, Hegel's modal argument acts as the seminal source-text for the theory of modal optimism developed in the following three chapters. It is in some respects difficult to wager to what extent Hegel himself would have been able to anticipate the vision of modal ontology that Part II explores, since this vision has benefited from contemporary modal and metaphysical insights that Hegel did not have access to when he wrote the *Logic*. By following through with the implications and inferences of Hegel's argument, there are ways in which the thesis from modal optimism extends us beyond Hegel.

As a defense against the objection that modal optimism commits us to contradictions and impossible beings, Chapter 4 presents a case for how constraint can be productive for possibility and how absolute constraint (absolute necessity) secures the constant proliferation, fluctuation, and contingency of this world. Chapter 5 examines the incompossibility problem in Leibniz, Hegel, and Deleuze. In this chapter, I argue that Hegel's modal theory offers a significant revision to Leibniz's claim that all possible worlds cannot come into existence. The final chapter, Chapter 6, fields some of the most substantial objections to modal optimism and attempts to defend Hegel's position from these detractors.

4

Necessity Amplifies Possibility: Hegel's Theory of Modal Transitivity

Commentators have largely recognized Hegel as a thinker who prioritizes necessity. As Hegel himself emphasizes, the term "science" in the subtitle "Science of the Experience of Consciousness" of the *Phenomenology*, as with the title *Science of Logic*, refers to the primacy of necessity in these works.[1] Necessity is one of the crucial elements of dialectical reasoning generally. The double meaning that Hegel attributes to *Aufhebung*, as both canceling and lifting up (SL 81-2, WL 113-4), comes from the force of necessity. The *Logic* is filled in this way with intense movement and necessity is its motor. Most commentators are clear on this point: the themes and transitions of the *Logic* are not random or contingent but emerge, instead, from the inherent design of internal critique and developmental necessity. The aim of this chapter is to argue that Hegel's commitments to necessity are equally commitments to possibility. While the textual interpretation I put forward of Hegel's dialectical account of possibility and necessity is not at odds with this general consensus of the primacy of necessity in Hegel's work, it offers a significantly different way to think about necessity. If necessity is not different from possibility, then the dynamic movements of the *Logic* are driven as much by the proliferation of possibilities as by the narrow path of necessity. In other words, the "science" of the *Logic* is a science *of possibility*.

Much has been said about Hegel's statement in the "Preface" to *the Elements of the Philosophy of Right* that "what is rational is actual and what is actual is rational."[2] What has been less discussed, but is equally interesting and contentious, is another claim that Hegel makes about the modal categories. Near the end of the "Real Modality" subsection of the "Actuality" chapter,

Hegel claims that "possibility and necessity are only seemingly different"[3] (*Möglichkeit und die Nothwendigkeit sind daher nur scheinbar unterschieden.*) (WL 211). If by this he means that everything possible is necessary, then this is one of the more provocative statements he makes, not only in the "Actuality" chapter, but in his corpus as a whole. While most of us agree to the axiom of necessity, which states that if something is necessary, then it is also possible ($N \supset P$),[4] Hegel's claim about the relationship between possibility and necessity becomes much more controversial if he also means that being possible makes something necessary ($P \supset N$). In other words, the entailment from necessity to possibility is usually taken for granted as obvious to everyone. That something is necessary presupposes that it also must have been possible. Possibility is in this sense a trivial condition for necessity. If p is necessary, then of course p is also possible. The controversy comes up, however, if we try to reverse the entailment, or, as I think Hegel does, argue for a bi-conditional equivalence ($N \equiv P$).[5] To say that everything possible equally entails its necessity leads to the seemingly absurd further consequence, which is not a position that Hegel ultimately endorses, that what is merely possible in the boundless sense of possibility (i.e., surreal monsters, unicorns, worlds where gravity goes up, non-adherence to the law of non-contradiction, and so on) is necessary and either is or will become actual.

Hegel acknowledges traditional definitions of necessity and possibility when he writes "what is necessary *cannot be otherwise*; but what is only *possible* can be [be otherwise]" (SL 484) (*Was nothwendig ist, kann nicht anders sein; aber wohl, was überhaupt möglich ist.*) (WLII 211). The question, then, is why he would go against this convention by redefining possibility and necessity dialectically in terms of each other, by claiming that the difference between not being otherwise and being able to be otherwise is only seemingly different, essentially by arguing that possibility and necessity are bi-conditional.

In this chapter, I explicate Hegel's claim that "possibility and necessity are only seemingly different." Although he complicates our common-sense definitions of possibility and necessity by exposing a dialectical relationship between these modal categories, Hegel does not thereby endorse the version of the claim "everything possible is necessary" that most people would find absurd, where the mere and boundless possibility of something would necessitate its emergence into actuality, as if everything that could be must be. What I propose, instead, is that Hegel has a theory of modal transitivity in mind. The basic idea behind modal transitivity is that necessity amplifies possibility and not only restricts it. We normally think of necessity and possibility as opposites in the sense that if something is necessary, it cannot be otherwise, whereas if something is possible, it can be otherwise. But Hegel undermines these common-sense definitions by arguing for a productive, bi-conditional entailment, with the exciting consequence that certain well-formed types of determinate necessity, while they restrict possibility in a superficial way, more importantly amplify and agitate what is immediately actual toward the actualization of greater amounts and more complex varieties of otherwise inaccessible possibilities.

To clarify this complicated dialectical relationship between possibility and necessity, I discuss the relationship between dialectics and bi-conditional entailment generally (in the section "Hegel's bi-conditional account of possibility and necessity"). I then discuss why the entailment from possibility to necessity (P ⊃ N) is usually perceived to be absurd (in the section "'Possibility entails necessity' is not absurd"), why the entailment from necessity to possibility (N ⊃ P) is usually perceived to be trivial, and how Hegel's dialectical account of modality revises our common-sense understanding of these entailments (in the section "'Necessity entails possibility' is not trivial"). I then outline two versions of modal transitivity: the access version, where necessity amplifies possibility by bringing access to otherwise inaccessible possibilities buried under the surface of this actual world (in the section "The necessity-access model"); and the production version, where necessity amplifies possibility by producing new possibilities that would not otherwise be there (in the section "The necessity-production model"). In a final section, I argue that Hegel's theory of modal transitivity is especially applicable to the domain of aesthetics as the free play of necessity and possibility, where spirit shines through the various mediums of the sensuous (in the section "Modal transitivity and aesthetics").

Hegel's bi-conditional account of possibility and necessity

One way to interpret Hegel's *Aufhebung* generally, and this statement "possibility and necessity are only seemingly different" specifically, is to view

Hegel as being involved with complex analysis about the logical nature of bi-conditional entailment. With the statement "possibility and necessity are only seemingly different," Hegel's point is not that possibility and necessity dissolve into complete, abstract identity, as if the two concepts were utterly the same. What Hegel has in mind, instead, is that the differences between the two concepts can only be understood from the entailment of each in the other. Dialectical thinking is, in this way, a detailed exposition of the nature of the bi-conditional relation. The reason why possibility and necessity only seem to be different is because each reciprocally entails the other. This makes possibility and necessity oppositional but at the same time co-relational. Insofar as each is, so is the other, in the specific sense that being possible entails being necessary, and being necessary entails being possible. The process of sublation, where each side is both the opposite of the other side as well as the emergence of the one as the other, is the process of speculative bi-conditional entailment, where each is the condition of the other to the point at which differences submerge into each other, with the result that the conditioning of each is the advancement (the rising up) of each as the other.

The task of analyzing possibility and necessity dialectically is the task of coming to terms with the interlocking meaning of each side of their bi-conditional entailment. When divorced from each other, the entailment from possibility to necessity appears to be absurd and the entailment from necessity to possibility appears to be trivial. This is the case because, as long as the two entailments are not brought together dialectically as a co-entailment, necessity appears to be an absurd condition of possibility, in the sense that the mere conjecture of the imagination necessitates whatever fanciful thoughts one has automatically into actuality; and, on the other side of this, possibility appears to be an obvious condition of necessity, in the simple sense that whatever is necessary must also be possible. But Hegel proposes that these entailments cannot be divorced from each other. When they are brought together dialectically as a bi-conditional, the entailment from necessity to possibility no longer appears to be absurd and the entailment from possibility to necessity no longer appears to be trivial. Let's begin with $P \supset N$ and show that this is not absurd. Then let's look at $N \supset P$ and show that, because the other side is not absurd, this side is not trivial, but has instead the exciting consequence that necessity turns out to amplify possibility.

"Possibility entails necessity" is not absurd

In a famous passage from the *Encyclopedia Logic*, Hegel also criticizes the entailment from possibility to necessity that most people would find absurd:

> Even the most absurd and nonsensical suppositions can be considered possible. It is possible that the moon will fall on the earth this evening, for the moon is a body separate from the earth and therefore can fall downward just as easily as a stone that has been flung into the air; it is possible that the Sultan may become Pope, for he is a human being, and as such he can become a convert to Christianity, and then a priest, and so on … Anything for which a ground (or reason) can be specified is possible. (EL 216)

As long as possibility remains merely formal and indeterminate, everything is boundlessly possible. The possibilities are boundless only because they have no association with necessity at all beyond the formal law of non-contradiction, and so their actualization is merely contingent. Even the most nonsensical suppositions are formally possible in this way. These suppositions become absurd, however, when we associate them with necessity. Of course it is formally possible that the moon could fall on the earth this evening. But it is equally absurd to assert that because this is formally possible, it is also therefore necessary for it to happen in actuality. Formal possibility is significantly different from necessity in this way. To assert that there is an entailment from the mere possibility of something to its necessity in actuality is to misunderstand the free openness of the imagination, on the one hand, and the determinate limitations of necessity, on the other.

In claiming that "possibility and necessity … are only seemingly different," Hegel does not endorse this direct and simple interpretation of the entailment, where possibility is open to everything and anything whatsoever, but if captured by necessity, forces the most absurd possibilities to emerge into actuality. What he does endorse, instead, is a real, determinate modal dialectic from possibility to necessity, where the possibilities of something are at first dispersed in others and can be actualized only through conditions, which require structures of determinate necessity within the environment of the real world. Aristotle has already called this type of possibility *dunamis*, but what is exciting, original, and controversial about Hegel's theory is that possibility and necessity are dialectically intertwined.

In contrast to what Hegel describes as the nonsensical version of the entailment, where the mere possibility of something necessitates itself in actuality, we can outline two dialectical ways to view the entailment as not being absurd: (i) All possibilities are necessary, but not necessarily actual; and (ii) for a determinate thing to be actual, it must become actual through conditions that are at first dispersed in others.

(i) All possibilities are necessary, but not all possibilities are necessarily actual: This variation assumes that all possibilities of a given determinate range necessarily exist, and that if any one strand of this range were not to exist, the actualization could not occur. This interpretation relies on a distinction between existence and actuality. All possibilities necessarily exist, but not all possibilities are necessarily actual. Most lie dormant under the surface of what is immediately actual. Most remain embedded in conditions and require necessity to bring about possibilities that are otherwise inaccessible and only distantly foreseeable. Based on this model, unicorns, monsters, and worlds where gravity goes up, all must exist. But their mere existence does not necessitate their actualization. This variation starts from the insight that every and any possibility whatsoever is constitutive for this actual world, that everything within an infinite range of possibilities must be given from the outset as part of the fabric of reality, and that any process of actualization whatsoever depends upon the equal existence of what does not become actual. By distinguishing between existence and actuality in this way, we are able to make sense of Hegel's claim that possibility and necessity only seem to be different. Insofar as possibility entails necessity, we can say that every possibility necessarily exists, even though only some of these become actual while others do not.

This variation explains why possibility entails necessary by proposing that although possibility must become actualized, there is no one determinate possibility that must become actual any more than any other. The moment of necessity in this variation appeals to the basic assumption that there must be something rather than nothing. But the variation also avoids the controversy that what is merely possible is necessary, or, similarly, that only certain determinate possibilities must become actual. Its strength relies on a level distinction between two types of determinateness, one where something must be determinate because being is, but also where there is no specific determinateness that should or must become actual. Since actuality immediately appears before us as the fact of existence, actualization cannot not happen; but this necessity where actualizing possibility cannot not happen makes no further claim to determinism, other than that something of a set of possibilities must become actual.

Or, Hegel might mean the more contentious claim that to posit a determinate range of possibilities commits something of this range to become actual. A claim like this one is more contentious because of its proximity to the claim that if something is merely possible, then it must become just that determinate actuality and nothing else (as if the mere possibility of a unicorn were to necessitate actual unicorns). But if Hegel is saying that only something of a given range of possibilities must become actual, but not that any one of these specific possibilities must emerge into actuality, then Hegel's position is still consistent and not absurd. One might say that the existence of the possibility of unicorns necessitates the actuality of horses, and likewise that the real actuality of horses posits in counter-distinction a whole variety of mythical equine possibilities, as a necessary contrast between the actual and the merely possible. This interpretation operates from the insight that actuality and possibility posit each other, are bound together, and that this bind is the bind of necessity. Houlgate makes sense of this insight by explaining that determinations, such as peace and war, require a conception of each other to be meaningful. Although we might think of war as the opposite of peace and of peace as its own self-subsisting state of being, the two really require each other, certainly in terms of definition, but also in terms of possibility, in that the possibility of being at peace is also a condition for the possibility of being at war. If the one is actual, then the other must of necessity be possible.[6]

(ii) For a determinate thing to be actual, it must become actual through conditions that are at first dispersed in others: This explanation of the entailment from possibility to necessity exposes the necessity in the movement from conditions to further actualities. In the "Actuality" chapter, Hegel claims that if something is a condition for something else, then it is an immediate actuality whose content as actual entails the possibility of other actuals (SL 483, WLII 209). If something initial results in actuality, this is because all of its conditions have become completely present. The possibility entails its necessity in the sense that possibilities are viewed as conditions that enable further actualizations through necessity. For example, insofar as a seed is the possibility of an oak tree, the mere possibility of the seed contains within it a teleological agent that directs the seed to emerge as the further actuality of the oak tree. Growth, movement, and vitality are all, in this sense, concrete expressions of the entailment from possibility to necessity. To posit the possibility is to posit the necessity of further actualizations as well. Of course, since the seed might not become an oak tree—because this process requires specific conditions (water, rich soil, sunlight, etc.), which might or might not come about—the entailment from possibility to necessity is not a forgone conclusion. But since the seed is a possibility only because it is the possibility *of the oak tree*, and since the oak tree can only emerge into actuality by way of a specific set of conditions, possibility really does entail necessity, not in the absurd way that the mere possibility of something entails its actualization, but in the real sense of possibilities, which through conditions necessitate the actuality of others.

"Necessity entails possibility" is not trivial

Non-dialectical thinking dictates that the entailment from necessity to possibility (N ⊃ P) is trivial, in the sense that being possible is an obvious and insignificant condition of being necessary, as per the analytic axiom of necessity, which states that "if p is necessary, then p is possible." However, on Hegel's account, just as the entailment from possibility to necessity turns out not to be absurd, so too the entailment from necessity to possibility turns out not to be trivial. There is, in effect, a direct correlation between the non-absurdity of P ⊃ N and the non-triviality of N ⊃ P. Because of the ways we have already outlined of viewing P ⊃ N coherently, we end up with a more robust theory of N ⊃ P, one in which necessity brings access to pre-existing possibilities but also generates possibilities that are not otherwise there.

In contrast to the version of the entailment that most people would find to be trivial, I put forward two interrelated models of the entailment from necessity to possibility. The first is the "necessity-access model." This model relies on the theory that necessity leads to access points for possibilities that are already embedded in the actual world as pre-existing and only need to be drawn out to be accessed concretely. The second model is the "necessity-production model." This model relies on the thesis that necessity creates new possibilities *ex nihilo*, that Hegel's one-world system is self-generating. While these two models are not mutually exclusive, the subtle distinction between accessing possibilities that are beyond barriers as opposed to producing possibilities that seem to come from nowhere helps us to uncover some of the important details of Hegel's vision of modal reality.

The statement "possibility and necessity are only seemingly different" is less problematic if we interpret the bi-conditional entailment between possibility and necessity to mean either:

1. All possibilities are necessary, but not all possibilities are necessarily actual. This leads to the necessity-access model. Based on this interpretation, the other side of the entailment (from necessity to possibility) comes from the insight that necessity brings access to otherwise inaccessible possibilities, which already exist.
2. It is necessary for possibility to become actual, but not in any specific way. This leads to the necessity-production model. Based on this interpretation, the other side of the entailment (from necessity to possibility) comes from the insight that necessity produces possibilities that are not otherwise there.

The necessity-access model

Let's borrow from the logical concept of transitivity to explain how this model of necessity-access works. Rudimentary logic shows us that if A entails B, and B entails C, then, by transitivity, A also entails C (as with the valid form of a pure hypothetical syllogism). Necessity brings access to possibilities in a similar way. What is immediately actual has embedded within it possibilities that only appear as possibilities when they are the conditions of others and of themselves as others. Necessity is the middle term, the directive at B to which

A would submit if A entails C. The point is not so much that the possibilities at C are only accessible through the middle term, but that when possibilities are embedded in the conditions, mediation is what draws them out. There are almost always other ways to access possibility than by the specific content of any one middle term. Still, as a basic generality, modal transitivity outlines the movement of conditional mediation for possibility. Although C might be accessible by any number of conditions or sets of conditions (B1, B2, and so on), it is nevertheless the necessity of any one of these that brings access to the possibility. Without this middle term, however flexible and fluid the alternative options of its determinate content might be, further possibilities cannot come about in actuality.

We can make sense of modal transitivity from Hegel's example of the seed growing into a tree. While it has real possibilities of its own, the seed does not have access to the same region of possibilities that it would find in itself as the tree. The seed cannot bud seeds, grow green leaves, or reach out to the sun. But through modal transitivity, the seed carries in it the tree's regions of possibility as well. Since these possibilities are only latent in the seed, the seed goes through the process of satisfying the conditions that would bring the tree about. By following the paths of its conditions, the seed gains access to possibilities that are already there, but that remain embedded and unrealized until the conditions are satisfied. These deeper layers of possibility that underlie the immediate actuality are part of the constitution of what things really are. Although they are not literally actual in the most immediate sense, unactualized possibilities exist in the depth of the conditions.

Depth and latency refer to similar processes of modal transitivity. Depth refers to the distance between something initial and the possibilities that it could come to access through conditions. Budding seeds or growing leaves are immediate possibilities in the tree, which, however, maintain depth insofar as they are also mediate possibilities in the seed as well. Depth is an explanatory concept for why possibilities that might seem absurd and definitively unactualizable nevertheless exist under the surface of what is immediately actual. When we claim that certain possibilities are absurd and definitively cannot be actualized, what we really mean is that these possibilities are so deeply embedded in the conditions that they appear as if insurmountably distant, as truly miraculous and strange. Latency, on the other hand, refers to the existence of possibilities that have not yet become realized in the conditions. Although growing leaves is a possibility in the seed itself, this remains latent in the seed, as a standing reserve is at-the-ready but has not yet fully come about. Although the child has a capacity to play the piano, this ability remains latent unless she learns from her instructor and practices consistently. Depth and latency have a layering effect. Not all potential actualities have the same amount of depth or carry the same latency within them. There is a certain layer of depth when the husk of corn grows from the seed in the field. But there is a deeper layer at work when the corn is ground into cornmeal, and this, in turn, gives energy and vitality to the people who eat it. The possibility of such vitality in the people is a possibility that already lies latent in the seed.

Modal transitivity appears not only in natural teleological examples, such as in the seed as the possibility of the tree, but in a much larger sense, as the basic movement of any condition whatsoever. Conditions are immediate actualities that have embedded within them the mediate possibilities of other actuals. To be a condition is to be the state of affairs of a relay process between necessity and possibility. The access-version of this supports the interpretation that while conditions are always only immediately this and not their others, in reality they are already disposed to be others, because in the immediate content of what they are lies the determination that they will become otherwise. In this sense, the possibilities embedded within conditions are merely dormant and at-the-ready. By going through the work of necessity, one comes to awaken possibilities that are already there.

The necessity-production model

Let's now turn to the necessity-production model of the entailment from necessity to possibility.

Proponents of the necessity-production model propose that although possibility must become actualized, there is no one determinate possibility that must become actual any more than any other. While the necessity-access model assumes that the possibilities are already embedded in the conditions, the necessity-production model presents the thesis that necessity itself generates new possibilities. The locus of the possibilities then lies not in the thing in question whose possibilities are presupposed from the outset as pre-existing, but in the power of necessity to manufacture possibilities that are not otherwise there. A does not already entail C (assuming that it can meet the requirements at B1, B2, and so on); necessity produces possibilities in the process of material actualization that are not otherwise there. In this sense, formal logic cannot fully anticipate this version of necessity since an act of creation can go in many different directions, since the results cannot be presupposed as embedded in the initial thing in question, and since the semantics of access cannot fully explain how the possibilities come seemingly *ex nihilo* into actuality.

From the terms of the necessity-production model, the seed does not automatically find the possibilities of the tree in the necessity of the soil, but risks that it might go in multiple directions from the soil. It finds in the soil the possibilities of itself that are the other of itself through growth, transformation, and adaptation. In this sense, the seed does not already have the possibilities of the tree latent in its own possibilities as the seed. Necessity is rather the source of contingent new creation. This version is less teleological and more open to indeterminateness and random selection. It also maps onto evolutionary theories better than the access-version might appear to do. Production is still about necessity, however, because there are only certain ways to establish a position that would lead in such indeterminate directions.

Hegel probably has both of these models in mind when he argues that possibility and necessity are not really opposite concepts, but that each entails the other. While there are subtle ways in which each model falls into conflicts with the other, we can interpret both of them together as offering a robust account of a generative bi-conditional entailment between possibility and necessity. When Hegel claims that "possibility and necessity are only seemingly different," he exposes a very large consequence about the nature of modal reality: it is necessity that entails the proliferation and plurality of possibilities.

In an attempt to present a few concrete examples from one specific sphere, I will turn to some suggestive remarks about the relationship between modal transitivity and aesthetics. I want to stress, however, that Hegel's theory is much broader than as an application to art alone. It applies to education in the sense that the restrictions of instruction bring about the possibilities of a learning process. It also applies to politics in terms of rights and laws, and ultimately to a deep ontological foundation about modal reality in general. What follows, then, is a sketch of the modal underpinnings of aesthetics, with the aim of showing one way out of many ways to apply this insight from the "Actuality" chapter. Necessity plays the role of dividing the possible from the actual. This one world contains every possibility within it. However, the world is divided and in conflict with itself. Even though every possibility exists in the expanded sense of the actual world containing everything whatsoever, not every possibility is actual *in the immediate sense*. Necessity compartmentalizes the possible from the actual. This saves Hegel from the threat of modal indeterminacy, as outlined in the Introduction of this book.

Modal transitivity and aesthetics

In the "Introduction" to his *Lectures on Aesthetics*, Hegel proposes that art should be treated scientifically. Although art appears to be involved with themes of chance, caprice, and whimsical imagination, as well as with aesthetic concepts such as the beautiful, the sublime, and the mimetic, which seem to be detached from the precise measurements and calculations of the natural and mathematical sciences, Hegel proposes, nevertheless, that the history and development of art unfold scientifically, that is, from the terms of necessity, and that art serves an important function, alongside religion and philosophy, as the exposition of spirit in the sensuous. According to Hegel, the various mediums of art (architecture, sculpture, painting, music, poetry, etc.) share the special quality of presenting spirit through the mediation of sensuous material. Spirit shines through the stone and gravity of architecture; it shines through the clay and tools of sculpture; it shines through the paint and canvas of painting; it shines through the instruments and voice of music; and it shines through the images and forms of poetry. Hegel divides the mediums of art into three historical periods. He argues that in the initial symbolic period spirit appears more sharply and definitively through the medium of architecture, that architecture then gives way to sculpture in the classical period, and that painting, music, and poetry become foundational for the romantic period of Hegel's time.

Hegel's discussion of the relationship between necessity and art primarily revolves around the necessary stages of development of spirit in the sensuous. But the connection between necessity and art also reveals that Hegel's theory of art as spirit in the sensuous is at the same time a theory of modal transitivity. Art opens up a "supersensuous world"[7] from the constraints and limitations of material necessity. The restrictions in the material are, in effect, a gateway for the further, transitive possibilities of spirit. That spirit rises up out of the material finds its modal equivalence in the amplification of possibility from the limitations of necessity.

Art movements demonstrate a wide variety of patterns and degrees of necessity as constraint, from strict adherence to classical ideals of symmetry and beauty to the more chaotic dissonance of atonal music and contemporary art movements that break from such classical ideals. For example, the constraints of an English sonnet can be construed to produce aesthetic contemplation that might not otherwise come about. To compose an English sonnet, the poet cannot write in an arbitrary way but restricts herself to the structure of the poem, to three quatrains and one couplet, to the rhythm of iambic pentameter, and to the conventional rhyme scheme of abab cdcd efef gg. But what is more important than these constraints, one could say, are the possibilities for aesthetic contemplation that come from these constraints. Adherence to the rules of the sonnet produce a specific character of beauty from the balance of the rhyme and measure. Although the precise coordination of rules might seem to go against the connotations of the merely possible as that which is open to anything and everything whatsoever, the formal constraints of a sonnet nevertheless lead the poet to a medium that one might not be able to approach by other means.

The thesis from modal transitivity extends as well to other forms of poetry. What makes a sonnet different from a haiku is the difference of necessity in the poems. The classic haiku has only three lines with a 5-7-5 syllable structure and typically conforms to the content restrictions of describing the experience of nature. These constraints reach a different domain of possibilities than what the constraints of the sonnet can reach. In other words, one requires various types of necessity for the proliferation of various types of possibility. We can say generally that each medium of art, and each sub-movement within it, and even each original style from each artist and each piece of artwork explore a different type of necessity and amplify, in turn, whole sets of possibilities which are uniquely aligned to the constraints of their medium.

In these examples from poetry, I emphasize the formal aspects of the necessity—the syllable structure, the rhyme scheme, etc. But this does not mean that necessity is always formal, or that modal transitivity requires a clear separation between form and content, where strict adherence to formal necessity generates new possibilities of content. Following Hegel's explanation in the "Introduction" to the *Logic* about how form and content mutually generate each other, we can see how both formal and content restrictions lead the poet to the sensuous expression of spirit, how the cultivation of the necessity, essentially, constructs the further possibilities of spirit, and how this is also equally the result of form and content together. It is *the medium itself*, not only the formal aspects, that must adhere to constraint for the sake of otherwise unobtainable developments of spirit. Art shares an important affinity to modal transitivity in this way.

One can find an almost self-conscious preoccupation with the very nature of necessity as constraint in art from contemporary art movements that aim to undermine classical ideals of symmetry and order. *A Void*, the lipogram novel by the Oulipo writer Georges Perec, which omits the letter "e" from the entire book, can be read as a meditation on the mechanics of constraint for the production of possibility. The Dogma 95 movement also contributes to an artistic demonstration of how necessity entails possibility. "The Vow of Chastity: Dogma Manifesto" establishes ten rules for filmmakers to follow in order to produce dogma films. It is certainly up for debate whether constraints such as no artificial lighting, artificial music, genres, or superficial plots could generate new possibilities for realism in film, but this, in any event, is the aim of the movement. These aesthetic examples expose how the free play of constraints leads to the imaginative creation of new possibilities as well as a theoretical realm of pure freedom. Their underlying aim is to expose the mechanics for how to generate possibilities. They thereby demonstrate the vast and complex concentration of possibility in actuality.

Art is exemplary in this way. Each medium sets up a specific range of constraints for the sake of new creation and further access to possibilities in the sensuous. Each work of art carries within it an adherence to rules that equally venture to expose the massive depth of possibility that lies directly under the surface of this actual world. One could say that aesthetics is the free play of constraint and possibility, whereas other spheres of life engage in the relationship between constraint and possibility with a concrete seriousness, without, however, achieving as fluid or far-reaching a movement between necessity and possibility. Art is the embodiment of spirit in the sensuous. Spirit springs forth out of the crude limits of materiality and restriction, out of the words and formal structure of the poem, out of the choreography and limitations of what a body can do in dance, and so on. That art is the free play of the bi-conditional entailment between possibility and necessity is both its advantage and its disadvantage. Art allows us to behold a great variety of constraints entailing possibility. It allows us to embody the spirit in the sensuous. But since it can only establish this through what Kant calls "purposiveness without a purpose,"[8] one could say that it only reaches certain domains of possibility through only certain types of constraint. This is the modal articulation of why Hegel claims that art is in a way lower than religion and philosophy. Art has the advantage of being able to explore the great depths of possibility from the material of the immediately actual. But it can do this only from the terms of one or another medium, and only as the free play of purposiveness that has no real force because it cannot fully make these possibilities emerge, but can only invoke them through image and feeling.

5

Leibniz, Hegel, and Deleuze on Incompossibility

The connotations of absolute necessity, which we established at the end of Chapter 3, position Hegel's theory of modality quite close to Spinozistic necessarianism. Spinozistic necessarianism, a prominent interpretation of Spinoza's modal ontology from around the time of Leibniz (1646–1716), draws from the supposition that since God is co-extensive with all of nature, every event is preordained and predetermined, and contingency itself is not a viable modal concept.[1] But in what follows, I argue that his vision of a dialectic between absolute necessity and absolute contingency saves Hegel from the charge of strict determinism leveled against Spinoza. What Hegel's modal ontology proposes, instead, are the exciting results that this actual world contains within it the most complex variety and abundance of possibilities, that this abundance comes as the result of a totalizing contingency, but also that most of what this actual world contains remains embedded in conditions and requires necessity to bring about otherwise inaccessible and unforeseeable possibilities.

Hegel's dialectic between absolute necessity and contingency offers an alternative account of the ontological status of unactualized possibilities than the account that Leibniz offers with his theory that God actualizes only the best of all possible worlds. It might seem that the primacy of absolute necessity as that which being always is exposes Hegel to a threat which Leibniz has made every intention to avoid. And yet, the contingency consequence of Hegel's dialectic leads him to what I believe is a genuine thesis about the abundance of possibility and nature of freedom, a thesis which offers a striking revision of Leibnizian perfection. Hegelian perfection maximizes possibility in one actuality, not by way of the exclusion of other less possible worlds, as Leibniz proposes, but rather by way of the real existence of the possible *qua* the possible, which can, to a limited extent, irrespective of contradiction, come to the surface of actuality.

First, I will summarize some of the main concepts of Leibniz's possible world theory—i.e., his principle of perfection, his distinction between absolute and hypothetical necessity, and the difference between compossibility and incompossibility. Then I will analyze two versions of the incompossibility problem and speculate about how Leibniz would have answered these challenges. The middle sections of this chapter establish what I see as Hegel's response to the incompossibility problem. Hegel articulates the problem through the interaction of his two interrelated conceptions of possibility, possibility as alternatives and possibility as a degree of quantity. By establishing Hegel's argument for why all possibilities must exist, through the interaction between these two conceptions of possibility, this chapter claims that Hegel's revision of Leibniz avoids some of the problems that Leibniz's modal ontology faces. The chapter also turns to Deleuze's answer to the question, why cannot all incompossible worlds also come into existence along with the actual world? I argue that from the perspective of Hegel, Deleuze's conception of the inclusion of the incompossible is too radical and has gone too far.

Leibniz and the thesis that God has actualized the best of all possible worlds

Leibniz claims that God has actualized the best of all possible worlds. This means that the world we live in is the most perfect of all worlds. This also means that God has chosen from an infinite variety of other worlds. The claim exposes a complex relationship between actuality and possibility. The world we live in is not the only possible world that could have been. God could have chosen a world that functions differently, with a different set of physical laws, a different trajectory of historical events, or a different cast of creatures. But God nevertheless chooses this world because, based on Leibniz's thesis, it is the most perfect of all worlds.

By claiming that God has actualized the best of all possible worlds, Leibniz establishes a principle of perfection and at the same time secures a moment of freedom and contingency in his system. If an infinite variety of other possible worlds were not projected in God's mind, then this actual world would not obtain perfection because it would not have an infinite variety of imperfect worlds to exclude. God picks this world from a magnitude of others as an expression of perfection. If God had not chosen among many, this world would not be relatively more perfect.

But this also means that the actual world is contingent. Because God could have chosen another world instead of this one, the world we have, and the events that occur within it, could have been otherwise. When we reflect on this, however, Leibniz's point about freedom might seem to be a specious amendment to God's omnipotence. After all, if God always brings into actuality only that which is most perfect, and if individual substances always act only in accordance with this principle, it might seem, as a number of prominent interpreters of Leibniz including Arthur O. Lovejoy, Nicholas Rescher, and David Blumenfeld have argued,[2] that Leibniz's allusions to freedom and contingency are not entirely genuine. However, Leibniz clarifies that God also chooses the principle of perfection, suggesting that God is indeed free to choose from any world at all, but ultimately, of free will, chooses to make the best one actual.

That God's creatures are free as well is perhaps a harder conclusion to justify. In the *Discourse on Metaphysics*, Leibniz says that they are inclined toward perfection rather than that they follow this principle of absolute necessity (DM 70). Agents pursue, according to Leibniz, goals that seem to be for the best, and pursue them from what seems to be their own volition. However, from God's perspective, the agent's volition is determined and couldn't be otherwise, since what an agent does is always for the best. Whether this is a satisfying answer or not, the claim that God has actualized the best of all possible worlds nevertheless leaves us with a distinct modality between the certainty of perfection, the exclusion of other possible worlds, and the role of freedom and contingency that comes along with this.

Leibniz's thesis stands in stark contrast to the threat of Spinozistic necessarianism. Spinoza represents for Leibniz an absolute determinism (TH 239). Because substance for Spinoza cannot depend by definition upon another for its existence, there can only be one substance, God, who, extended through attributes and expressed through modes, is the coincidence of all of nature. Since God is perfect, and since it is more perfect to be actual than to be merely possible, everything possible is actual. God is, therefore, the instantiation, through pantheism, of every possibility in actuality. Since God extends through all of nature, God does not project unactualized possibilities standing in reserve as a remainder. But this also obfuscates the distinction between actuality and possibility. If God is co-extensive with all of nature, there is no place for unactualized possibility. In contrast, Leibniz avoids this complication and rejects Spinozistic necessarianism by arguing for an infinite series of unactualized possible worlds projected in God's mind.[3]

Absolute and hypothetical necessity

Division thirteen of the *Discourse on Metaphysics* supports the conclusion that there is genuine freedom in this actual world by positing a distinction between two types of necessity (DM 70-1). On the one hand, Leibniz defines absolute necessity (he also calls this metaphysical necessity) as that the contrary of which would imply contradiction, such as the squaring of a triangle or the proposition that two plus two equals five.[4] However, Leibniz claims that much of our experience falls under the category of contingency, in the sense that it would not be impossible if the contrary were to have existed instead. Adam-the-sinner (PE 29) and Caesar-crossing-the-Rubicon (DM 71) exist in this world, and yet there would be no contradiction if their contraries, Adam-the-non-sinner or Caesar-not-crossing-the-Rubicon, were to have existed instead. If their contraries were impossible, this would return Leibniz to the threat of Spinoza, to the conclusion that all events must follow the strict course of fate, that God has already determined the future direction of all things without the chance of contingency. By claiming that their contraries are not impossible, Leibniz demonstrates contingency and thereby complicates the theory that God necessarily brings only the best of all possible worlds into existence. On the one hand, contingent things follow a course of events that is certain, since God always knows what will happen. On the other hand, God's creatures are still contingent in a restricted sense, since God chooses them freely and lets the creatures of this world choose for themselves what is always the most perfect (DM 70).

One might assume from this that there is no concept of necessity behind why contingencies exist and why their contraries do not exist. However, Leibniz proposes that contingent actualities are still about truth and that as contingent truths they follow the logic of hypothetical necessity (or what he also calls physical necessity) (DM 70-1). The contrary of hypothetical necessity does not imply contradiction. But it still implies imperfection. Since the actual world would be less perfect if Adam-the-non-sinner were to have existed instead of Adam-the-sinner, the contingent facts of existence are implicated in necessity after all because the world would be less perfect if these things were to have been otherwise. "For even if the world is not metaphysically [absolutely] necessary," Leibniz explains in "On the Ultimate Origination of Things," "in the sense that its contrary implies a contradiction or a logical absurdity, it is, however, physically [hypothetically] necessary or determined, in the sense that its contrary implies imperfection or moral absurdity" (PE 151).

Blumenfeld articulates this point about hypothetical necessity quite well in his essay "Freedom, Contingency, and Things Possible in Themselves." Blumenfeld explains that if God always actualizes what is most perfect, then Leibniz must rely on hypothetical necessity rather than absolute necessity. The projection of other possible worlds serves as evidence that God could have chosen otherwise. However, if God's aim is to bring into actuality the most perfect of all possible worlds, his free choice binds him by hypothetical necessity to the principle of perfection. If the actual world is absolutely necessary, then "everything that occurs," Blumenfeld explains, "occurs necessarily."[5] But if the actual world is hypothetically necessary, the position attributed to Leibniz, then everything occurs necessarily if and only if God prefers perfection.

The reason why God excludes alternative possibilities is not because he is incapable of bringing these worlds into existence, but because the mere fact of their existence would mar the actual world and reduce it to imperfection. God brings into existence the best combination of substances, and thereby the most possible reality in one actuality, only if God excludes alternative worlds from existence. By projecting an infinite variety of alternative worlds, Leibniz retains a concept of freedom and exposes the open multiplicity of the possible while at the same time arguing for the necessary exclusion of these projected worlds, since their co-existence would throw the world into imperfection.

Leibniz and the ontological status of unactualized possibilities

Leibniz claims that it would not be a contradiction if God were to have brought a different world into existence instead of this one. He supports this conclusion by recognizing that God houses infinite possible worlds in the mind. Leibniz thereby upholds a subtle distinction between existence in God's mind and existence in actuality. Leibniz does not flesh out this distinction fully, but his theory nevertheless operates from the division between these two realms of existence. Because he supports his conclusion in this way, one inevitably asks, what is the difference between existing in God's mind and existing in actuality?

The actual world exists both in God's mind and in actuality, while other possible worlds exist only in God's mind. God chooses the actual world and brings it into existence. This endows it with a higher ontological status than other possible worlds. The actual world is, in effect, rooted more deeply in existence. The kind of existence that is only in God's mind is merely a projection of the existence of less perfect worlds.

Leibniz's position on whether alternative possible worlds exist or not is in some ways ambiguous. In paragraphs 43 and 44 of *the Monadology*, for example, he claims that mere possibility contains truth and reality insofar as it is an element that contributes to the constitution of essences. "God is not only the source of existences, but also that of essences insofar as they are real, that is, or the source of that which is real in possibility ... without [God] there would be nothing real in possibles, and not only would nothing exist, but also nothing would be possible (PE 218)." On the face of it, passages such as this one suggest that, for Leibniz, there is something weighty and real about the unactualized possibilities in God's mind. They function to not only demonstrate God's freedom, as the debris that is left of what God could have chosen, but also contribute to the understanding's grasp of essences. But if we put this ambiguity aside, Leibniz is in other ways quite clear: unactualized possibilities do not exist in as significant a way as the actual world exists. Certainly, they have some ontological status as projections in God's mind. But one could equally say that outside of being projections in this way, unactualized possible worlds do not really exist, not in the way that actuality exists.

The compossible and incompossible relation

God projects every iteration of everything, from the minutest details of how particular events could have gone otherwise to the most magnificent alternatives of science fiction worlds that function from radically different sets of physical laws and contain every imaginable form that life could take. By actualizing the best of all possible worlds, God excludes all iterations of other worlds from existence, causing a relation of divergence to occur. However, by bringing this one actual world into existence, God also causes a relation of convergence to occur. Leibniz uncovers an unusual relation, compossibility, by claiming that everything in this actual world is an expression of God. In *Philosophical Papers and Letters*, he writes:

> Not all possibles are compossible. Thus, the universe is only a certain collection of compossibles, and the actual universe is the collection of all existing possibles, that is to say, those which form the richest composite. And since there are different combinations of possibilities, some of them better than others, there are many possible universes, each collection of compossibles making up one of them.[6]

One might think of the universe as an odd collection of independent objects, people, forces, colours, shapes, and so on, but Leibniz suggests with his unusual relation of compossibility that the universe is "all of one piece, like an ocean" (TH 131). An ocean has an indeterminate variety of waves. Waves are of various sizes and strengths, and peak and crest at various tempos. But each wave is the ocean itself. Certainly, each piece of a puzzle contributes to the puzzle as a whole, and there is a way in which a puzzle is nothing other than the totality of its pieces. But a wave is not just a piece of the ocean. Each wave is the whole ocean, only from one or another angle. Similarly, Leibniz says that each individual substance is at the same time an expression of the whole world.

Compossibility presents a logic in which each monad expresses everything, and in which the whole universe, insofar as it is a world, is thoroughly interconnected.[7] In the "Monadology," Leibniz argues that each thing is a perspective of everything. "Every body," he writes, "is affected by everything that happens in the universe, to such an extent that he who sees all can read in each thing what happens everywhere, and even what has happened or what will happen."[8] But there is a limitation to this. Each monad expresses the whole world that comes along with it. But this means that each can express only that with which it converges. A monad does not express those other worlds which could have been but which diverge from this one. Incompossibility, then, has to do with infinite sets of infinite series that diverge from this world. Since God only projects the possibility of these other worlds, the ontological status of unactualized possibilities is, for Leibniz, of a lower grade than that of the actual world.

The compossibility relation, therefore, replaces the concept of actualized possibility in the sense that this actual world is a thoroughly interconnected series of individual substances. It also explains the interior connections within an infinite variety of other possible worlds in the sense that each alternative world is also self-coherent and all of one piece. However, the compossibility relation is not synonymous with the concept of possibility in the sense that although God projects many possible worlds, these alternative worlds are not compossible with the actual world.[9] Each possible world is compossible with itself. This is, in effect, what makes each world a world.[10] But each world is also incompossible not only with the infinite variety of other possible worlds, but with the actual world as well. One must then think of expression rather than identity relations between things. Each monad expresses the whole world with which it stands connected, but some do this more clearly than others, leading to a subtle theory of individuation. However, compossibility is not the same as possibility; otherwise, the unrestricted inclusion all possible worlds would lead to the compossibility of every other world with this world, which, as John Earman emphasizes in his reading of Leibniz,[11] would render this actual world into a massive compossible relation of disharmony and chaos, verging on modal indeterminacy.

Why do other incompossible worlds seem to be better than this one?

Leibniz's unusual relation of compossibility, and the equally unusual relation of divergence that follows from this, leads directly to the incompossibility problem in the literature on Leibniz. On my estimation, the two most prominent versions of the problem stem from the questions: (1) If this is the best of all possible worlds, then why do other incompossible worlds seem to be better than this one? And (2) why cannot all incompossible worlds come into existence as part of the constitution of this actual world? As a way to elucidate the incompossibility generally, I will briefly outline these two versions of the problem, although it is the second version that I want to take up in detail and compare with Hegel and Deleuze.

Leibniz can be seen to anticipate the first version of this problem through his responses to the question: if this is the best of all possible worlds, then why does it seem to contain so much pain and suffering, so many natural and manmade disasters, and why can we imagine other possible worlds that do not exhibit these problems? There are various ways to interpret Leibniz's response to this challenge. At one end of the spectrum is the being-over-nothing interpretation. This interpretation proposes that the only reason why this world is better than other worlds is because this world is actual while other worlds are merely possible. At the other end of the spectrum is the essence-in-existence interpretation. This interpretation proposes that some amount of pain and suffering must be included in this world in order to harmonize the simplest means with the most complex results.

The being-over-nothing interpretation appeals to the same modal commitment that Saint Anselm appeals to in his ontological argument when he claims that it is more perfect to be actual than to be merely possible.[12] Being is better than non-being, existence is better than non-existence, and actuality is better than mere possibility. Because this is the world that is, it is relatively better than other worlds which could have been but are not.[13] The prescriptive basis of this claim, that it is better to be than not to be, establishes nothing more about perfection than that actualized possibility stands higher than unactualized possibility. From the terms of this interpretation, Leibniz is not claiming that the content of this world is any better than other worlds. He is only claiming that its status as actuality makes it relatively more perfect than any world whose status is merely possible. One advantage of this interpretation is that Leibniz thereby avoids the problem of evil. If God has actualized the most perfect world, then why does evil seem to exist in this world? Why do some of the other possible worlds seem to be morally better than this one? In response, Leibniz writes in the *Theodicy*: "It is true that one may imagine possible worlds without sin and without unhappiness ... but these same worlds again would be very inferior to ours in goodness ... You must judge with me *ab effectu*, since God has chosen this world as it is" (TH 133).

The disadvantage of the being-over-nothing interpretation, however, is that it can offer no criteria for calculating perfection other than the ontological privilege of actuality over possibility. But Leibniz also argues that perfection has to do with maximizing possibility in actuality and that maximizing possibility has to do with quantifying essence in existence. Taking up the other end of the spectrum, then, is the essence-in-existence interpretation. This is the theory that by actualizing the best of all possible worlds, God has brought into existence as much of essence as can be brought into actuality. Leibniz states this prominently in his 1697 essay "On the Ultimate Origination of Things": "Of the infinite combinations of possibilities and possible series, the one that exists is the one through which the most essence or possibility is brought into existence" (PE 150).

This interpretation operates from a definition of essence in terms of individual substance as that which can take on predications but which cannot be the predicate of another subject. To bring essence into existence is to express clearly and without confusion that the predicate is contained in the subject. Essence is about the expression of something insofar as it is the expression of everything, that is, insofar as each substance includes the whole universe within it. "We may call," Leibniz writes in division sixteen of *Discourse on Metaphysics*, "the concept that includes everything we express and that expresses our union with God himself ... our essence" (DM 76). Perfection, then, has to do with the degree of essence in existence. An actuality is more perfect, the more of essence it contains in its existence. Leibniz also explains this in terms of possibility. That which is the most perfect contains as much of possibility as can be contained in its existence. In one of the most revealing sentences of "On the Ultimate Origination of Things," Leibniz defines essence in terms of possibility and defines existence in terms of perfection or degree of essence: "Just as possibility is the foundation of essence, so perfection or degree of essence (through which the greatest number of things are compossible) is the foundation of existence" (PE 151). In this sense he uses the terms essence and possibility interchangeably. It follows that since God is the only substance whose essence and existence are the same, God contains not only a degree of essence, but the entirety of essence, in one existence.

In the being-over-nothing interpretation, the only reason why this world is better than other worlds is because actualized possibility is of a higher status than unactualized possibility; but, in the essence-in-existence interpretation, the actual world is better than other possible worlds because the maximum amount of essence exists in this world. If the actual world is the most perfect world because it contains the most essence in existence, then there are many permutations of possibility, some with more essence, some with less essence, and God has actualized that one series of permutations with the most possibility in it.

We might think of how an individual thing could have a maximum amount of possibility within it, but Leibniz suggests that it is not a question of each individual thing being the best of all, but rather of the whole aggregate or series of things existing together as the best of all possible worlds. In a different way from how the being-over-nothing interpretation does this, the essence-in-existence interpretation also thereby attempts to avoid the problem of evil. "Some adversary ... will perchance answer ... that the world could have been without sin and without sufferings; but I deny that then it would have been *better*. For it must be known that all things are *connected* in each one of the possible worlds" (TH 131). Although in other possible worlds there might have existed individual things that are more perfect (or creatures that sin less), Leibniz maintains that the reason why God has brought this world into existence is because the best possible aggregate of things exist within it. The question of maximizing possibility is then not about how each individual thing expresses possibility in actuality, but rather about how this actual world expresses the most possibility as a series of things.[14]

To bring about as much of essence in one existence, that is, to express as much of possibility in one actuality, Leibniz subscribes to the strategy of simplest means for maximum ends. "God ... has chosen the most perfect [world]," Leibniz writes, "that is to say the one that is both the simplest in hypotheses and the richest in phenomena" (DM 64). Perfection is as much about simplicity at the starting point as it is about complex variety in the result. In division five of the *Discourse on Metaphysics*, he offers a number of examples and metaphors to explain this strategy. He says that to act with perfection is like the geometer, the architect, the householder, the machinist, or the author who, each in their own way, produces the richest and most abundant outcome from the simplest means and with the least effort (DM 62-3). In "On the Ultimate Origination of Things," Leibniz says that if someone were to direct us to walk from place A to B without designating any specific path, we would prefer the "easiest or shortest" path. Invoking a modal version of Ockham's razor, he proposes that if we were to think of the actual world as one single plot of land, we would prefer to build "the most pleasing building possible" on this land because this is the minimum cost for the maximum effect. And within this building (since there would only be one building), it would follow that we should find a way to maximize the space within it, to build as many rooms as possible, and to make each room as elegant as possible (PE 151).

Nicholas Rescher offers an insightful analysis of the opposition inherent in the strategy of simplest means for maximum ends. Perfection comes from a dialectic that synthesizes the simplest means, or laws as Rescher describes them, with the richest ends and the most abundant phenomena. "It is," Rescher writes,

> a striking feature of Leibniz's criterion of world perfection that the two operative factors are *opposed* to one another and pull in opposite directions ... Clearly, the less variety a world contains—the more monotonous and homogeneous it is—the simpler its laws will be; and the more complex its laws, the greater the variety of its phenomena must be to realize them. Too simple laws produce monotony; too varied phenomena produce chaos. So these two critical factors of order and variety are by no means cooperative, but stand in a relationship of mutual tension and potential opposition. Perfection overall is, for Leibniz, a matter of combining harmonizing and balancing two distinct factors.[15]

Rescher proposes that, for Leibniz, perfection comes from the harmonizing of an otherwise oppositional dualism between simplicity and complexity. Rescher could have taken this dialectical analysis further if he had concluded that as opposites these two factors are indeed in cooperation with each other, that perfection is produced, essentially, from the cooperation of integrating simplicity at the start with complexity at the end. This will become, as we will see, a major commonality between Leibniz's and Hegel's approach to perfection. Looking ahead, we can already visualize in Hegel's theory of conditions a similar strategy of simplest means for maximum ends, one that realizes perfection through the integration of opposites, of actualities that are also the possibilities of other actuals. But this commonality will only become apparent through an analysis of the incompossibility problem in Leibniz and a proposed revision of this problem in Hegel.

Why cannot all incompossible worlds come into existence?

A second version of the incompossibility problem raises further challenges, however, challenges which Leibniz cannot be seen to have fully anticipated. When we ask the question, what is the principle behind why worlds diverge and why cannot all incompossible worlds also come into existence?, we realize that there is an ambiguity at the heart of Leibniz's distinction between the compossible and the incompossible. On the one hand, Leibniz privileges the maximum amount of possibility in his conception of perfection. The world that has the most possibility within it, in other words, the most essence in existence, is the one that God actualizes. However, on the other hand, with the incompossibility relation, God excludes the vast majority of what is possible through the process of a bifurcation with the actual.

Commentators of Leibniz have come up with two primary interpretations to establish a rationale for the origin of this division, and therefore to save Leibniz from the inconsistency. Some commentators—including Jaakko Hintikka, Benson Mates, and Nicholas Rescher[16]—propose that the principle of non-contradiction is the main reason behind why God excludes incompossible worlds from existence. This is often referred to as the logical interpretation. Although God projects, for example, an alternative world where Adam does not sin, it would be a matter of contradiction if the actual world were to include both Adam the sinner and Adam the non-sinner. Moreover, since the whole world in which Adam does not sin would come along with Adam the non-sinner, it would be incomprehensible to imagine how these worlds, as well as an infinite variety of others, could combine together. If what is possible must adhere to the principle of non-contradiction, what is impossible, then, is that which logically contradicts itself. The world in which Adam does not sin cannot be made compossible with the world in which Adam sins, much in the way that, logically, A cannot be both A and not A.

As James Messina and Donald Rutherford present it in "Leibniz on Compossibility," the strength of the logical interpretation is that it precisely delimits the compossible from the incompossible and thereby secures Leibniz's modal ontology from Spinoza's.[17] But the logical interpretation also exhibits a number of shortcomings. Foremost, it places a restriction on God in the sense that God can then only actualize what is logically coherent, and must admit a limitation insofar as he cannot also actualize across contraries. As Deleuze emphasizes in his reading, the logical interpretation conflicts not only with God's unlimited power, but also with the whole notion of the compossible relation. The reason why compossibility is an unusual relation, says Deleuze, is because its source of individuation comes through expression and relative clarity rather than through the more intuitive thesis that things are simply different in kind from other things. Although Leibniz frequently endorses a principle of non-contradiction in his analysis of formal and absolute necessity, where it would be a contradiction if the opposite of a necessity were also to be true, his privileging of hypothetical necessity further suggests a more complicated approach to non-contradiction, one that, at least to some extent, upholds contraries without the erasure of non-contradiction.

The other primary solution to this second version of the incompossibility problem comes by way of the lawful interpretation, popularized by Gregory Brown, Ian Hacking, J. A. Cover, and John O'Leary-Hawthorne, among others.[18] Leibniz claims that when God brings the actual world into being, he brings with it not only an infinite series of compossible substances, but also a series of laws that help to form the world's consistency and determinateness. Commentators who appeal to the lawful interpretation propose that the physical laws of each world are what divide compossibility from incompossibility. One advantage of this interpretation is that if laws are the real source of the compossible–incompossible division, this frees God from the otherwise problematic limitation that he would not be able to actualize across contraries. For the lawful interpretation, there is nothing inherently inconsistent about a world that contains contrary iterations of the same individual substance. It is simply a matter of whether a given set of laws can harmonize the perfections of the world better than others. Laws are what limit compossibility and distinguish the compossible from the merely possible. They are the basic order of things. The interconnections of compossibility and the whole notion of a world as well would be inconceivable without the laws that govern these connections. Brown's version of the lawful interpretation emphasizes this well when he claims that perfection and harmony are in direct ratio with each other. The more harmony there is, the greater the perfection, and vice versa. Brown cites Leibniz's argument in division six of *Discourse on Metaphysics* that God always attributes an order to everything and that nothing could ever be extraordinary or chaotic for God (DM 63-4).[19]

The lawful interpretation also exhibits a number of shortcomings. Messina and Rutherford point out that it does not fully target the problem of incompossibility as it is presented in the question why cannot all possible worlds come into existence along with the compossible world?[20] It leaves a certain mystery at the origin of the division between the compossible and the incompossible. It is this mystery that any purported solution to the incompossibility problem was supposed to have explained. Listing an algorithm of laws instead of the principle of non-contradiction leaves the lawful interpretation vulnerable to the same ambiguity that had presented us with the problem in the first place. After all, if God's aim is to bring into actuality the maximum amount of possibility, then why would he not be able to envisage a series of laws that maximally include the possible in the actual, rather than a series of laws that overtly exclude most of what is possible? The logical interpretation, at any rate, has at least offered an answer to this question. By making all iterations of all substances "per se" compossible, as Messina and Rutherford mention in objection to a thesis put forward by Cover and O'Leary-Hawthorne,[21] proponents of the lawful interpretation are forced to rely on an undefined algorithm to explain divergence, one that is presupposed rather than explained.

In "Leibniz and the Puzzle of Incompossibility," Jeffrey K. McDonough also critically analyzes the logical and lawful interpretations. McDonough claims that the incompossibility problem (he calls it a "puzzle") arises from the incompatibility between the "thesis of maximization," which states that God creates as much being as he can; the "thesis of independence," which states that a substance cannot depend upon another for its existence but receives its existence only from the essence of its form; and the "thesis of alternatives," which states that because God is free, he chooses between an infinite variety of possible worlds.[22] McDonough argues that the logical and lawful interpretations can only establish compatibility between two of these theses, but cannot establish compatibility between all three theses at once.[23] The logical interpretation makes sense of the theses of maximization[24] and alternatives, but at the expense of independence. The logical overstates the role of the compossible connection within each world, making it impossible for God to entertain the transworld substitution of a substance with other possible world mates, thereby disregarding one of the main tenets of substance for Leibniz, that its essence cannot depend upon another substance for its existence. In contrast, the lawful interpretation makes sense of the theses of independence and alternatives, but at the expense of maximization. The point from McDonough is that if laws were not to dictate the order of each world, God would be free to maximize even more possibility. I find Rescher's and Brown's analysis[25]—that a harmony between simple laws and complex phenomena is what generates perfection—more convincing than McDonough's analysis on this particular point. But McDonough's overall intention is certainly well-founded of exposing why both the logical and the lawful interpretations cannot make sense of all three theses at once.

There is a branch of McDonough's alternative proposal, the "packing strategy," that effectively addresses this version of the incompossibility problem. This version of the incompossibility problem stems from the question, *if this world is perfect because it contains the most possibility within it, then why does it exclude alternative possible worlds from existence?* Would it not be more perfect to affirm the existence of these worlds too? McDonough's packing strategy proposes that God intends "to pack" as much of essence into one existence, much like a traveler packs a bag as tightly as possible to optimize carrying the most things in the least amount of space.[26] In response to what he calls the debate about "infinite idealist worlds" (which comes from a theory of incorporeal substance in later Leibniz), McDonough visualizes a significantly inclusive version of compossibility, but one which still retains the exclusion of infinite sets of alternative possible worlds, and so continues to save Leibniz from the threat of Spinoza, and, in a different sense, the threat of modal indeterminacy.[27] McDonough entertains a compossible world that maximizes possibility by including all of the various perfections of every other possible world within it. It contains all of the possibilities of other worlds, but since these other worlds do not contain it, this massive compossible world still excludes the imperfection of all other worlds. In this sense, it maximizes possibility by including all of the incompossible worlds within it. But, at the same time, it satisfies the criteria of alternatives because all other worlds diverge from it by being exclusive rather than inclusive. It is, in effect, better than all of the others simply because it includes them even while they exclude all other worlds from their series. Hegel's response to the incompossibility problem in Leibniz follows along these same lines. I will develop Hegel's argument as a way of exploring this third version of the incompossibility problem.

Hegelian revisions to the incompossibility problem in Leibniz

Hegel's "Actuality" chapter offers a powerful way of describing the incompossibility problem and an important solution to this problem as well. The version of the incompossibility problem that presents itself in Hegel has to do with recognizing that there are really two separate conceptions of possibility at work in Leibniz's claim that this is the best of all worlds. These two conceptions of possibility are (1) possibility as a disjunction of alternative actualities and (2) possibility as a degree of quantity.[28] The first conception of possibility operates from the insight that although possibility offers a boundless multiplicity of alternatives, whatever emerges into actuality excludes most of what is possible at the point of actualization. Actualization is, from this disposition, the upholding of one actuality at the expense of a multiplicity of other possibilities. These alternative possibilities then stand against this actual world as counterfactual iterations of what could have been actual if actuality were to have been otherwise.

However, possibility as a degree of quantity offers a second, equally plausible conception of what possibility means. We experience degrees of possibility in our everyday lives. We say that certain decisions contain more possibility within them and that other decisions take possibilities away from us.[29] This conception of possibility operates from the insight that more or less possibility can exist in one actuality, that there are ways to harness higher concentrations of possibility, and that if being is the coincidence of actuality and possibility together, then this world is the most perfect of all worlds, not because it excludes other worlds from existence, but because it includes within it every possibility whatsoever.

One of Hegel's primary contributions to the incompossibility problem in Leibniz comes not only from his recognition that these two conceptions of possibility are distinct from each other and should not be conflated with each other, but also from Hegel's account of how possibility as a degree of quantity develops as a natural consequence from the more immediate, obvious conception of possibility as alternatives. Hegel's articulation of the incompossibility problem in Leibniz takes the following form: On the one side, Leibniz's claim that God actualizes the best of all possible worlds assumes a conception of possibility as alternatives. God actualizes the best of all possible worlds by excluding the contrary nature of possibility from actuality. That world is best that excludes the alternative possibility of other less perfect worlds. However, on the other side, Leibniz's claim assumes a conception of possibility as greatest quantity. To bring about the best of all possible worlds, God actualizes the greatest amount of possibility in one reality. This division of possibility is problematic because one is left to wonder why God would exclude possibility if the aim is to bring into existence the maximum quantity of possibility in one actuality. In one usage, Leibniz wants to include the possible to the greatest extent. However, in the other usage, he wants to exclude the possible from the actual. The charge against Leibniz, then, is that these two conceptions of possibility are left conflated and unanalyzed, and that this is what causes the incompossibility problem to arise in the first place.

What is innovative about Hegel's modal ontology is that he not only anticipates these two conceptions of possibility, but also exposes how one conception develops from the other as an argument. Hegel's modal argument begins from an initial conception of possibility as alternatives, similar to Leibniz's thesis of infinite sets of infinite world. From this disposition, there is no way to actualize the form of possibility itself, but always only some aspect of the possible at the exclusion of others. This exclusion of the possible from the actual is what Leibniz refers to as incompossible worlds. But Hegel then claims—and this is the important point—that what is excluded from actuality becomes reintroduced as a greater quantity of possibility in actuality. Hegel's conception of possibility as a degree of quantity builds directly from his initial conception of possibility as the projection of alternatives.

We can view the development from alternatives to greatest quantity as Hegel's solution to the incompossibility problem in Leibniz. Although unactualized possibilities are at first excluded from the actual, they also become reintroduced through conditions to maximize possibility. A stone is just a stone. But it is also the possibility of all sorts of other actualizations, of becoming a statue, a street, a hammer, and so on. Activating conditions means including possibilities that at first remain under the surface of what is immediately actual. In this way, Hegel offers a solution to the incompossibility problem by arguing that the two conceptions of possibility are not only distinct, but that a maximum degree of possibility is produced from the initial conception of possibility as diverging accounts of actuality. What diverges as the merely possible becomes reincorporated as contrary possibilities in an expanded version of actuality. Since conditions are both possibility and actuality together, to actualize across conditions is to actualize a larger extent of possibility's negativity and therefore a greater degree of possibility in actuality. Leibniz, on the other hand, keeps these conceptions of possibility separate from each other. He claims that the world God brings into existence is the one with the most possibility within it, but also that all other possible worlds diverge from it at the point of actualization.

Everything turns on the question of the ontological status of unactualized possibilities. For Leibniz, unactualized possibilities exist only as projections in God's mind and otherwise do not exist. But Hegel states clearly in his explication of formal possibility that possibilities really do exist as part of the basic constitution of modal reality. "Everything possible has existence" (SL 480, WLII 205). Hegel thereby upgrades the ontological status of possibility from mere projection in God's mind to real existence. Of course, Hegel is not the only thinker since Leibniz to have prioritized the role of unactualized possibility. Deleuze also elevates the role of possibility through his reconception of modal concepts in terms of virtuality. Borges's wonderful story, "The Garden of Forking Paths," presents a literary account of what it would mean to bring all possibilities whatsoever into existence. Philip K. Dick's vision of science fiction, especially in his novel *The Man in the High Castle*,[30] promotes a subgenre of alternative history, along with other novels such as Eric Flint's *Sixteen Thirty Two*. As Rescher points out,[31] this revival of the status of unactualized possibility has also gained scientific backing in recent years through the theory of quantum mechanics, and has gained credence as well in the analytic tradition through David Lewis's plurality of worlds thesis. The debate between Meinong, Russell, and Quine over the question of non-existent objects offers yet another fruitful discussion of the ontological status of unactualized possibilities in the analytic tradition.

Hegel's claim that every possibility exists is nevertheless original because it leads to an immanent theory of perfection that makes the two conceptions of possibility productive and cogenerative. Leibniz argues that there is an untraversable distance between the actual world and other possible worlds. Hegel claims that this distance is immanently traversable. Embedded unactualized possibilities exist under the surface of what is immediately actual. Although ultimately absolute modality collapses all distances between actuality and possibility, this type of modality nevertheless arises from real modality, which still maintains a modicum of distance through its explanations of how this distance is traversable. Unactualized possibilities still remain embedded in the conditions of immediate actualities and need to be drawn out to become actual. Hegel offers this, in effect, to satisfy Leibniz's requirement that not all possibilities can be actual. Actuality and possibility become transitional concepts. Since conditions are both actuality and possibility together, they allow for an amount of freedom and choice, insofar as what is immediately actual might or might not come to the realization of further actualizations.

Hegel offers a one-world theory. This world, the only world there is, contains an infinite variety of other world-like composites within it. For Leibniz incompossible worlds transcend the actual, but for Hegel, world-like composites stand embedded within the determinate content of this actual world, even though they are in large part inaccessible from the immediate state of conditions. Accessibility and inaccessibility, then, replace incompossibility. Leibniz's multi-world system is transcendent; God chooses the best of all possible worlds; all other worlds are products only of God's mind and therefore transcend this world and do not exist in a significant ontological sense. Hegel's theory presents a dialectic account of transcendence and immanence; an infinite variety of possible world-like composites exist in a significant ontological sense as immanent to this world.

If we put aside these differences, the perfection thesis that comes from Hegel's theory of conditions can still be explained in terms of Leibniz's strategy of simplest means for maximum ends. One comes to maximize possibility by actualizing across the negativity of what is immediately present, thereby reaching an actuality of the whole process. As the conditions fall under, the actuality that rises up is both itself and possibility because it has come to include within itself the negative aspects of possibility. Actualization is of a higher status the more effectively one can actualize the negative side of possibility, and not only the positive. Since this process requires precision, in his descriptions of real necessity, Hegel can be seen to explore a special version of Leibniz's simplest means for maximum ends, one where particular conditions lead to maximum effects, and where from the sacrifice and integration of immediate actualities, a rich actualization of the whole possibility process appears before us. Like Leibniz's metaphor of a single building with the most elegant rooms, Hegel's material actualization follows directives in the conditions toward a certain concentration of possibility in one actuality. Even if we put aside Leibniz's theological assumption that God measures all things and brings only the best combination of these into actuality, we can still recognize in Hegel the theory that actuality is perfect because there exists an infinite concentration of the possible in it. Higher and lower concentrations of possibility appear through various patterns of conditions; but there is also a way in which this world is always perfect, whether what has emerged contains a high degree of concentration or not, simply because all possibilities exist within it. And yet, by upgrading unactualized possibilities to the status of existence, Hegel significantly changes the conceptual terrain between necessity and contingency. For Hegel, what is immediately possible in actuality must undergo a series of limitations and determinations in order to induce the further possibilities of others. But this also means, as we have already discussed in Chapter 4, that the same entailment that begins from the restriction of possibility leads to otherwise inaccessible possibilities.

The objection from the inclusion of divergence

If accessibility replaces incompossibility, one consequence of this is that Leibniz's diverging incompossible worlds become, for Hegel, immanently accessible within this actual world. But this would seem to leave Hegel with one massive compossible world of disharmony and chaos, returning us to the threat of modal indeterminacy.[32] Before conceding this, however, we should recognize that Hegel does not exactly collapse the incompossible into the compossible, but rather complicates the relation between the two by arguing that the incompossible is part of this world. Making the incompossible into an infinite compossible relation is problematic since there are then no compartments between things, no guiding rules, and therefore no limitations to generate determinate being. But since accessibility replaces incompossibility for Hegel, to include divergence does not exactly mean to make one massive compossible world. The accessibility relation establishes real limitations, however temporary and transgressible, which lead, in turn, to compartments, distinction, and determinate being.

As another iteration of this objection, proponents of Leibniz might also object that actualizing contraries in conditions does not really commit Hegel to the claim that all possibilities exist, nor does it commit him to the thesis that what diverges nevertheless exists in a greater sense of reality. Actualizing through conditions could be viewed, in contrast, as a normal effect of convergence in a world. In this sense, the contraries that become integrated through conditions are not unactualized possibilities but are rather part of the existence of what is already actual. To actualize conditions is, from this objection, not really about actualizing alternative worlds. It is just a feature of the actual world and part of the mechanics of convergence.

I maintain that either this facet of the objection does not take Hegel's strong claim about absolute necessity seriously enough, or revising the term "compossibility" to include conditional actualization commits Leibniz to a controversial interpretation of his modal ontology. If actualizing conditions is a normal effect of convergence in a world, Leibniz would have to be committed to the claim that the actual world expands (and contracts) in perfection. But there are significant debates about this in the literature on Leibniz, referred to as the question of the striving possibles.[33]

The objection from modal elitism

The debate outlined in Chapter 4 about whether possibilities already exist or whether necessity produces them *ex nihilo* as a spontaneous act of creation presents us with a second, interrelated debate about whether we are able to make normative claims about the degrees of possibility. To claim that a tiger has a numerical degree of possibility that is greater than that of an inert stone does seem to be problematic since it could be construed as modal elitism, where instantiations of actuality are stronger or better than others and where weaker instantiations should be avoided or discarded. This objection has the following form: Let us assume that greater possibilities exist under the surface of this actual world, and that the function of necessity causes the actual world to undergo a constant pressure to expose as much of possibility as can be presented in actuality. Would it then not be better, as a normative claim, to secure in actuality a set of entities that embody higher concentrations of possibility than to let lower concentrations of possibility linger in the actual? To state this again in ontological terms, does being emerge into actuality to greater extents as it realizes higher forms of life, culture, and rationality? And if this is the case, are we able to measure entities in the world in terms of possibility in such a way that we might direct actuality toward more possibility, and thereby exclude what we deem to be lower concentrations of possibility?

Since the theory of modal optimism extends beyond Hegel in many ways, let us put aside the question of whether Hegel himself might have endorsed this description of modal elitism, as some of his writings about history and religion suggest, and focus instead on what the exact connotations of a dialectic between absolute necessity and contingency reveal to us. The objection from modal elitism assumes that entities in the world can be endowed with numerically higher or lower concentrations of possibility, and then asks about the precision or imprecision of such an evaluation. But there is a misconception at the root of this interpretation of possibility concentration. Possibility becomes concentrated in actuality, not because numerically better entities exist at the expense of others, but because actualization exposes itself to the negativity of the possible, to the promise that this actual world contains within it what it is not. Possibility can be measured not so much in terms of stronger, better, or more complex positive entities, such as one might claim about a tiger as opposed to a stone. One can draw up a case for how certain entities contain more possibility within them. But to do this is to stop short of the contingency consequences of absolute necessity. To do this is to stop short of the ontological claim—which is really the heart of the matter—that this actual world is all of one piece because it contains everything whatsoever as part of what it is, without excluding the possible at all. The ontological significance of modal optimism comes from a recognition that this actual world contains not only higher or lower degrees of concentration but total concentration. While the local level of relative necessity and real conditions faces a number of difficult objections about how to evaluate degrees of possibility when determinate actualities are placed in contrast with each other, the ontological level does not face these same problems. Insofar as each entity—the tiger, the mouse, the stone, and so on—is being itself, each contains within it the total concentration of possibility. Insofar as each is the radical contingency of pure being, each contains the same amount of possibility, both sides together, that is, the maximum amount, the totality.

A more significant version of this objection presents itself when we recognize that the ontological level threatens to trivialize the consequences of modal optimism by reducing all determinate things to the pure possibility of being. If all determinate beings can refer back only to the pure being of absolute possibility, as Hegel's final conclusion to the "Actuality" chapter suggests, this would seem to take away the meaning of the distinction between necessity-access and necessity-production. Then the same conclusion can be made about dark matter as can be made about the complexities of human civilizations and the vast varieties of ecosystems produced from nature. Then it does not make a difference whether sets of possibilities entail huge networks of otherwise inaccessible possibilities or whether being itself fails to produce even the most insignificant and futile advancements of possibility. Then it does not make a difference whether the immediacy of this actual world resembles a bleak dystopia of grey, one-dimensional, lifeless bodies that have no chance to grasp the immense circuits of life and order that are teeming under surface of the actual world. If being always already contains the most perfect expression of possibility in every instantiation of actuality, this does seem to trivialize the motivation that agency desires the perfection of possibility over any one-sided instantiation in actuality, and that at the broadest ontological level being itself endeavors to express the greatest amount of possibility and to let as much of this emerge at the surface of actuality as can be maintained.

This version of the objection from modal elitism is certainly more serious, if we assume that determinate entities in the world—the stone, the tiger, or anything else—can be measured in terms of the concentration of possibility in actuality. But there are better resources to field this objection when we remember that Hegel is not primarily talking about how determinate entities contain more or less possibility than other entities, but rather that certain structures of organization and processes of actualization bring access to more possibility than others. Take an example from Hobbes, who upholds an inference from the state of nature to the social contract. Although living in a state of nature produces possibilities of war and promotes the freedom to do crime, the set of possibilities that are available for actualization are nowhere near as abundant or far-reaching as the multiple sets of possibilities we gain when we lay down arms against each other and establish rules for civil society. Even though some of the possibilities of a state of nature are lost in the transference, the social contract offers a higher platform for a more adequate expression of the possible *qua* the possible.

Or, to take another example from daily life, one might say that lying in bed in depression does yield a variety of possibilities in its own right, which come from the entailment of the conditions that make depression possible and result in subtle variations of mood and disposition, even resulting in the extreme possibilities of suicide. Depression produces unique possibilities, which happiness, boredom, love, etc. cannot directly approach. Nevertheless, proponents of modal optimism subscribe to the normative claim that the reason why adverse moods or states, such as depression as opposed to happiness, or decay as opposed to growth, are adverse is because they do not produce possibilities as effectively as their positive counterparts. Although depression generates a variety of possibilities for pain, misery, and self-abuse, proponents of modal optimism defend the claim that some forms of organization, such as political, ecological, and aesthetic structures, set up better avenues for possibilities than others. Generally speaking, the modal reason why we place positive and negative evaluations on terms such as happiness or depression is because some states of being increase the ranges and abundances of possibility, while other states decrease them. Since our normative claims arise from our evaluations of how processes of actualization are more or less successful at uncovering latent possibilities, the problematic connotation of modal elitism is then less significant.

Fielding this response to the objection from modal elitism presents us with a hybrid reading between necessity-access and necessity-production, which I believe anticipates some of the most exciting implications of Hegel's dialectic from absolute necessity and contingency. By absolute necessity, every possibility is already embedded in the actual world, and in this one respect, everything that could happen is already predetermined to happen. However, since what absolute necessity includes is the possible *qua* the possible, what is predetermined on the one hand is really open contingency as well. There is an association of linear development from the standpoint of relative necessity. The necessity embedded in the determinate conditions of things requires determinate activation to draw out possibilities that are already present in the thing in question. There is a normative claim attached to this, that certain structures of organization yield more open prospects for possibilities. But the necessity of absolute necessity works differently because it is circular and not only linear. It generates free movement and therefore avoids the problems of evaluation altogether because every set of every series already exists within its field. Actualizations, then, can appear as if from nowhere. They are produced as if from the inexplicable chaos of creation. They already exist only in the sense that everything is, by absolute necessity, already included in and as being. But they can also be produced without seeming to be predetermined, anticipated in advance, or directed by rational evaluations. This is what Hegel means when he claims that being can appeal only to itself, that being is the reason for itself. Necessity generates possibilities. It brings access to what is already there, latent and buried in the depths of the actual. But it thereby also produces these possibilities *ex nihilo* from the indeterminacy of being itself. Like clots or folds in the thrown existence of the actual, possibility *qua* possibility appears through the movement of necessity.

Deleuze and the question of the ontological status of incompossibilities

We can interpret Deleuze as initiating an even more radically inclusive relation of incompossibility when, in his discussions of Leibniz, he inquires about what it would mean to bring all incompossible worlds into existence. This line of inquiry is similar to the inclusive actualization of contrary possibilities that motivates Hegel's theory of conditions in the sense that Hegel and Deleuze both anticipate a model of actualization that recognizes the existence of alternative possibilities as part of the constitution of reality. However, Deleuze's version of this inquiry begins from the claim that pre-individual singularities, in a way similar to Leibniz's monads, exist in a more originary position than individuated things do, whereas Hegel's version arrives at the inclusion of possibilities as a result of his conclusion, as a way of undermining the assumption that the identity of something does seem to exclude its opposite. Deleuze claims that the law of identity and the law of non-contradiction are derivative principles, derived from incompossibility,[34] that singularities take up the more primary position, and that this origin prior to contradiction affirms difference and lets contraries co-exist without exclusionary disjunction. Does Hegel place too much importance on the formal impossibility of actualizing contrary possibilities as what spurs his method toward inclusive substance? Or has Deleuze gone too far in attempting to actualize incompossibles all at once?

On the one hand, as Deleuze remarks, Hegel's treatment of contradiction does seem to be significantly distinct from the kind of affirmative difference that Deleuze promotes. Hegel offers a modal application of this productive thesis about contradiction, insofar as it is the formal impossibility of actualizing contrary possibilities that spurs the actual toward greater concentrations of possibility. Deleuze, in contrast, treats contradiction as a mere derivation of pre-individual singularities. But on the other hand, Hegel and Deleuze can both be construed to come to a strikingly similar revision of Leibniz's incompossibility problem. Both recognize that ontology requires a disposition beyond the conception of things and toward a conception of affirmative multiplicity, where contraries co-exist without becoming excluded from one another. To recognize this commonality between Hegel and Deleuze, it will help to explicate briefly from Deleuze's sixteenth series of *The Logic of Sense*.[35]

In the sixteenth series, Deleuze claims that there are two levels of actualization, one that actualizes across convergences, but another that actualizes across divergences.[36] The first level is the more primary one (in the sense of genesis) because we can see in the actualization of convergences the basic constitution of what a world is and of how it functions. Each world is made up of an infinite series of singularities. Deleuze's theory of singularities comes out of an argument that the transcendental field does not begin from the ego, the individual, or consciousness (as Husserlian phenomenologists often believe), but begins prior to this in a field of pure materiality from which persons and objects of consciousness are merely derivations. This is an important and complicated argument in Deleuze's work, but, for our purposes, we only need to establish that singularities exist at a pre-individual level, that each world is made up of an infinite series of these singularities, and that the definition of world is based on how each series converges.

The first level of actualization corresponds to Leibniz's conception of compossibility as a converging series of pre-individual monads, where each monad expresses the whole world but from a limited perspective. One of Leibniz's great insights, on Deleuze's account, is that since the monad expresses the whole world with which it stands connected, there is a more originary relation than that things are separate from things. The reason why the compossibility relation precedes the principles of identity and non-contradiction is because each singularity is itself an aspect of everything with which it stands connected. Deleuze emphasizes that it is the logic of expression that contains the reason for why identity and contradiction are derivative concepts, and why pre-individual singularities are more originary. Expression is thoroughly inclusive in nature, since even what a monad cannot express clearly is nevertheless included along with what it can express clearly. And yet it still upholds a subtle principle of individuation between clarity and obscurity.

However, when Leibniz says that the monad expresses everything, he only means that it expresses everything with which it stands connected as a world. The relation of inclusion that Deleuze attributes to Leibniz's compossibility only goes so far (LS 172). Leibniz's monad does not express other worlds which are possible but not compossible. Deleuze emphasizes that because of divergence, compossibility is not only the relation of an infinite series, but also the relation of a finite series as well. It is infinite in the sense that each monad expresses the infinite series with which it stands connected. But it is also finite in the sense that it is limited by the infinite divergence of other worlds. Deleuze invokes the image of a summit to describe how each singularity is both the expression of an infinite series that converges in a world and equally the expression of the finite limitation that marks the divergence between one world and an infinity of other worlds (LS 61). We can also make sense of this in terms of basic numbers. If we divide whole numbers into two infinite series of odd and even sets, we can imagine a scenario in which the infinite odds is compossible, and the infinite evens is also compossible, but the relation between the two infinite sets of numbers is nevertheless incompossible, which, in effect, posits a finite limit between the two limitless series.

Divergence, therefore, also marks the division between a small infinite and a large infinite. Although each compossible world is infinite, each is only the small infinite in the sense that its limitless series is also limited by the equally limitless series of others. Since there are infinite sets of infinite series, it is the divergence of incompossible worlds that exhibits the large infinite. But what this interplay between the infinite and the finite also exposes is that small infinites can occur within a large infinity. A large infinity is made up of an infinite set of small infinites, which are each limited by, but at the same time combine with, each other.

Deleuze takes exception to Leibniz's point about the exclusion of incompossible worlds from existence. This is the crucial point of departure from Leibniz, just as it is for Hegel. Deleuze claims instead that one can also actualize across divergences, initiating an affirmation of disjunction rather than a rejection of it. In one of the most revealing passages from the twenty-fourth series of the *Logic of Sense*, Deleuze writes:

> Leibniz ... makes use of this rule of Incompossibility in order to exclude events from one another. He made a negative use of divergence of disjunction—one of exclusion. This is justified, however, only to the extent that events are already grasped under the hypothesis of a God who calculates and chooses, and from the point of view of their actualization in distinct worlds or individuals. It is no longer justified, however, if we consider the pure events and the ideal play whose principle Leibniz was unable to grasp, hindered as he was by theological exigencies. (LS 172)

Deleuze claims that if we leave behind the assumptions about God as an external source who calculates and chooses the most perfect world, we come to recognize a second level of actualization, one that actualizes across divergences and therefore authorizes the co-existence of incompossible worlds. By taking God out of the picture, we extend the original relation of inclusivity to worlds that diverge as well as to worlds that converge. Without dissolving the small infinite into the large, we nevertheless come to actualize across divergence as well as convergence.

What does it mean to make divergence "an object of affirmation?" (LS 114, 172). Does this mean that the world in which Adam sinned can affect the world in which Adam did not sin? If we retain the assumption that, strictly speaking, our world is the only actual one, and that all other worlds which diverge from our own do not enjoy the same ontological status, then the answer must be no. However, once we take God out of the picture, we come to what Deleuze calls the pure events of pre-individual singularities. This leads us to the primary modal problem for Deleuze: what is the ontological status of the disjunction between worlds?

The affirmation of divergence explains how one and the same event can have many different futures. At the moment when Caesar pauses before the Rubicon, he can either cross the river or not cross it. Various compossible worlds come along with each decision. There is the world in which Caesar marches his troops across the river, Pompey flees to Greece, and civil war starts. There is also the world in which Caesar goes alone to Rome, and an entirely different set of events then occur. Now, from the stance of what has already happened, it might seem as if, no matter which event comes about, the opposite of this event cannot also have occurred. But from the stance of the future, that Caesar can and can *not* cross the Rubicon affirms a multiplicity of incompossible worlds. By affirming the divergence of the event, this lets the event be a free act that has an open future. If there is no God who can see everything that will ever happen, then one and the same event can have many different futures, then Caesar can and can *not* cross the Rubicon, and this is not determined ahead of time from some external source, but is instead a free act of contingency generated from multiplicity.

That Caesar crosses and does not cross the Rubicon only becomes contradictory if we assume that because the event has taken its course, the other worlds that diverge are then oppositional and cannot also have happened. But insofar as the event has a future, the possibilities that diverge from the event nevertheless constitute the multiplicity of the event, in much the same way that each compossibility is made up, at the first level of actualization, not of an odd collection of disassociated things but of the entire series of all things that come along with each. That Caesar crosses and does not cross the Rubicon exposes the event as having many futures, which, on its own, is not self-contradictory because the event itself is constituted by this divergence. Like convergence, divergence is also "all of one piece."

To affirm divergence does not mean to reduce all divergence to a series of convergence, as if the affirmation were a matter of making what diverges conform to the given principles of a converging series. To make divergence an object of affirmation is rather to include divergence as divergence, and to think from the terms of an actuality (what Deleuze calls virtuality and what can be attributed to Hegel as the expanded actuality of absolute actuality) that can include the alterity between other worlds as part of the constitution of an event. Just as each singularity expresses the whole world with which it belongs, each likewise expresses a multiplicity of other worlds which diverge from it at the point of actualization. Each singularity belongs not only to that one infinite series with which it converges, but equally to that infinite set of series with which it diverges. Caesar's decision to cross the Rubicon belongs not only to that world where Pompey flees and civil war starts. The decision also belongs to those incompossible sets of worlds where Caesar crosses the river alone or does not cross it at all. If the decision were not also to belong to innumerable incompossibles, the event would have no distinct differences in possibility, and the notion of compossibility itself would break down.

Deleuze ultimately claims that the disposition of things, individuals, personhood, and consciousness results in a derivative way from the synthetic unity of actualizing across divergences.[37] While the first level of actualization yields the analytic unity of pre-individual singularities, where each singularity is an expression of the whole series, the second level yields the synthetic unity of indeterminate and what Deleuze calls vague concepts—not only the world in which Adam sinned or the world in which Adam did not sin, but also Adam the indeterminate who appears as the result of actualizing across the differences of Adam-the-sinner, Adam-the-non-sinner, and an infinite variety of others (LS 114). In this way, the steps Deleuze outlines from the first level of actualization to the second are a proof for why the principle of contradiction and the relation of exclusion that come out of this are derivative relations, relations that presuppose the more originary relation of inclusion. Since the disposition of things appears only in the result of actualizing across divergences, the relation of contradiction appears as only one of many possible relations, and only after one recognizes the affirmation of difference. More than this, since the synthetic unity that makes indeterminate concepts possible is the unity of pre-individual singularities, the indeterminate concepts that result from actualizing across divergence are concepts of these singularities, not generalities in the more traditional sense of genus and instance.

Hegel and the incompossibility problem in Deleuze

Although Deleuze proposes a very different type of argument than Hegel does for a modal ontology that recognizes unactualized possibilities as part of the basic constitution of reality, we can also see in Deleuze's starting point of pre-individual singularities and in Hegel's conclusion from inclusive substance the same powerful insight about the nature of affirmative multiplicity. Hegel's argument begins from the formal impossibility of actualizing alternative possibilities within one actuality, and from the concept of possibility as alternatives. Because something can be identical only with itself, it cannot be both itself and the opposite of itself, at least not formally. But since for Hegel the possibilities of things are always contained in the context of others, literally as the immediate actuality of what these things are not, actualization happens across contraries and from a disposition that is inclusive rather than exclusive. This can be interpreted as Hegel's mediated, indirect solution for how to affirm the existence of unactualized possibility and for how to affirm the divergence of incompossibility as part of the modal fabric of reality. Even though Deleuze offers a more direct, and in a way more radical, theory for why all incompossible worlds come into existence, the two philosophers nevertheless share important ontological commitments.

Hegel and Deleuze both argue for the priority and real existence of unactualized possibilities as constitutive of the actual world. Both present a case for why the possibility that diverges still helps to form our conception of modality. Hegel would have accepted Deleuze's account of why each existent is the expression of totality. Deleuze uses the language of expression and clarity from Leibniz's definition of the monad, while Hegel retains the language of existence and essence; still, the relation of inclusivity, where something is both itself and the other, is an important conceptual point in both arguments. Hegel would have also accepted the claim that modality requires the inclusion of differences which are no longer, strictly speaking, contrary to one another. This results in a logic where contradiction no longer has an exclusionary influence.

Hegel can also be construed to resist certain aspects of Deleuze's argument. Hegel would have resisted the theory that contradiction can only be derived secondarily from a field of pre-individual singularities. Contradiction is rather like a motor that motivates Hegel's central argument. Deleuze's theory of inclusion can be viewed as too extreme when he claims that modal reality begins from pre-individual singularities, and that identity and contradiction are laws that can only govern logic after consciousness and thinghood have been derived in a secondary sense from these singularities.

Hegel would also have resisted Deleuze's thesis that incompossibles come into actuality all at once and without further mediation. By describing a process of material actualization where contraries become integrated to the point of non-opposition and non-contradiction, Hegel recognizes the actualization of incompossibles only to a limited extent. Hegel's premises from Real Modality offer strategies for how to overcome the formal impossibility of actualizing contrary possibilities. However, these strategies limit the actualization of incompossibles because they require mediation, where the reason why immediate actualities are the possibilities of other actuals is because they are conditions, because they go through various sacrifices, transitions, and dispersions in order to sustain in a volatile and temporary way the negativity of the possible. On the other hand, Deleuze claims that because an event can have many incompossible futures, and because these futures really exist in the constitution of the event itself, incompossibles are actualizable all at once and without limitation. That Hegel would have resisted this version of incompossibility is clear enough from his choice to omit temporality from his modal analysis.

While these points of resistance make Hegel and Deleuze incompatible in a number of ways, Deleuze's revision of Leibniz is nevertheless of primary importance for this modal analysis of Hegel. Deleuze makes it possible to anticipate the kind of logic that Hegel presents in the absolute necessity premises of his modal argument. Under the logic of affirmative multiplicity, each thing is both itself and the other of itself, yet this no longer leads to contradiction because the negativity of the possible has become included as what the actual is. In this sense, affirmative multiplicity has removed all contingency from the field, but this only happens because it has come to include all contingencies whatsoever. This necessitates that each existent in the field is both a determinate thing, differentiated from all others, and yet everything that the field could possibly be. This reading of Hegel comes out of Deleuze's ideas about the affirmation of divergence because Deleuze establishes a model for how to think multiplicity and difference that is not under the influence of contradiction. Although Hegel derives this type of multiplicity from an earlier conclusion about the contradiction of multiple possibilities in one actuality, he nevertheless finds as the result of his argument from modality the same position where difference no longer carries over into contradiction.

6

Totality and Transformation: More Objections and Consequences

Modal optimism is the theory that this actual world contains infinite sets of infinite possibilities within it. One of the main objections to this theory comes by way of a challenge about contradiction. If Hegel's accessibility relation stands in for incompossibility, the consequence of this is that Leibniz's diverging incompossible worlds become real and actualizable within this world. But this would seem to leave Hegel with one massive compossible world of disharmony, chaos, and contradiction, or, at any rate, with incompossible worlds compressed within the actual world to the point of breaking the definition of "world." Is Hegel's commitment to the existence of unactualized possibilities a commitment to impossible beings and absurd *aporias*? Proponents of modal optimism upgrade the ontological status of unactualized possibilities by claiming that every possibility whatsoever exists. It might seem as if upgrading the status of unactualized possibilities to the level of existence commits us to the seemingly non-existent objects, events, and worldmates of the pure imagination, such as the visionary creativity of science fiction stories, as well as the more subtle counterfactual projections of other literary genres, projects for us. What is even more problematic, however, is that the immanent conception of modal reality that comes from the co-primacy of possibility and actuality as transitional concepts would seem to promote a very difficult consequence to accept, that contradictions really exist, such as that a square triangle is a real shape or that an event can and must realize all of its possible outcomes. Leibniz effectively avoids these problems by maintaining an ontological hierarchy between the existence of this actual world and the mere projection of alternative possible worlds. Divergence and incompossibility keep the world from splicing together all of the possible iterations of all other worlds and events. This saves Leibniz's theory from the endless contradictions, inconsistencies, and incoherencies that might otherwise seem to come from a modal theory that upholds all incompossible worlds as sharing the same ontological status as the actual one.

One of the primary aims of this book has been to answer the question of how we can conceive of a dialectical account of modal reality, one that does not rely on modal priority or, as in the case of Leibniz, transcendent world separation, but one that nevertheless makes sense as a viable description of modal reality while avoiding the pitfalls of modal indeterminacy. This book explores Hegel's argument that, far from leading to indeterminacy and absurdity, as some critics might assume, the modal contradiction that forms between actuality and possibility makes up a fundamental aspect of modality, leading to a coherent one-world theory that views the modal concepts as thoroughly transitional.

This chapter outlines further objections and consequences to Hegel's theory. Modal optimism faces two more of its most significant objections in determinism and radical transformation. Leibniz's model does not face these same objections since his theory assumes that incompossible worlds diverge from the actual world and do not exist in reality. But to replace incompossibility with a significantly different relation, accessibility, leads to the conclusion that this world is all of one piece in the maximum sense that all fractured world-like composites dividing from this actual world are also part of the basic constitution of this world. We are therefore confronted with an unusual kind of totality. If accessibility replaces incompossibility, then this actual world contains everything and excludes nothing. The consequences of this kind of totality are unusual because if we are no longer able to posit a transcendent realm that stands outside of this actual world, rigidity, on the one side, and absurd transformations, on the other side, would seem to be the basic characteristics of a world that operates from the principles of modal optimism. If this actual world contains an infinite variety of other world-like composites within it, it appears thus as a purely immanent world devoid of exteriority. Because absolute necessity includes everything in every which way, this modal theory must respond to the significant objections: (1) that because it is a totality it suffers from rigid confinement, and, paradoxically, (2) that the most absurd variety of transformations would seem likely to occur within it. Leibniz is safe from both of these objections because he promotes a world-totality that maintains exterior, infinite sets of ontologically diminutive possible worlds. The theory of world-totality that Hegel's argument inspires must account for why total inclusion does not mean fatal determinism and specious freedom. This theory must also account for why such an inclusive principle of connectivity, which lets everything exist together, does not make the transformations occurring within it absurd.

The objection from determinism

The reason why modal optimism is an optimism is because every possibility already exists within the world. Complex varieties of possibility stand latent under the surface of this actual world and are immanently traversable through conditions. But this picture also presents us with the problem of an immanent kind of totality. If there are no other worlds to transcend this actual world, if all world-like composites already belong within this actual world, the question arises of whether this vision of modal reality can sustain a genuine account of freedom. Opponents might object that even though modal optimism celebrates possibility under the rubrics of divergence and difference, the primacy of immanence inherent in Hegel's one-world theory nevertheless leads to suspicions about underlying determinism. Taken to the extreme, Hegel's one-world theory provokes connotations of totalitarianism, authoritarianism, and elitism associated with overbearing political and social structures that cause only certain combinations and avenues of determinate being to realize themselves in actuality.

We have already discussed one version of this objection, the version that Leibniz attributes to Spinoza. If everything possible is already actual, then the world has no chance to be otherwise than how it already is. This version of the objection assumes that although possibility and actuality are transitional concepts, one can still imagine all sorts of possibilities that exceed the extent of actuality and that cannot become present in the world. Determinism then arises because the set of possibilities in actuality is only one set of many possible sets. Since actuality embodies all of the possibilities of the set, Leibniz maintains that there is no principle of movement within this set, and, moreover, that other regions of determinate being are definitively excluded from the actual world. Since other combinations and avenues of determinate being are completely impossible, Leibniz rejects this version of modal reality, where the world contains every possibility, but since the set of possibilities that it contains exhausts itself, it cannot become otherwise.

At first glance, the term absolute necessity suggests to an uninitiated reader of the *Logic* that Hegel's theory of modality is quite close to the kind of determinism that Leibniz would whole-heartedly reject. "Absolute necessity," Hegel claims, "is the truth into which actuality and possibility return" (SL 487, WLII 215). Even if we take Hegel to mean something more subtle than common-sense intuition would admit—which tends to equate absolute necessity with fatal determinism and the untenable thesis that everything possible is actual, predetermined, and cannot be otherwise—the claim that actuality and possibility withdraw into each other still sounds a lot like a kind of rigid totalizing from which there are no further options for things to be otherwise.

This would be a plausible reading of absolute necessity if the only consequence where that possibility necessarily withdraws into actuality. But contrary to this, Hegel claims that actuality and possibility withdraw into each other. He does not put forward the unilateral conclusion that everything possible is actual, but rather the bilateral conclusion that actuality and possibility are mutually transitional. Insofar as the necessity of all possibilities in actuality equally entails further permutations of possibility, absolute necessity enters into a dialectical relationship with contingency, leading to the further consequence that absolute necessity is an agitator of free movement. Modal optimism therefore avoids the objection from determinism because the inclusivity principle of absolute necessity includes not only the possibilities that seem to be apparent in this actual world, but every possibility whatsoever. Taken in this light, totality is not the exhaustion of all determinate being or the foreclosure of some finite set of possibilities. Totality describes a relation that holds the positive and the negative together as one. Absolute necessity is a totality in the sense that it contains the negativity of the possible as part of the constitution of being.

Although the objection from determinism can be disarmed in this way, the more extreme version of this objection, the objection from determinism, mounts a further problem than the one that we have outlined in terms of Leibniz. Determinism poses the problem of whether there is still free choice and free movement in Hegel's theory, or whether conditions block spontaneity and freedom from constraint. When Hegel claims that possibility and necessity only seem to be different, he endorses a kind of freedom that is about the generation of possibilities. To be free means to generate possibilities that are not immediately apparent in actuality. This is what he means at the conclusion of the "Actuality" chapter when he talks about the "free actualities" of "absolute conversion" (SL 487-8, WLII 216). But this modal iteration of freedom also raises concerns about whether we are ever free from the conditions that make us possible, or whether we are always only directed by the forces of compulsive necessity toward greater expanses of possibility in actuality. Since this objection exposes a related debate about the nature of freedom, I will entertain Isaiah Berlin's version of the objection from determinism as it concerns Hegel in his seminal essay "Two Concepts of Liberty."

There are two kinds of freedom in Berlin's analysis. Berlin defines negative freedom as a freedom from the constraints that impede upon an agent's ability to choose between a variety of alternative options.[1] Berlin attributes this conception of freedom to the kind of liberty found in the political philosophies of Hobbes, Mill, and Bentham, among others. It is arguably the most common-sense definition of freedom since it invokes associations of spontaneous free acts of will and, on the other side of this, social laws and physical obstacles that would obstruct movement and decision, such as being confined to a prison. Berlin contrasts negative freedom with positive freedom. He defines positive freedom in terms of self-realization, rationality, and the commitment to follow the commands of one's true self.[2] Whereas negative freedom is a freedom "from" obstacles, positive freedom is a freedom "for" the self-realization of a rational order that comes by way of following social laws and specific directives. Berlin attributes this conception of positive freedom to the kind of liberty found in Kant, Fichte, Marx, Freud, and especially Hegel, who can be seen to epitomize the argument that only by way of necessity and constraint are we free.

As compelling and persuasive as this positive conception of freedom might appear to be, Berlin warns us that the application of positive freedom to determinate spheres of social life, especially politics, can lead to regimes that many of us would consider to be the opposite of freedom, namely to totalitarianism.[3] Since self-constraint is the vehicle for self-realization, when this constraint is applied to others, even if this is applied with good intentions, it effectively undermines the kind of freedom that many of us hold to be dear to our hearts, the freedom not to be restricted by others.

It is certainly up for debate whether Hegel's specifically modal claim that necessity is what generates possibility results in a similar positive conception of freedom that Berlin has in mind, and whether this in turn leads to the problematic application in political life that prepares the way for a rigid and dogmatic adherence to laws and rules. Hegel's modal iteration of freedom as the expression of possibility concentration does seem to share commonalities with Berlin's description of positive freedom. Conditions act as a kind of rational command that limit the immediate range of possibility, and yet since one gains greater concentrations of possibility, what is initially a limitation becomes revealed as freedom.

Berlin's example of a musician under the constraints of composition presents a similar relationship.[4] The musician follows the precise patterns of the composition but, through cultivation and education, eventually internalizes these and no longer views them as constraints or as the loss of freedom. However, Berlin's example falls short, I think, of approaching the modal insights from Hegel, since Berlin does not seem to fully recognize that it is the constraints themselves that make the possibilities what they are. Berlin claims that once she has "assimilated the pattern of the composer's score," the musician no longer views these patterns as commands but internalizes them as part of her own free movement. But what Berlin does not explain is that the pattern of the score is itself the possibility of music, that the musician would not be able to play, and that music itself would not be possible, without some adherence to the conditions, patterns, and constraints that make it possible. This, in effect, is the additional insight that comes from Hegel's modal iteration of freedom, and in one way separates him from Berlin's characterization of Hegel's positive freedom.[5]

Whether modal optimism really presents us with a modal iteration of Berlin's positive freedom is one kind of question. Whether modal optimism disregards all aspects of Berlin's description of negative freedom, or whether gaining access to embedded possibilities can also be construed as spontaneous freedom is another kind of question. I think that there are good reasons to believe that negative freedom is still significantly part of the conceptual framework by which necessity generates possibility, that, in effect, being free from conditions is one of the results of accessing conditions. We can interpret Hegel in this way to conceive of positive freedom as involving a robust conception of negative freedom. Negative freedom is an essential feature for Hegel of any genuinely positive freedom.

One reason why Berlin attributes positive but not negative freedom to Hegel is because of Hegel's obvert rejection of spontaneous freedom in the introduction to *Elements of the Philosophy of Right*. Here, Hegel illustrates how the necessity of laws and rules, and, in a less strict sense, how cultural traditions and intimate social relations help to generate further possibilities of civil society. "The common man," Hegel explains, "thinks that he is free when he is allowed to act arbitrarily, but this very arbitrariness implies that he is not free."[6] Hegel's stance might seem to be overly conservative, like a paternal father curbing the spontaneous freedom of his children. But the sentiment of Hegel's argument is really that freedom comes from the activation of conditions, rather than from an actualization that rejects conditions. Certainly, there is a modicum of freedom gained from the spontaneous act against any conditional necessity. But since following the paths of conditions leads to the actuality of possibilities that are not otherwise accessible, it is often better to forego the immediate possibilities of actuality for the sake of gaining access to higher concentrations of possibility in actuality.

Many passages of the *Introduction to the Philosophy of History* make Hegel look like a communitarian. The state appears as the house of freedom. Citizens follow the commands of the law so that they can maintain a cultivated version of freedom, ultimately to act spontaneously and to lack constraints. We can read Hegel's political treatise as a demonstration of how the state comes to actualize this goal of freedom, first in terms of property, then in terms of rights, and finally in terms of ethical substance and world history. By following the necessary forms of rationality, we release ourselves from the constraints of the external world, precisely where we come to recognize the unity of our particular desires in the universal. This communitarian version of Hegel might seem to be overly conservative and paternalistic, requiring that free action can only come about through the limitation of rules, and that freedom depends upon certain necessary and sufficient conditions of rationality. But we can also recognize a more moderate stance than this. Although there are cases where strict laws might be the only option to establish a position from which we can access possibilities, there are also many cases where something less severe than laws might also work, such as in the sphere of intimate relationships, where a more porous and dynamic set of conditions helps intimacy to flourish.

If conditions are porous and various, and if they sometimes lead to further possibilities for spontaneous movement and free choice, then modal optimism does not obviously succumb to the objections from determinism. As the Hegel scholar Paul Franco effectively demonstrates, Berlin is driven to the conclusion that Hegel cannot think spontaneous freedom from an overly simplistic premise, that rationality commands us in only one determinate way, and not in various ways.[7] If Berlin's conclusion were correct, then when we think from the terms of conditions, there would always be only one precise way to gain access to possibilities that are embedded in the immediacy of actuality.

But since the abundance of possibility and the variety of complexity are some of the primary consequences of modal optimism, there is no reason to come to Berlin's conclusion about Hegel. As we saw from our analysis of the aesthetic spheres of life in Chapter 4, limitations not only deter us but also prepare the way for a more abundant variety of alternative possibilities and for a greater sense of free movement and free choice. The possibilities and alternatives one has in a civil society greatly outnumber the immediate possibilities one has in a state of nature. Likewise, the formal constraint of the sonnet can be interpreted to induce a free state of aesthetic contemplation, giving us a glimpse into the infinite variety of the possible itself. And there is also no reason to conclude—and this is the essential criticism of Berlin—that these richer and more abundant states of alternative choice can only be accessed by way of a singular and therefore determinate pathway through the conditions. If infinite sets of infinite series of possibilities exist embedded in the immediate actuality of this world, we can also assume that there is a vast multiplicity of pathways that bring access to these embedded possibilities.

This is not to imply that negative freedom is all that we have once we gain access to greater concentrations of possibility, or that the whole issue of positive freedom is of only secondary interest. The point is that these positive and negative aspects of freedom are significantly intertwined in Hegel's theory of conditions. Conditional actualization initiates a plurality and abundance of possible outcomes and yet also directs us into the depths of otherwise unreachable contents of being. Certain forms of organization, such as social contracts or the rights of property in terms of political thought, or such as material constraints in terms of aesthetics, open up the immediate surface of the actual to simultaneous collections and gathering points of possibility (i.e., negative freedom), but in doing this they also reach deeper into the conditional expanse by traversing the great extent of being (i.e., positive freedom).

Hegel's language about how absolute necessity lets actualities "go free" (WLII 216) offers textual evidence to support this interpretation that positive and negative freedom are intertwined as part of the conceptual framework of modal optimism. Absolute necessity is the total restriction of all possibilities within a field. But because this amounts to the total inclusion of possibility, the effect of this severe restriction is, rather, an exponential agitation of free movement as well as new formulations of content. What the absolute necessity constraint sets free is the principle of connectivity, allowing everything to connect with everything else without the threat of exclusivity at the law of non-contradiction. Everything can and must connect in every possible way with every other thing, because the only reason for being, ultimately, is being itself. Necessity is, in this respect, a conception of freedom.[8]

This conclusion about the connectivity of everything opens the way for a different kind of objection. Insofar as being is just being, the most radical transformations of free contingency must also be possible. Whereas the objection from determinism claims that there is not enough movement in a world that contains every possibility within it, the objection from radical transformation claims that there is too much movement in a world in which everything connects to everything else.

The objection from radical transformation

Radical transformation refers to a kind of transformation, or becoming otherwise, which appears to be impossible. I will address both a weak and a strong version of this objection. The weak version objects to the claim that determinate entities can become radically different from what they are. The strong version objects to the claim that something unthinkable or unimaginable could occur in actuality. The weak version is weaker than the strong version because it objects to the radical transformation of determinate entities that already exist, or can be imagined to exist, within the content of this actual world. In contrast, the strong version is stronger because it objects to the radical contingency that this actual world could become otherwise in unthinkable ways, even beyond the stance of what is merely possible. Transformations such as a goat becoming a tree or worlds where gravity goes up and monsters roam the earth are at stake in the weak version. Sheer apophatic alterity is at stake in the strong version. First, let us hear the weak objection and responses to this before we hear the strong objection.

The weak version operates from the assumption that, although y either exists or could possibly exist, it is impossible for x to become y if this requires a radical transformation. Someone thinking through this version has the following train of thought: It seems hard to imagine how all possibilities could exist embedded within immediate actuality. It is one thing to say that the possibilities of the tree lie embedded within the possibilities of the seed. But it is much more problematic to claim that any and all possibilities stand within this world, that the seed, for example, could become a goat or anything at all. This world contains untraversable limitations. What is actually here cannot become anything but must follow a set of physical, social, and environmental laws that allow for only limited degrees of transformation. Even with Darwinian principles in play, a goat could never become a tree or something radically different from what it is simply because the range of her real possibilities, embedded in her identity, contains limitations that are in effect insurmountable. While there might indeed be ambiguity and imprecision about the parameters of these limitations, depending on the context and the entities involved, there are nevertheless obvious restrictions to one's possibilities, and it would be absurd to assert otherwise. Could it be that Hegel's accessibility thesis includes some but not all possibilities within it, and that many things that are possible—e.g., supernatural forces or worlds where gravity goes up—do not exist? This limitation, at any rate, would save Hegel from the seemingly absurd consequence that every possibility whatsoever lies embedded under the surface of what is immediately actual.

The implications of accessibility supply us with a good response to the weak version of the objection from radical transformation. Accessibility and inaccessibility, effectively, replace impossibility for Hegel. A given entity can radically transform into anything else, but this is not absurd, because the principle of accessibility carries with it certain real limitations, stabilizing transformations within a normalcy of consistency, while offering internal explanations for why transformations occur when they do occur. Hegel's thesis is less problematic when we take into account the complex barriers that some conditional actualizations must face to turn from existence into actuality. For the seed of a tree to become a goat would require such a distant set of conditions that it might seem absurd even to entertain such a transformation from the disposition of what is immediately actual. Absurdities aside, even the most distant, seemingly improbable possibilities of transformation still exist embedded under the surface of what is immediately actual. In this way, distance and complexity save Hegel from the weak version of the objection of radical transformation.

If we were to accept the limitations that the weak version of the objection proposes, this would return Hegel to Leibnizian exclusion, where only some possibilities exist and are actual while others diverge and do not exist. To accept that certain possibilities are impossible would revert Hegel's claim about absolute necessity to a milder claim about hypothetical necessity. Other worlds would remain not only inaccessible from the actual world, but completely impossible. But I contend that radical transformation should be embraced as a significant consequence of a genuinely transitional conception of actuality and possibility. The consistency factor of conditional constraints mitigates what would otherwise seem to be an absurd conclusion from Hegel, that every possibility—whatsoever—exists. Constraints are constantly in play at a local level, limiting, at least temporarily, what can and cannot be. Being is not determinate being, has no meaning, and is devoid of possibility, only if it is not constantly meditated by the constraints of real necessity. At this local level of real necessity, transformations must still follow the specific patterns of determinate being. Not anything at all, but only specific determinateness, can be produced from actualizing across conditions.

But this limitation is only a limitation of distance and access. If we forget for a moment how complicated and obscure it would be to bring certain actualizations about, radical transformations really can occur. Entities really can become radically different, assuming that the conditions that would make these transformations possible were to come into place. The seed really can become anything at all. Hegel's argument for this comes from his claim that being refers only to itself. Being is the ultimate reason why things are what they are. Being shines through in the seed just as it does in the goat. That the seed might become a goat, or anything at all besides a tree, appears to us to be absurd only because the conditions that would have to come about to gain access to the transformation are more deeply and distantly embedded in the actuality. They nevertheless exist as part of what the seed can be, since the seed is the same as all other determinate things, namely being. This is the powerful consequence of absolute necessity as free contingency.

The strong version of the objection from radical transformation is more difficult to disarm, however. This objection takes the following form: If you claim that every possibility exists in this actual world, then you are also committed to the possibility that this actual world could become radically transformed even beyond all conception. Then you are committed to the paradoxical conclusion that even apophatic alterity—what cannot be thought or said—is also embedded within this actual world. This commitment is absurd, however, since it conflicts in the most basic way with the nature of actualization. Possibility itself represents an unthinkable position. It appears as the absence of all actuality, of any actualization whatsoever, but it appears as such only as the trace of a remainder that could never be set down in the positive terms of actuality because it maintains absolutely no association with actuality. The term "absolute possibility" (SL 486, WLII 213) suggests, nevertheless, that you are committed to such a radically inclusive form of actualization as to one that attempts, however absurdly, to actualize even what cannot be associated with actuality. This is a more severe objection to modal optimism because it operates from a place beyond thought and reality. Would it not be better to recognize that this actual world necessarily excludes the radical transformations of apophatic possibilities?

As background to this stronger objection, we should discuss for a moment the history of the term "apophaticism" in the Western tradition. Plato and Neo-Platonic philosophers (Plotinus, Porphyry, Proclus, and Damascius) outlined a debate about the relationship between being and the One. They discussed questions such as whether the One is beyond being or whether it remains a predicate of being, because nothing can exist beyond being. The Judeo-Christian world bore witness to a theological development of apophaticism in the form of "negative theology." Negative theology is the thesis that there can be no proper name for God and that God can only be described through negation. Some of the main interlocutors of negative theology include Dionysius the Aeropagite, Moses Maimonides, Meister Eckhart, and Nicholas of Cusa. This tradition has helped to shape contemporary discussions about the nature of radical alterity in the work of Levinas and Derrida, among others. The question of apophatic possibility, then, is a modal question about the relationship between being and radical alterity that harkens back to these Greek and Judeo-Christian debates about the inconceivable, the infinite, and the absolutely Other.[9]

There are at least two ways to work around the stronger version of this objection, which states that transformations beyond the scope of what can be thought or named are absurd. The first is to claim that since Hegel consistently emphasizes contextualized actuality as the origin of all further possibilities, possibility is always only an account of actuality, which means that there is no such thing as an inconceivable possibility. Transformations, as radical as they might seem to be, can only occur from the standpoint of what is immediately actual. This actual world can become anything at all, but only insofar as it stands in a coherent relation to itself as immediately actual. Actuality can transform in the most radical of ways assuming that the right conditions come into place to make these transformations happen; however, actuality cannot become other than itself in these transformations. This world could become a world in which gravity goes up and monsters roam the earth, because even the most radically distant possibilities maintain a basic level of consistency—that this world is identical-with-itself, no matter what happens.

It might seem that this first way of responding to the strong objection leaves us with a more restricted form of modal optimism. Our actual world contains every possibility within it if and only if these possibilities can become actualized. Every conceivable possibility remains immanent to this actual world. But to claim that every possibility is immanently conceivable is to exclude sets of possibilities that diverge from this actual world because they are inconceivable. Yet if we take his insights about the origin of possibility in actuality seriously, Hegel's best rebuttal to this might simply be to assert that there can be no such thing as a possibility beyond all association with actuality. Possibilities are always formed from the actualities that precede them.

Although this first way around the objection can be interpreted not to exclude possibilities, it can be seen to inhibit the totalizing effect of absolute necessity. Possibility itself remains impossible. It can only be set down in the terms of the actual. This limits Hegel's theory to only that which can be identified, no matter how radically different, in the actual. We might conclude from this that Hegel is anti-apophatic in the sense that this first response leaves no space for the possibility of what we cannot think or conceive of, that is, of what no condition could ever bring about. But I maintain that there is also a second more controversial way to work around the strong version of radical transformation, one that includes even the most discordant apophatic possibilities as part of the constitution of this actual world. This second response comes by way of reinterpreting how totality functions in absolute necessity. Although this response is more controversial, in my estimation, it is also a more exciting response to the strong objection from radical transformation because it interprets the term "absolute contingency" without further qualification.

Absolute necessity includes everything. But the consequence of this is absolute contingency. To understand this consequence, we must reconceive of what totality means. The term totality typically suggests connotations of exhaustion, finitude, and completion. Apophatic possibility eludes all forms of actualization, cannot be made finite or exhaustible, and therefore appears only as a trace of what cannot appear, as a remainder that could never be included in this actual world. These connotations direct us to a kind of totality that contains everything by excluding that which cannot be said, the fragment, the ineffable, the absolute other of the system. But to apply this kind of totality to the Hegelian dialectic between absolute necessity and absolute contingency throws us into a productive paradox. If the actual world does not contain even the most radical transformations of apophatic possibility, then it does not contain every possibility whatsoever. However, if we concede that the actual world can transform into even that which cannot be thought or seemingly be brought about in reality, we succeed only in reducing the alterity of what cannot be thought to what can be thought. In other words, if we claim that this actual world contains even that which cannot be brought about in actuality, we take what is radical out of the transformation and turn it into something realizable, however distantly, in actuality.

Our response to this version of the objection can only come by way of recognizing that there is a significantly different conception of totality at work in Hegel's necessity-contingency dialectic. In contrast to the kind of totality that contains everything as a way of completing and exhausting that which it contains, there is also a kind of totality that contains everything because it contains its opposite, its negation, as part of the constitution of what it is. This, in effect, is the more Hegelian kind of totality. Even the radical transformations of apophatic possibility exist embedded in this world, not because they could come about in actuality, but because to include them is the only way to maintain a genuine theory of absolute necessity. That this actual world could become unthinkably otherwise is, in this sense, paramount to the theory of modal optimism. This actual world contains within it even the absurd possibility of its own impossibility. This is a significant consequence of Hegel's dialectic. The foreclosure of every possibility as part of the constitution of this actual world is at the same time the free movement of absolute contingency. Why? Because to include everything requires, as the most essential member of the set, that which cannot, and could never, be included as part of it.

Notes

Introduction

1 Some strands of Buddhism can be interpreted to embrace the emptiness and indeterminacy that come from the complete and unmediated unity of actuality and possibility. For example, see Casey Rentmeester's comparative analysis of the Huayan Buddhist's modal theory underlying the story of the god Indra's net in "Leibniz and Huayan Buddhism: Monads as Modified *Li*?" *Lyceum* 13, no. 1 (2014): 36–57.

2 The debate between Aristotle and the Megarians is a debate about the nature of *dunamis*, the Greek term which is usually translated as "potentiality." I will retain the term "potentiality" from here on in when referring to the Greek conception of *dunamis*, but I will use the term "possibility" when discussing Modern modal theories, such as Leibniz's and Hegel's. There are certainly important differences between the two terms. Potentiality gives off the connotation of power, capacity, real determinateness, and teleological design, whereas possibility tends to refer to the more formal aspects of modality. In the modal passages of the *Logic*, Hegel can be interpreted to refer to potentiality as "real possibility," and contemporary continental philosophers, such as Giorgio Agamben, call for a return to potentiality as the primary concept. For the sake of presenting a coherent conceptual trajectory across the ancient and modern worldviews, however, I will use the terms "potentiality" and "possibility" as roughly synonymous, even though some of the subtleties of the modal discussions are lost when this consistency is upheld.

3 Charlotte Witt helpfully divides Aristotle's refutation of the Megarians into three distinct arguments. *The Techne Argument* covers rational agents and acquired arts such as the art of building. Contrary to the Megarians, Aristotle claims that *dunamis* does not simply go away when the acquired art is inactive. Likewise, an agent does not gain an art inexplicably, but only from practice and repetition over a period of time. In contrast, *the Perception Argument* concerns irrational nature that has the passive capacity to be perceived. Aristotle rejects the Megarian conclusion that nature only exists when it is perceived. In this argument,

Aristotle also mentions the active capacity of exercising perception, such as with the example of sight—we do not become blind as soon as we look away. Witt also divides Aristotle's text into a third argument, *the Immobility Argument*, which establishes Aristotle's primary criticism: the Megarians are unable to account for movement from one activity to another because they think *dunamis* does not exist. Charlotte Witt, *Ways of Being: Potentiality and Actuality in Aristotle's Metaphysics* (Ithaca: Cornell University Press, 2003), 24–30.

4   Kant's criticism of St. Anselm's argument appears in the chapter "On the Impossibility of an Ontological Proof of God's Existence" in Immanuel Kant, ed. *Critique of Pure Reason*, translated by Paul Guyer and Allen W. Wood (Cambridge: Cambridge University Press, 1998), 563–68. For a detailed analysis of Kant's claim that being is not a predicate and that nothing is added to the content when something possible becomes actual, see Nicholas F. Stang, *Kant's Modal Metaphysics* (Oxford: Oxford University Press, 2016), 74–77.

5   In the first section of book *Theta* (9.1), Aristotle presents a precise and extremely detailed breakdown of the various ways in which potentiality is a source of change or movement in the actual. There are arguably ten senses of potentiality as motion to be drawn out of the text. (1) An agent can actively move or change an other, as when a builder builds a building. Or (2) an agent can move or change itself *as if it were other to itself*, as when I walk, I pivot and use my joints to push off myself. Aristotle also lists two parallel senses of passive potential, as when (3) a thing is capable of being moved by an agent that is not itself or when (4) a thing is capable of being moved by the agency of itself. The notion that an agent can be resistant to change and sustain itself in the face of agency produces two further senses of potentiality, as when (5) a thing is insusceptible to change in the face of an exterior agent (i.e., refuses to change for the worse) or when (6) a thing is insusceptible to change caused by its own inner agency (e.g., when someone resists temptation). Adding even more detail and complexity, Aristotle goes on to list four more senses of potentiality as motion through the normative distinction between whether something acts *well* or *badly*, as when (7) a thing acts upon another *well* (e.g., the fire burns dry wood *well*, but burns green or wet wood *badly*) or when (8) a thing acts upon itself *well*, or, again, in terms of passive potentiality, as when (9) a thing is acted upon by another *well* (e.g., as when the wood has the capacity to be burnt *well* or *badly*) or when (10) a thing is acted upon by itself *well*. As is typical of Aristotle's writing, the text becomes amazingly complex the more closely we explicate it (CWA 1046a9–35).

6   Aristotle points out that the Greek word for actuality, *energeia*, has the associations of "action" and "work" built into it. Hegel must have had this insight from Aristotle in mind when he recognizes in the real modality passage of the *Logic* that the German word for actuality, *Werklichkeit*, has the word *werken* in it, which can be translated into English as *to work* or *to act*. Hegel's catchphrase from this passage, "what is actual can act" (SL 482)—*was wirklich is, kann wirken* (WLII 208)—should be understood from the context of Aristotle's parallel statement "actuality is action." Lampert also highlights Hegel's catchphrase and suggests that Hegel is making use of a productive pun on the German. See Jay Lampert, "Hegel on Contingency, or, Fluidity and Multiplicity," *Bulletin of the Hegel Society of Great Britain* 51, no. 2 (2005): 74–82, 76. The pun does not come across as well in English as it does in Greek or German, but it still does come across to some extent. "Actuality" has the verb "to act" built into it. The play on words conveys that actuality is not as static as it has come to be thought, but should be recognized as the process of action and emergence as much as it is the end or the result of an activity. Heidegger no doubt draws on this same play on words in his 1931 lectures when he claims that for Aristotle *energeia* is the expression of the movement of potentiality. Martin Heidegger, *Aristotle's Metaphysics Θ 1–3*, translated by Walter Brogan and Peter Warnek (Indianapolis: Indiana University Press, 1995).

7   Jonathan Barnes translates *logos* as "formula" while Makin translates it as "account." Stephen Makin, translator, *Aristotle Metaphysics Book Θ*. By Aristotle (Oxford: Clarendon, 2006), 10.

8   I have relied on Witt's commentary as a guide to Aristotle's distinction between eternal and perishable substances. Witt, *Ways of Being*, 89–94.

9   Heidegger's reversal of modal priority in *Being and Time*, Agamben's analysis of the modal paradox underlying the paradox of the sovereign in *Homo Sacer*, and Stiegler's claim that modern industrial society bears witness to a disorienting overabundance of possibility in *Technics and Time* name some of the most prominent recent modal theories from the continental tradition that attempt to critically assess the actuality-primacy of Aristotle. See Martin Heidegger, *Being and Time*, translated by John Macquarrie and Edward Robinson (New York: Harper & Row, 1962), 63. Also see chapter 3, "Potentiality and Law" of Giorgio Agamben, *Homo Sacer: Sovereign Power and Bare Life*, translated by Daniel Heller-Roazen (Stanford: Stanford University Press, 1998), 39–48. Stiegler's account of modal priority appears in chapter 6, "Technoscience and Reproduction," of Bernard Stiegler, *Technics and Time, 3: Cinematic Time and the*

Question of Malaise, translated by Stephen Barker (Stanford: Stanford University Press, 2010), 187–224.
10 Martin Heidegger, *Being and Time*, 63. The German is "*Höher als die Wirklichkeit steht die Möglichkeit.*"
11 For an extended discussion of Heidegger's distinction between *eidos* in Aristotle and his own being-toward-death teleology, see Nahum Brown, "Aristotle and Heidegger: Potentiality in Excess of Actuality." *Idealistic Studies* 46, no. 2 (2017): 199–214.
12 In contrast to two-world metaphysical systems built on a model of *ascending* transcendence (i.e., ideal types in the heavens and the earthly realm), as well as three-world systems that posit both an above and below, there are also two-world metaphysical systems built on a model of *descending* transcendence. The horror fiction of H.P. Lovecraft offers a literary example of this branch. In his story "The Call of Cthulhu," Lovecraft presents a fictional vision of reality in which the "terrifying vistas" of the most horrific, monstrous underworld teem below the surface of our everyday world. H.P. Lovecraft, *The Fiction—Complete and Unabridged* (New York: Barnes & Noble, 2008), 355–79.
13 Generally, my discussion in this section, "Possible worlds are separate from each other," builds from Nicholas Rescher's summary of possible world theories in the "Introduction" of his book *On Leibniz*. Rescher offers an extremely helpful overview of some of the main models of world separation, including conceptions from the ancient Atomists, David Lewis, Jorge Luis Borges, and the Everett-Wheeler theory in quantum mechanics. In this way, Rescher situates Leibniz's modal theory within historical and contemporary debates about the nature of possible worlds. Although I build from Rescher's summary, my analysis develops a number of different insights. Rescher does not mention Hegel or Deleuze in his discussion, and he does not explore the distinction between modal priority and world separation as two responses to the problem of modal indeterminacy. In contrast to Rescher, who focuses on Leibniz, my aim is to situate Hegel's modal theory within the history of possible world theories. For his summary of modal theories, see Nicholas Rescher, *On Leibniz: Expanded Edition* (Pittsburgh: University of Pittsburgh Press, 2013), 10–14.
14 Hermann Diels and Walther Kranz, *Die Fragmente der Vorsokratiker* (Berlin: Weidermann, 1903), 68 A 40. This quote appears in English in G.S. Kirk and J.E. Raven (trans.), *The Presocratic Philosophers* (Cambridge: Cambridge University Press, 1957), 411. It also appears in Rescher, *On Leibniz*, 10–11.

15 James Warren draws out the ethical implications of the Atomists' position in "Ancient Atomists on the Plurality of Worlds," *The Classical Quarterly*, New Series 54, no. 2 (2004): 354–65.
16 Warren, "Ancient Atomists on the Plurality of Worlds," 359.
17 "These possibilities only subsist, as it were, and do not exist." Rescher, *On Leibniz*, 8. Rescher interprets Leibniz's position more definitely as non-existence elsewhere when he writes "with the one single and extraordinary exception of the actual world, [the infinite manifold of possible worlds] do not exist, save as ideas in the mind of God." Rescher, *On Leibniz*, 3.
18 Rescher claims that for Leibniz this is the "irreconcilable distinctness of the different spaces of different possible worlds." Rescher, *On Leibniz*, 16. My analysis of the Atomists' conception of space and how this differs from Leibniz's conception is indebted to Rescher's excellent account of this in *On Leibniz*, 14–19.
19 David Lewis, *On the Plurality of Worlds* (Malden: Blackwell Publishing, 1986), vii.
20 Lewis, *On the Plurality of Worlds*, 7.
21 Lewis, *On the Plurality of Worlds*, 4.
22 Lewis, *On the Plurality of Worlds*, 2.
23 Lewis, *On the Plurality of Worlds*, 92–96.
24 Lewis, *On the Plurality of Worlds*, 93.
25 In his comprehensive study of the history of indeterminacy, Moss discusses Aristotle's point about the indeterminacy of meaning. See Gregory S. Moss, "The Emerging Philosophical Recognition of the Significance of Indeterminacy" in *The Significance of Indeterminacy: Perspectives from Asian and Continental Philosophy*, Routledge, 9.
26 Aristotle also says this in section 9 of *De Interpretatione* (18b4–5), near his discussion of the sea battle.
27 The Hegel scholar Richard Dien Winfield proposes as much in his article "Negation, Contradiction, and Hegel's Emancipation of Truth, Right, and Beauty," unpublished. Winfield claims that the connection for Aristotle between contradiction and indeterminacy is an assumption that is only finally overturned with Hegel.
28 Jorge Luis Borges, *Labyrinths: Selected Stories and Other Writings* (New York: New Directions, 1962), 37. Deleuze mentions Borges's story in *The Fold*, 70–71. Also see Rescher, *On Leibniz*, 11–12.

29 I develop this analysis of Deleuze's conception of modal reality, and his relation to Leibniz and Hegel, in Chapter 5 of this book, "Leibniz, Hegel, and Deleuze on Incompossibility."
30 Unless otherwise noted with the abbreviation SL, all translations of Hegel's *Science of Logic* are my own. When this abbreviation is listed, the translation comes from George di Giovanni's *The Science of Logic* (Cambridge: Cambridge University Press, 2010). Generally, I have consulted and benefited from both di Giovanni's 2010 translation and Miller's 1969 translation.
31 I establish the intellectual background for this book in a companion volume, *Hegel's Actuality Chapter of the* Science of Logic: *A Commentary* (Lanham: Lexington Books, 2018). This commentary offers a close premise-by-premise textual account of Hegel's argument from modality as it appears in the "Actuality" chapter. I will not repeat the same detail of the analysis nor discuss the secondary literature at great length here, but I direct my readers to this other work for a more comprehensive textual discussion of Hegel's argument.
32 For a detailed explanation of Hegel's revaluation of Kant's idealism in terms of the *Doctrine of Essence*, see Michael Baur, "Sublating Kant and the Old Metaphysics: A Reading of the Transition from Being to Essence in Hegel's *Logic*," *The Owl of Minerva* 29, no. 2 (1998): 139–64.
33 Johann Wolfgang von Goethe. *Werke*, edited by Erich Trunz, 14 vols. (Munich: Beck, 1998), 245. The English version appears in Johann Wolfgang von Goethe, *Selected Verse*, edited by D. Luke (Harmondsworth: Penguin, 1964), 197.
34 In "With What Must a Science Begin," Hegel clarifies that, on the one hand, the *Phenomenology* clears the way for the project of the *Logic*, but that, on the other hand, it is not a presupposition for the *Logic*, since this would otherwise conflict with Hegel's theory that the *Logic* is a presuppositionless science.

Chapter 1

1 G.R.G. Mure, *A Study of Hegel's Logic* (Oxford: Oxford University Press, 1950), 33.
2 For analysis of the syntax of the opening line "being, pure being," see David Gray Carlson, *A Commentary to Hegel's Science of Logic* (New York: Palgrave Macmillan, 2007), 9. As a source of this analysis, Carlson cites Andrew Haas, *Hegel and the Problem of Multiplicity* (Evanston: Northwestern University Press, 2000), xxiii.

3 Michael Rosen, *Hegel's Dialectic and Its Criticism* (Cambridge: Cambridge University Press, 1982), 143.
4 William Maker, *Philosophy without Foundations: Rethinking Hegel* (Albany: SUNY Press, 1994), 94–96.
5 Houlgate, *The Opening of Hegel's Logic*, 272–74. Houlgate points to Wolfgang Wieland as another commentator who interprets the transition through the external source of a subject who thinks. Wolfgang Wieland, "Bemerkungen zum Anfang von Hegels Logik" in *Seminar: Dialektik in der Philosophie Hegels*, edited by R.P. Horstmann (Frankfurt am Main: Suhrkamp Verlag, 1978), 194–212.
6 Houlgate, *The Opening of Hegel's Logic*, 274.
7 For criticism of the thesis-antithesis-synthesis in Hegel, see Gustav E. Mueller, "The Hegel Legend of 'Thesis-Antithesis-Synthesis'" in *The Hegel Myths and Legends*, edited by John Stewart (Evanston: Northwestern University Press, 1996), 301–05.
8 Also see Houlgate's argument in "Does Hegel Have a Method?" for why the opening of the *Logic* cannot presuppose dialectical thinking. Houlgate, *The Opening of Hegel's Logic*, 32–35.
9 Songsuk Susan Hahn, *Contradiction in Motion: Hegel's Organic Concept of Life and Value* (Ithaca: Cornell University Press, 2007), 32.
10 Hahn, *Contradiction in Motion*, 32.
11 Heidegger, *Being and Time*, 22–24.
12 Heidegger, *Being and Time*, 21.
13 Rosen, *Hegel's Dialectic and Its Criticism*, 144–48.
14 Rosen, *Hegel's Dialectic and Its Criticism*, 146.
15 Rosen, *Hegel's Dialectic and Its Criticism*, 147.
16 Rosen, *Hegel's Dialectic and Its Criticism*, 150–52.
17 Translation modified.
18 Errol E. Harris, *An Interpretation of the Logic of Hegel* (Lanham: University Press of America, 1983), 94.
19 I retain Miller's translation "determinate being" for "*Das Dasein.*" Di Giovanni translates this as "existence," but in doing this, he loses the word play between "*Sein*" and "*Dasein.*"
20 For example, compare with Fichte's first principle "I am I" in Johann Gottlieb Fichte, *The Science of Knowledge*, translated by Peter Heath and John Lachs (Cambridge: Cambridge University Press, 1982).
21 William Desmond, *Hegel's God: A Counterfeit Double?* (Aldershot: Ashgate Publishing, 2003), 79.

22 Desmond, *Hegel's God*, 83.
23 At the beginning of the *Logic*, Hegel describes the last movement of indeterminate being, the "Sublation of Becoming," as "inherently self-contradictory" (SL 81, WL 113). But since contradiction does not emerge until much later in the *Logic* (Book 2, Section 1, Chapter 2), this statement from Hegel should seem premature in terms of the development of the *Logic*. The language that initiates the *Logic* is for the most part quite strict but Hegel does sometimes assume the language of latter chapters.

Chapter 2

1 George di Giovanni, "Reflection and Contradiction. A Commentary on Some Passages of Hegel's Science of Logic," *Hegel-Studien* 8 (1973): 132.
2 In her 2010 article about contradiction, Karin de Boer defends Hegel against Karl Popper's criticism that Hegelian logic threatens to undermine scientific reasoning. De Boer proposes that Hegel's treatment of contradiction does not violate the "formal requirements of valid propositions"; instead, it targets "modes of thought" and the dynamic relations of dialectics. Karin de Boer, "Hegel's Account of Contradiction in the Science of Logic Reconsidered," *Journal of the History of Philosophy* 48, no. 3 (2010): 345. For Karl Popper's criticism, see "What is Dialectic?" *Mind* 49 (1940): 418.
3 Bertrand Russell, *Our Knowledge of the External World: As a Field for Scientific Method in Philosophy* (New York: Routledge, 2009), 198. This sentence is also quoted in Robert Pippin, "Hegel's Metaphysics and the Problem of Contradiction," Journal of the History of Philosophy 16, no. 3 (1978): 303.
4 Bertrand Russell, *History of Western Philosophy* (London: Routledge, 2004), 796.
5 Di Giovanni mentions Hartmann's criticism in "Reflection and Contradiction," 131. For the original source, see Eduard von Hartmann, *Über die dialektiche Methode* (Berlin: Carl Duncker's Verlag, 1868).
6 For criticism of Brandom's position, see Stephen Houlgate, "Phenomenology and *De Re* Interpretation: A Critique of Brandom's Reading of Hegel," *International Journal of Philosophical Studies* 17, no. 1 (2009): 29–47. Also see de Boer's analysis of "asymmetrical contradiction" in "Hegel's Account of Contradiction in the *Science of Logic* Reconsidered," 369. She claims that Hegel's theory of "self-contradiction" is distinct from the earlier "classical period of non-contradiction." De Boer, "Hegel's Account of Contradiction in the *Science of Logic* Reconsidered," 364.

7   Pippin, "Hegel's Metaphysics and the Problem of Contradiction," 303.
8   Hahn, *Contradiction in Motion*, 24.
9   Hahn, *Contradiction in Motion*, 24.
10 Karin de Boer, *On Hegel: The Sway of the Negative* (New York: Palgrave Macmillan, 2010), 93.
11 De Boer, *On Hegel*, 95.
12 Graham Priest, "The Logical Structure of Dialectic," unpublished. For an introduction to the theory of dialetheism, see the chapter "Dialetheism" in Graham Priest, *In Contradiction: A Study of Transconsistent Logic* (Oxford: Clarendon Press, 2006), 3–8.
13 Priest, "The Logical Structure of Dialectic," unpublished, 1. Priest also discusses the logical nature of dialectics in "Dialectic and Dialetheic," *Science and Society* 53, no. 4 (1989): 388–415. Also see his analysis of Hegel in Graham Priest, *Beyond the Limits of Thought* (New York: Cambridge University Press, 1995).
14 Miller translates *der Schein* as "illusory being" (Hegel, 1969, 394). Di Giovanni translates *der Schein* literally into the English word "shine" (SL 341, WLII 17).
15 Hegel's discussion of identity and contradiction also appears in other works. See G.F.W. Hegel, *The Encyclopaedia Logic*, translated by T.F. Geraets, W.A. Suchting, and H.S. Harris (Indianapolis: Hackett Publishing, 1991), 179–88; G.F.W. Hegel, *Jena System, The, 1804–5: Logic and Metaphysics*, translated by John W. Burbidge and George di Giovanni (Kingston: McGill-Queens University Press, 1986), 136–38; and G.F.W. Hegel, *Lectures on Logic*, translated by Clark Butler (Bloomington: Indiana University Press, 2008), 132–40. For the sake of this project, my analysis focuses primarily on how this argument plays out in the Greater Logic.
16 Translation modified.
17 In his explication of the identity and contradiction passages of the *Logic*, Winfield claims that it is the "formula $A = A$" that distinguishes identity from earlier determinations of being, such as something, finitude, the one, etc. Winfield, *Hegel's Science of Logic: A Critical Rethinking in Thirty Lectures* (Lanham: Rowman & Littlefield, 2012), 171.
18 Translation modified.
19 For Hegel's subsequent discussion of parts and wholes, see "The Relation of Whole and Parts" (SL 450–55, WLII 166–71).
20 Slavoj Žižek claims that this transition comes about because one side of the opposition is also the universal: "We pass from opposition to contradiction through the logic of what Hegel called 'oppositional determination': when the universal, common ground of the two opposites 'encounters itself' in its

oppositional determination, i.e., in one of the terms of the opposition." Slavoj Žižek, *Tarrying with the Negative* (Durham: Duke University Press, 1993), 132.
21 I reference the Miller translation here. Hegel, *Hegel's Science of Logic*, 440–41 (SL 383, WLII 77).
22 This drawing of the square of oppositions is taken from the *Internet Encyclopedia of Philosophy*. https://www.iep.utm.edu/sqr-opp/ (accessed April 13, 2019).
23 Pippin, "Hegel's Metaphysics and the Problem of Contradiction," 309.
24 Pippin, "Hegel's Metaphysics and the Problem of Contradiction," 309.
25 Pippin, "Hegel's Metaphysics and the Problem of Contradiction," 310.
26 Pippin, "Hegel's Metaphysics and the Problem of Contradiction," 310.
27 Lampert, "Speed, Impact and Fluidity at the Barrier between Life and Death: Hegel's Philosophy of Nature." *Angelaki* 10, no. 3 (2005): 145–56.
28 Lampert, "Speed, Impact and Fluidity at the Barrier between Life and Death," 148.
29 Lampert, "Speed, Impact and Fluidity at the Barrier between Life and Death," 149.
30 Lampert, "Speed, Impact and Fluidity at the Barrier between Life and Death," 148.
31 Lampert, "Speed, Impact and Fluidity at the Barrier between Life and Death," 151.
32 Lampert, "Speed, Impact and Fluidity at the Barrier between Life and Death," 151.
33 Lampert, "Speed, Impact and Fluidity at the Barrier between Life and Death," 151.

Chapter 3

1 My analysis of Hegel on the possibility *not to be* draws from Agamben's distinction between the *can* and the *can not* in "On What We Can Not Do." See Giorgio Agamben, *Nudities*, translated by David Kishik and Stefan Pedatella (Stanford: Stanford University Press, 2011), 43–45.
2 I take this distinction from Aristotle, who warns us not to conflate *can not* and *cannot*, when he explains in *De Interpretatione* that the opposite of "it is possible for something to be" is not "it is possible for something not to be," but rather "it is not possible (impossible) for something to be" (CWA 21a34–22a12). If somebody has the capacity to walk, Aristotle points out, this person can choose to walk or

not to walk. It would be a mistake to say that when this person chooses not to walk, this person cannot walk.
3   Heidegger, *Being and Time*, 63.
4   The "Potentiality and Law" chapter of Agamben's *Homo Sacer* offers an ontological-modal basis for the political sovereign paradox in the form of an analysis of Aristotle's *Metaphysics* book *Theta* over the constitutive ambiguity between whether actuality or potentiality is more primary. For my explanation of this argument, see Nahum Brown, "The Modality of Sovereignty: Agamben and the *Aporia* of Primacy in Aristotle's *Metaphysics* Theta," *Mosaic* 46, no. 1 (2013): 169–82.
5   Stiegler, *Technics and Time, 3*, 202–07.
6   This chapter is a condensed version of my monograph, Hegel's Actuality Chapter of the *Science of Logic*: A Commentary. I direct readers to this book for a more detailed explication of Hegel's chapter and for a more thorough examination of the secondary literature on the "Actuality" chapter. Generally, the commentaries that I have found most helpful include John W. Burbidge, *Hegel's Systematic Contingency* (New York: Palgrave Macmillan, 2007); George Di Giovanni, "The Category of Contingency in the Hegelian Logic," in *Art and Logic in Hegel's Philosophy*, edited by W.E. Steinkraus (Atlantic Highlands: Humanities Press, 1980), 179–200; Dieter Henrich, "*Hegel's Theorie über den Zufall*," in *Hegel im Kontext* (Frankfurt: Suhrkamp, 1971); Stephen Houlgate, "Necessity and Contingency in Hegel's *Science of Logic*," *Owl of Minerva* 27 (1995): 37–49; Franz Knappik "Hegel's Modal Argument against Spinozism: An Interpretation of the Chapter 'Actuality' in the *Science of Logic*," *Hegel Bulletin* 36, no. 1 (2015): 53–79; Lampert, "Hegel on Contingency, or, Fluidity and Multiplicity," 74–82; Béatrice Longuenesse, *Hegel's Critique of Metaphysics* (Cambridge: Cambridge University Press, 2007); Herbert Marcuse, *Hegel's Ontology and the Theory of Historicity* (Cambridge: MIT Press, 1987); Pirmin Stekeler-Weithofer, "Hegel on Reality as a Modal Notion," in *Hegel's Analytic Pragmatism*. Unpublished. Accessed online: http://www.sozphil.unileipzig.de/cm/philosophie/files/2012/11/StekelerHegelsAnalyticPragmatism.pdf (accessed September 25, 2018); Christopher Yeomans, *Freedom and Reflection: Hegel and the Logic of Agency* (Oxford: Oxford University Press, 2012).
7   Burbidge explains this when he writes, "that the actual incorporates the possible specifies its difference from the apparently synonymous terms: 'being' and 'existence.'" Burbidge, *Hegel's Systematic Contingency*, 17. Also see John W. Burbidge, *The Logic of Hegel's Logic* (Peterborough: Broadview Press, 2006), 75.

8   Melvin Fitting and Richard L. Mendelsohn, *First-Order Modal Logic* (Dordrecht: Kluwer Academic Publishers, 1998), 5.
9   Hegel's analysis of the positive side of possibility begins formally in this way as truth verification, but it also carries over into the "Real" subchapter as the determinate, teleological drive of something possible as predisposed to become actual. One of Hegel's favorite examples of the "real" possibility *to be actual* appears in the organic life passages of the *Logic* and the *Philosophy of Nature* as the seed's predisposition to become an oak tree.
10 Burbidge, *Hegel's Systematic Contingency*, 19.
11 Lampert, "Hegel on Contingency, or, Fluidity and Multiplicity," 75.
12 I use the phrases "the possible *itself*" and "possibility *qua* possibility" interchangeably. These phrases refer to the sides of possibility as one unity, A and -A together, that something possible both *can* and *can not* be.
13 Houlgate explains this facet of real possibility quite effectively when he writes: "It may well be possible in itself for me to be the tallest person in the world; however, it is clearly not possible for me to be the tallest person, to the extent that there are, and always will be, others who are taller than I." Houlgate, "Necessity and Contingency in Hegel's *Science of Logic*," 40. Given that Houlgate is around 6 feet tall, in the context of a world of people, some of whom are taller than he is, it is not really possible for Houlgate to be the tallest person in the world.
14 In the subsequent section of the *Logic*, the "Relation of Substantiality," Hegel will call this relation of absolute conversion between actuality and possibility "actuosity" (*Actuosität*) (SL 490, WL 220). Actuosity is a development upon the absolute conversion of actuality and possibility because it emphasizes not only the self-movement of substance, but also the tranquility of this movement.
15 For Aristotle's discussion between primary and secondary substances, see Chapter 5 of the "Categories" (CWA 2a13–4b20).
16 Lampert outlines this result when he claims that absolute necessity is "the interaction of all forces in every possible way—such that what *is* must continue to generate and envelop ever differing possibilities." Lampert, "Hegel on Contingency, or, Fluidity and Multiplicity," 75.

Chapter 4

1   Hegel defines "science" in terms of "necessity" in the "Introduction" to the *Phenomenology* when he writes: "Because of this necessity, the way to Science

is itself already *Science*, and hence, in virtue of its content, is the Science of the *experience of consciousness*" (PS 56). He also writes in "With What Must the Beginning of Science Be Made?" of the *Logic*: "The *Phenomenology of Spirit* is the science of consciousness, its exposition ... consciousness has the *concept* of science, that is, pure knowledge, for its result. To this extent, logic has for its presupposition the science of spirit in its appearance, a science which contains the necessity, and therefore demonstrates the truth, of the stand-point which is pure knowledge and of its mediation" (SL 46–47, WL 67).

2   G.F.W. Hegel, *Elements of the Philosophy of Right*, translated by Allen W. Wood (Cambridge: Cambridge University Press, 1993), 20. For a detailed discussion of Hegel's statement "what is rational is actual and what is actual is rational," see Béatrice Longuenesse's chapter "What Is Rational Is Actual" of *Hegel's Critique of Metaphysics*. Also see M.W. Jackson, "Hegel: The Real and the Rational," in *The Hegel Myths and Legends*, edited by John Stewalt, 19–41.

3   I use the Miller translation for this sentence: Hegel, *Hegel's Science of Logic*, 549. Di Giovanni translates this as "possibility and necessity are only *apparently* distinguished" (SL 484).

4   For an explanation of the "axiom of possibility" and the related "axiom of necessity," see G.E. Hughes and M.J. Cresswell, *A New Introduction to Modal Logic* (London: Routledge, 1996), 28. For a variation from necessity to actuality: "if p is necessary, then p is actual," see Fitting and Mendelsohn, *First-Order Modal Logic*, 9–10. Aristotle uncovers a similar inference when he recognizes, in book 13 of *De Interpretatione*, that it would be impossible for something actual not to have been possible. "From being of necessity there follows capability of being." This can be referred to as the "actuality axiom," which states that if p is actual, then necessarily p is possible (CWA 23a18).

5   I am using symbolic notation here loosely: "$N \supset P$" stands for "if p is necessary, then p is possible." "$P \supset N$" stands for "if p is possible, then p is necessary." "$N \equiv P$" stands for "if p is necessary, then p is possible, *and*, if p is possible, then p is necessary." This notation is not meant to be truth functional, but is merely shorthand for the conditional and bi-conditional entailments of possibility and necessity as they are established in this chapter.

6   Houlgate, "Necessity and Contingency in Hegel's *Science of Logic*," 43.

7   G.F.W. Hegel, *Hegel's Aesthetics: Lectures on Fine Art*, translated by T.M. Knox, Volume 1 (Oxford: Clarendon Press, 1975), 8.

8   Immanuel Kant, *Critique of the Power of Judgment*, translated by Paul Guyer and Eric Matthews (Cambridge: Cambridge University Press, 2000), 120.

Chapter 5

1. I am not claiming that critics who hold this view of Spinoza believe that Spinoza has to deny that God contains the most complex variety and abundance of possibility. I am only claiming that such critics assume that Spinoza understands God from the stance of necessarianism.
2. Arthur O. Lovejoy, *The Great Chain of Being* (Cambridge: Harvard University Press, 1936). Rescher, *On Leibniz*. David Blumenfeld, "Freedom, Contingency, and Things Possible in Themselves," *Philosophy and Phenomenological Research* 49, no. 1 (1988): 81–101.
3. I realize that Spinoza scholars might find this reading of Spinoza to be superficial and in ways inaccurate. My intention is only to present the interpretation of Spinoza that Leibniz and debates about Leibniz have relied upon in order to develop their own arguments and objections. Whether Leibniz has accurately portrayed Spinoza or not goes beyond the scope of this analysis.
4. Although it might not seem obvious why two plus two equals five would be a direct contradiction, that is, why a world could not exist in which two plus two does not equal four, Leibniz maintains that there are a set of basic truths which cannot be otherwise but for which no concrete reason could ever be given. For his distinction between basic and derivative truths, see "On Freedom" (PE 96). Leibniz does offer a clear example in "On Freedom and Possibility" of how mathematics can demonstrate contradiction, such as that the part cannot be equal to itself and the whole: "[Suppose] someone were to look for a number which multiplied by itself is 9 and also added to 5 makes 9. Such a number implies a contradiction, for it must, at the same time, be both 3 and 4, that is, 3 and 4 must be equal, a part equal to the whole" (PE 21). However, he seems to suggest that even the law of non-contradiction cannot be given as the reason for why basic truths must exist.
5. Blumenfeld, "Freedom, Contingency, and Things Possible in Themselves," 93.
6. G.W. Leibniz, *Philosophical Papers and Letters*, translated by Leroy E. Loemker (Chicago: Chicago University Press, 1956), 662.
7. Hegel's theory of absolute actuality presents us with a similar kind of logic, where each instance of a thing is at the same time an expression of the totality.
8. "The Monadology" (PE 221).
9. Russell's explanation of the distinction between the possible and the compossible is very helpful. Bertrand Russell, *The Philosophy of Leibniz* (London: Routledge, 1900), 67. Also see Brown's discussion of Russell's explanation in Gregory Brown,

"Compossibility, Harmony, and Perfection in Leibniz," *Philosophical Review* 96, no. 2 (1987): 172–203, 177.

10 In the *Theodicy*, Leibniz defines world as "the whole succession and the whole agglomeration of all existent things" (TH 132).

11 If all possible relations are compossible, "the compossible relation threatens to become trivial, i.e., the individual concepts C_1 and C_2 are compossible if and only if C_1 is possible and C_2 is possible, in which case there is only one possible world, a world of maximum disharmony." John Earman, "Perceptions and Relations in the Monadology," *Studia Leibnitiana* 9, no. 2 (1977): 212–30, 220. Also see Brown's discussion of this in "Compossibility, Harmony, and Perfection in Leibniz," 180.

12 Saint Anselm's argument can be rendered as: (1) Anyone can conceive of the possibility that God exists. (2) To conceive of the possibility of God is to conceive of a being that is better than any other being. (3) It is better to be actual than to be merely possible. (4) Therefore, God is actual and not merely possible. Anselm, *Basic Writings*, translated by Thomas Williams (Indianapolis: Hackett Publishing, 2007), 81–83.

13 Deleuze also mentions this interpretation. "If this world exists, it is not because it is the best, but because it is rather the inverse; it is the best because it is, because it is the one that is" (FLB 68).

14 As an alternative reading, one can see in "On the Ultimate Origination of Things" (PE 151) the argument that maximum possibility also stands at the origin of what makes each thing determinate and makes each thing exhibit the content that it has. This argument appears in Leibniz's language about how each thing "strives to exist" with the most possible essence. Each determinate thing takes its form from the principle that it should express the most of its essence as can be expressed in one existence. The principle of maximum possibility is then the reason why each thing is what it is. The reason why the triangle has the shape that it has is because this shape maximizes possibility. However, even if this reading is plausible, one can still maintain that the maximum possibility principle is about how one composite series of things is better than other incompossible series. It is then not the case that the isolated triangle that is not in relation to any world exhibits the most possibility; Leibniz's point would remain that the determinate content of things exhibits the maximum amount of possibility only insofar as each thing is the expression in a composite of the whole world. For a discussion of whether Leibniz's doctrine of the striving possibles is consistent in his system, see David Blumenfeld, "Leibniz's Theory of the Striving Possibles," *Studia Leibnitiana* 5, no. 2 (1973): 163–77.

15 Rescher, *On Leibniz*, 28.
16 Jaakko Hintikka, "Leibniz on Plenitude, Relations, and the 'Reign of Law,'" in *Reforging the Great Chain of Being*, edited by S. Knuuttila (Dordrecht: Springer, 1972), 259–86; Benson Mates, "Leibniz on Possible Worlds," *Critica* 4, no. 10 (1970): 123–27; Rescher, *On Leibniz*.
17 James Messina and Donald Rutherford, "Leibniz on Compossibility," *Philosophy Compass* 4, no. 6 (2009): 962–77, 964–65. Incidentally, they promote what they call the cosmological interpretation as a solution to the incompossibility problem. The cosmological solution comes from the criteria that for a world to be a world, it must remain spatially and temporally consistent. Messina and Rutherford claim that what makes a world compossible is a "unified spatiotemporal and causal order." Messina and Rutherford, "Leibniz on Compossibility," 974.
18 Brown, "Compossibility, Harmony, and Perfection in Leibniz"; Ian Hacking, "A Leibnizian Theory of Truth," in *Leibniz: Critical and Interpretative Essays*, edited by Michael Hooker (Minneapolis: University of Minnesota Press, 1982), 185–95; J.A. Cover and John O'Leary-Hawthorne, *Substance and Individuation in Leibniz* (Cambridge: Cambridge University Press, 1999).
19 Brown, "Compossibility, Harmony, and Perfection in Leibniz," 179.
20 Messina and Rutherford, "Leibniz on Compossibility," 966–67.
21 Messina and Rutherford, "Leibniz on Compossibility," 966; Cover and O'Leary-Hawthorne, *Substance and Individuation in Leibniz*, 137.
22 Jeffrey K. McDonough, "Leibniz and the Puzzle of Incompossibility: The Packing Strategy," *Philosophical Review* 119, no. 2 (2010): 135–63, 137–40.
23 McDonough, "Leibniz and the Puzzle of Incompossibility," 139–43.
24 As we will see from my claims about Hegel's revisions of the incompossibility problem, I do not think that the logical interpretation can establish the maximization thesis well either, since it ultimately excludes a huge vista of possibility, that is, the possibility of actualizing contraries.
25 Rescher, *On Leibniz*, 27–30 and Brown "Compossibility, Harmony, and Perfection in Leibniz," 195–99.
26 McDonough, "Leibniz and the Puzzle of Incompossibility," 145–46.
27 McDonough, "Leibniz and the Puzzle of Incompossibility," 152–53.
28 I outlined these two conceptions of possibility in the "Introduction" to this book, in the section "Hegel's Two Conceptions of Possibility."
29 The act of making a decision suggests that the quantity of possibility is relative to an agent's interest, and that certain decisions lead to more while other decisions lead to less possibility, such as when one decides to travel, etc. Although agency is certainly an important factor for a conception of possibility as a surging and

receding degree of quantity, modal optimism also commits us to an ontological claim that the surface of being itself contains degrees of quantity.

30 Also see Philip K. Dick, "If You Find This World Bad, You Should See Some of the Others," 1977. Reprinted in *The Shifting Realities of Philip K. Dick: Selected Literary and Philosophical Writings*, edited by Lawrence Sutin (New York: Vintage Books, 1995), 233–58.

31 Rescher, *On Leibniz*, 10–14.

32 Earman, "Perceptions and Relations in the Monadology," 220. Also see Brown, "Compossibility, Harmony, and Perfection in Leibniz," 180.

33 Christopher Shields is one commentator who argues against this interpretation. See "Leibniz's Doctrine of the Striving Possibles," *Journal of the History of Philosophy* 24 no. 3 (1986): 343–57. Also see Blumenfeld, "Leibniz's Theory of the Striving Possibles" and Lloyd Strickland, "Leibniz on whether the World Increases in Perfection," *British Journal for the History of Philosophy* 14, no. 1 (2006): 51–68.

34 Deleuze describes this original relation as "vice-diction" rather than contradiction. "Between the two worlds there exists a relation other than one of contradiction … It is vice-diction, not contradiction" (FLB 67). Cf. "The notion of Incompossibility is not reducible to the notion of contradiction. Rather, in a certain way, contradiction is derived from Incompossibility" (LS 111).

35 Although chapter 5 of Deleuze's *The Fold* is explicitly about incompossibility in Leibniz, I find the "Sixteenth Series" of *The Logic of Sense* to contain the primary argument from Deleuze.

36 There are a number of related concepts to incompossibility from Deleuze's corpus, including the virtual, the dice-throw, and the desiring machine. For the virtual, see "Memory as Virtual Coexistence," in Gilles Deleuze, *Bergsonism*, translated by Hugh Tomlinson and Barbara Habberjam (New York: Zone Books, 1991), 51–72. Also see Gilles Deleuze, *Difference & Repetition*, translated by Paul Patton (New York: Columbia University Press), 1994, 208–14. For the dice-throw, see Gilles Deleuze, *Nietzsche and Philosophy*, translated by Hugh Tomlinson (New York: Columbia University Press, 1983), 25–27. For the desiring machine, see Gilles Deleuze and Félix Guattari, *Anti-Oedipus: Capitalism and Schizophrenia*, translated by Robery Hurley, Mark Seem, and Helen R. Lane (Minneapolis: University of Minnesota Press), 1983, 8–50.

37 Turning to Husserl's "Fifth Cartesian Meditation," Deleuze proposes that while the first level of actualization presents us with *die Umwelt*, the second level presents us with *die Welt*. The second level discovers something that the first

level cannot find, the ego whose consciousness transcends each serial grouping of converging worlds. "The Ego as knowing subject appears when something is *identified* inside worlds which are nevertheless incompossible, and across series which are nevertheless divergent" (LS 113).

Chapter 6

1 Isaiah Berlin, *Four Essays on Liberty* (Oxford: Oxford University Press, 1969), 122–31.
2 Berlin, *Four Essays on Liberty*, 131–34.
3 Berlin, *Four Essays on Liberty*, 144.
4 Berlin, *Four Essays on Liberty*, 141.
5 Franco claims, effectively I think, that Hegel's concept of freedom does not really correspond to Berlin's account of Hegel in terms of positive freedom. For Franco's discussion of this, see Paul Franco, *Hegel's Philosophy of Freedom* (New Haven: Yale University Press, 1999), 180–82.
6 Hegel, *Elements of the Philosophy of Right*, 49.
7 Franco, *Hegel's Concept of Freedom*, 182. Cf. Berlin, *Four Essays on Liberty*, 145.
8 While this result of open contingency where everything can and must connect in every possible way with everything else follows directly from Hegel's conclusions about "Actuality," his commitment to free movement is harder to read into Hegel's arguably less left-leaning social-political theory. The results from "Actuality" can in this way be viewed as an alternative version of Hegel, although there is still something fruitful about its application in terms of his political work.
9 For a comprehensive analysis of the history of apophatic thinking in the West from Plato to Derrida, see William Franke, *On What Cannot Be Said: Volume 1: Classic Formulations* (Notre Dame: University of Notre Dame Press, 2007); Franke, William. *On What Cannot Be Said: Volume 2: Modern and Contemporary Transformations* (Notre Dame: University of Notre Dame Press, 2007).

Bibliography

Agamben, Giorgio. *Homo Sacer: Sovereign Power and Bare Life*, translated by Daniel Heller-Roazen. Stanford: Stanford University Press, 1998.

Agamben, Giorgio. *Nudities*, translated by David Kishik and Stefan Pedatella. Stanford: Stanford University Press, 2011.

Anselm. *Basic Writings*, translated by Thomas Williams. Indianapolis: Hackett Publishing, 2007.

Aristotle. *The Complete Works of Aristotle*, in two volumes, edited by Jonathan Barnes. Princeton: Princeton University Press, 1984.

Baur, Michael. "Sublating Kant and the Old Metaphysics: A Reading of the Transition from Being to Essence in Hegel's *Logic*." *The Owl of Minerva* 29, no. 2 (1998): 139–64.

Berlin, Isaiah. *Four Essays on Liberty*. Oxford: Oxford University Press, 1969.

Blumenfeld, David. "Freedom, Contingency, and Things Possible in Themselves." *Philosophy and Phenomenological Research* 49, no. 1 (1988): 81–101.

Blumenfeld, David. "Leibniz's Theory of the Striving Possibles." *Studia Leibnitiana* 5, no. 2 (1973): 163–77.

Borges, Jorge Luis. *Labyrinths: Selected Stories and Other Writings*, edited by Donald A. Yates and James E. Irby. New York: New Directions, 1962.

Brandom, Robert B. *Tales of the Mighty Dead: Historical Essays in the Metaphysics of Intentionality*. Cambridge: Harvard University Press, 2002.

Brown, Gregory. "Compossibility, Harmony, and Perfection in Leibniz." *Philosophical Review* 96, no. 2 (1987): 172–203.

Brown, Nahum. "Aristotle and Heidegger: Potentiality in Excess of Actuality." *Idealistic Studies*, 46, no. 2 (2017): 199–214.

Brown, Nahum. Hegel's Actuality Chapter of *the Science of Logic*: A Commentary. Lanham: Lexington Books, 2018.

Brown, Nahum. "Indeterminacy, Modality, Dialectics: Hegel on the Possibility *Not to Be*." In *The Significance of Indeterminacy: Perspectives from Asian and Continental Philosophy*, edited by Robert H. Scott and Gregory S. Moss, 104–23. New York: Routledge, 2018.

Brown, Nahum. "Is Hegel an Apophatic Thinker?" In *Contemporary Debates in Negative Theology and Philosophy*, edited by Nahum Brown and J. Aaron Simmons, 107–30. Cham: Palgrave Macmillan, 2017.

Brown, Nahum. "The Modality of Sovereignty: Agamben and the *Aporia* of Primacy in Aristotle's *Metaphysics* Theta." *Mosaic* 46, no. 1 (2013): 169–82.
Brown, Nahum. "Transcendent and Immanent Conceptions of Perfection in Leibniz and Hegel." In *Transcendence, Immanence, and Intercultural Philosophy*, edited by Nahum Brown and William Franke, 183–206. Cham: Palgrave Macmillan, 2016.
Brown, Nahum. "Why Do Contradictions Sink to the Ground? A Re-Examination of the Categories of Reflection in Hegel's *Logic*." *Journal of Speculative Philosophy* 33, no. 4 (2019): 628–43.
Brown, Nahum. "Why Is Being Nothing? An Apophatic Reading of Hegel's Opening to the *Logic*." *Frontiers of Philosophy in China* 13, no. 4 (2018): 508–34.
Burbidge, John W. *Hegel's Systematic Contingency*. New York: Palgrave Macmillan, 2007.
Burbidge, John W. *The Logic of Hegel's Logic*. Peterborough: Broadview Press, 2006.
Carlson, David Gray. *A Commentary to Hegel's Science of Logic*. New York: Palgrave Macmillan, 2007.
Cover, J.A. and John O'Leary-Hawthorne. *Substance and Individuation in Leibniz*. Cambridge: Cambridge University Press, 1999.
De Boer, Karin. "Hegel's Account of Contradiction in the *Science of Logic* Reconsidered." *Journal of the History of Philosophy* 48, no. 3 (2010): 345–73.
De Boer, Karin. *On Hegel: The Sway of the Negative*. New York: Palgrave Macmillan, 2010.
De la Durantaye, Leland. *Giorgio Agamben: A Critical Introduction*. Stanford: Stanford University Press, 2009.
Deleuze, Gilles. *Bergsonism*, translated by Hugh Tomlinson and Barbara Habberjam. New York: Zone Books, 1991.
Deleuze, Gilles. *Difference & Repetition*, translated by Paul Patton. New York: Columbia University Press, 1994.
Deleuze, Gilles. *Nietzsche and Philosophy*, translated by Hugh Tomlinson. New York: Columbia University Press, 1983.
Deleuze, Gilles. *The Fold: Leibniz and the Baroque*, translated by Tom Conley. Minneapolis: University of Minnesota Press, 1993.
Deleuze, Gilles. *The Logic of Sense*, translated by Mark Lester. New York: Columbia University Press, 1990.
Deleuze, Gilles and Félix Guattari. *Anti-oedipus: Capitalism and Schizophrenia*, translated by Robery Hurley, Mark Seem, and Helen R. Lane. Minneapolis: University of Minnesota Press, 1983.
Desmond, William. *Hegel's God: A Counterfeit Double?* Aldershot: Ashgate Publishing, 2003.

Di Giovanni, George. "The Category of Contingency in the Hegelian Logic." In *Art and Logic in Hegel's Philosophy*, edited by W.E. Steinkraus, 179–200. New Jersey: Humanities Press, 1980.

Di Giovanni, George. "Reflection and Contradiction. A Commentary on Some Passages of Hegel's Science of Logic." *Hegel-Studien* 8 (1973): 131–61.

Dick, Philip K. "If You Find This World Bad, You Should See Some of the Others." 1977. Reprinted in *The Shifting Realities of Philip K. Dick: Selected Literary and Philosophical Writings*, edited by Lawrence Sutin, 233–58. New York: Vintage Books, 1995.

Dick, Philip K. *The Man in the High Castle*. London: Vintage Books, 1962.

Diels, Hermann and Walther Kranz, *Die Fragmente der Vorsokratiker*. Berlin: Weidermann, 1903.

Earman, John. "Perceptions and Relations in the Monadology." *Studia Leibnitiana* 9, no. 2 (1977): 212–30.

Fichte, Johann Gottlieb. *The Science of Knowledge*, translated by Peter Heath and John Lachs. Cambridge: Cambridge University Press, 1982.

Fitting, Melvin and Richard L. Mendelsohn. *First-Order Modal Logic*. Dordrecht: Kluwer Academic Publishers, 1998.

Flint, Eric. *1632*. Riverdale: Baen Books, 2000.

Franco, Paul. *Hegel's Philosophy of Freedom*. New Haven: Yale University Press, 1999.

Franke, William. *A Philosophy of the Unsayable*. Notre Dame: University of Notre Dame Press, 2014.

Franke, William. *On What Cannot Be Said: Volume 1: Classic Formulations*. Notre Dame: University of Notre Dame Press, 2007.

Franke, William. *On What Cannot Be Said: Volume 2: Modern and Contemporary Transformations*. Notre Dame: University of Notre Dame Press, 2007.

Goethe, Johann Wolfgang von. *The Metamorphosis of Plants*. Cambridge, MA: MIT Press, 2009.

Goethe, Johann Wolfgang von. *Selected Verse*, edited by D. Luke. Harmondsworth: Penguin, 1964.

Goethe, Johann Wolfgang von. *Werke*, edited by Erich Trunz, 14 vols. Munich: Beck, 1998.

Haas, Andrew. *Hegel and the Problem of Multiplicity*. Evanston: Northwestern University Press, 2000.

Hacking, Ian. "A Leibnizian Theory of Truth." In *Leibniz: Critical and Interpretative Essays*, edited by Michael Hooker, 185–95. Minneapolis: University of Minnesota Press, 1982.

Hahn, Songsuk Susan. *Contradiction in Motion: Hegel's Organic Concept of Life and Value*. Ithaca: Cornell University Press, 2007.

Harris, Errol E. *An Interpretation of the Logic of Hegel*. Lanham: University Press of America, 1983.

Harris, H.S. *Hegel: Phenomenology and System*. Indianapolis: Hackett Publishing, 1995.

Hartmann, Eduard von. *Über die dialektiche Methode*. Berlin: Carl Duncker's Verlag, 1868.

Hegel, G.F.W. *Elements of the Philosophy of Right*, translated by Allen W. Wood. Cambridge: Cambridge University Press, 1993.

Hegel, G.F.W. *The Encyclopaedia Logic*, translated by T.F. Geraets, W.A. Suchting, and H.S. Harris. Indianapolis: Hackett Publishing, 1991.

Hegel, G.F.W. *Hegel's Aesthetics: Lectures on Fine Art*, translated by T.M. Knox, Volume 1. Oxford: Clarendon Press, 1975.

Hegel, G.F.W. *Hegel's Phenomenology of Spirit*, translated by A.V. Miller. Oxford: Oxford University Press, 1977.

Hegel, G.F.W. *Hegel's Science of Logic*, translated by A.V. Miller. Amherst: Humanity Books, 1969.

Hegel, G.F.W. *Introduction to the Philosophy of History*, translated by Leo Rauch. Indianapolis: Hackett Publishing, 1988.

Hegel, G.F.W. *Jena System, The, 1804–5: Logic and Metaphysics*, translated by John W. Burbidge and George di Giovanni. Kingston: McGill-Queens University Press, 1986.

Hegel, G.F.W. *Lectures on Logic*, translated by Clark Butler. Bloomington: Indiana University Press, 2008.

Hegel, G.F.W. *Lectures on the History of Philosophy: Volume 3, Medieval and Modern Philosophy*, translated by E.S. Haldane and Frances H. Simson. Lincoln: University of Nebraska Press, 1995.

Hegel, G.F.W. *Philosophy of Nature*, translated by A.V. Miller. Oxford: Oxford University Press, 1970.

Hegel, G.F.W. *The Science of Logic*, translated by George di Giovanni. Cambridge: Cambridge University Press, 2010.

Hegel, G.F.W. *Werke in zwanzig Bänden*. Frankfurt am Main: Suhrkamp Verlag, 1969.

Hegel, G.F.W. *Werke in 20 Bänden mit Registerband: Gesamte Werkausgabe—5: Wissenschaft der Logik I*. Frankfurt am Main: Suhrkamp Verlag, 1986.

Hegel, G.F.W. *Werke in 20 Bänden mit Registerband: Gesamte Werkausgabe—6: Wissenschaft der Logik II*. Frankfurt am Main: Suhrkamp Verlag, 1986.

Heidegger, Martin. *Aristotle's Metaphysics Θ 1–3*, translated by Walter Brogan and Peter Warnek. Indianapolis: Indiana University Press, 1995.

Heidegger, Martin. *Being and Time*, translated by John Macquarrie and Edward Robinson. New York: Harper & Row, 1962.

Heidegger, Martin. *Poetry, Language, Thought*, translated by Albert Hofstadter. New York: Harper & Row, 1971.

Henrich, Dieter. *Hegel im Kontext*. Frankfurt: Suhrkamp, 1971.

Hintikka, Jaakko. "Leibniz on Plenitude, Relations, and the 'Reign of Law.'" In *Reforging the Great Chain of Being*, edited by S. Knuuttila, 259–86. Dordrecht: Springer, 1972.

Hobbes, Thomas. *Leviathan*. Indianapolis: Hackett Publishing, 1994.

Houlgate, Stephen. "Necessity and Contingency in Hegel's *Science of Logic*." *Owl of Minerva* 27, no. 1 (1995): 37–49.

Houlgate, Stephen. *The Opening of Hegel's Logic: From Being to Infinity*. West Lafayette: Purdue University Press, 2006.

Houlgate, Stephen. "Phenomenology and De Re Interpretation: A Critique of Brandom's Reading of Hegel." *International Journal of Philosophical Studies* 17, no. 1 (2009): 29–47.

Hughes, G.E and M.J. Cresswell. *A New Introduction to Modal Logic*. London: Routledge, 1996.

Husserl, Edmond. *Cartesian Meditations*, translated by Dorion Cairns. The Hague: Martinus Nijhoff Publishers, 1960.

Hyppolite, Jean. *Logic and Existence*, translated by Leonard Lawlor and Amit Sen. Albany: SUNY Press, 1997.

Kant, Immanuel. *Critique of Pure Reason*, translated by Paul Guyer and Allen W. Wood. Cambridge: Cambridge University Press, 1998.

Kant, Immanuel. *Critique of the Power of Judgment*, translated by Paul Guyer and Eric Matthews. Cambridge: Cambridge University Press, 2000.

Kirk, G.S. and J.E. Raven (trans.). *The Presocratic Philosophers: A Critical History with a Selection of Texts*. London: Cambridge University Press, 1957.

Knappik, Franz. "Hegel's Modal Argument against Spinozism: An Interpretation of the Chapter 'Actuality' in the *Science of Logic*." *Hegel Bulletin* 36, no. 1 (2015): 53–79.

Lampert, Jay. "Hegel on Contingency, or, Fluidity and Multiplicity." *Bulletin of the Hegel Society of Great Britain* 51, no. 2 (2005): 74–82.

Lampert, Jay. "Speed, Impact and Fluidity at the Barrier between Life and Death: Hegel's Philosophy of Nature." *Angelaki* 10, no. 3 (2005): 145–56.

Leibniz, G.W. *Discourse on Metaphysics and Other Writing*, edited by Peter Loptson. Toronto: Broadview Editions, 2012.

Leibniz, G.W. *Philosophical Essays*, translated by Daniel Garber and Roger Ariew. Indianapolis: Hackett Publishing, 1989.

Leibniz, G.W. *Theodicy*, translated by E.M. Huggard. Charleston: BiblioBazaar, 2007.

Leibniz, G.W. *Philosophical Papers and Letters*, translated by Leroy E. Loemker. Chicago: Chicago University Press, 1956.

Levinas, Emmanuel. *Totality and Infinity*, translated by Alphonso Lingis. Pittsburgh: Duquesne University Press, 1969.

Lewis, David. *On the Plurality of Worlds*. Malden: Blackwell Publishing, 1986.

Longuenesse, Béatrice. *Hegel's Critique of Metaphysics*, translated by Nicole J. Simek. New York: Cambridge University Press, 2007.

Lovecraft, H.P. *The Fiction—Complete and Unabridged*. New York: Barnes & Noble, 2008.

Lovejoy, Arthur O. *The Great Chain of Being*. Cambridge: Harvard University Press, 1936.

Macdonald, Iain. "Adorno's Modal Utopianism: Possibility and Actuality in Adorno and Hegel." *Adorno Studies* 1, no. 1 (2017): 2–12.

Maker, William. *Philosophy without Foundations: Rethinking Hegel*. Albany: SUNY Press, 1994.

Malabou, Catherine. *The Future of Hegel: Plasticity, Temporality and Dialectic*, translated by Lisabeth During. London: Routledge, 2005.

Marcuse, Herbert. *Hegel's Ontology and the Theory of Historicity*, translated by Seyla Benhabib. Cambridge, MA: MIT Press, 1987.

Makin, Stephen (trans.). *Aristotle Metaphysics Book Θ*, by Aristotle. Oxford: Clarendon, 2006.

Mates, Benson. "Leibniz on Possible Worlds." *Critica* 4, no. 10 (1970): 123–27.

McDonough, Jeffrey K. "Leibniz and the Puzzle of Incompossibility: The Packing Strategy." *Philosophical Review* 119, no. 2 (2010): 135–63.

McTaggart, John and Ellis. *A Commentary on Hegel's Logic*. New York: Russell & Russell 1910.

Messina, James and Donald Rutherford. "Leibniz on Compossibility." *Philosophy Compass* 4, no. 6 (2009): 962–77.

Michelini, Francesca. "Hegel's Notion of Natural Purpose." *Studies in History and Philosophy of Biological and Biomedical Sciences* 43, no. 1 (2012): 133–39.

Moss, Gregory S. "The Emerging Philosophical Recognition of the Significance of Indeterminacy." In *The Significance of Indeterminacy: Perspectives from Asian and Continental Philosophy*, edited by Robert H. Scott and Gregory S. Moss, 1–47. New York: Routledge, 2018.

Mure, G.R.G. *A Study of Hegel's Logic*. Oxford: Oxford University Press, 1950.

Nancy, Jean-Luc. *Hegel: The Restlessness of the Negative*, translated by Jason Smith and Steven Miller. Minneapolis: University of Minnesota Press, 2002.

Perec, Georges. *A Void*, translated by Gilbert Adair. London: Vintage Publishing, 2008.

Pippin, Robert. "Hegel's Metaphysics and the Problem of Contradiction." *Journal of the History of Philosophy* 16, no. 3 (1978): 301–12.
Popper, Karl. "What Is Dialectic?" *Mind* 49 (1940): 403–26.
Priest, Graham. *Beyond the Limits of Thought*. New York: Cambridge University Press, 1995.
Priest, Graham. "Dialectic and Dialetheic." *Science and Society* 53, no. 4 (1989): 388–415.
Priest, Graham. *In Contradiction: A Study of Transconsistent Logic*. Oxford: Clarendon Press, 2006.
Priest, Graham. "The Logical Structure of Dialectic," unpublished.
Rentmeester, Casey. "Leibniz and Huayan Buddhism: Monads as Modified *Li*?" *Lyceum* 13, no. 1 (2014): 36–57.
Rescher, Nicholas. *On Leibniz: Expanded Edition*. Pittsburgh: University of Pittsburgh Press, 2013.
Rosen, Michael. *Hegel's Dialectic and Its Criticism*. Cambridge: Cambridge University Press, 1982.
Russell, Bertrand. *History of Western Philosophy*. London: Routledge, 2004. Originally published by George Allen & Unwin, 1946.
Russell, Bertrand. *Our Knowledge of the External World: As a Field for Scientific Method in Philosophy*. New York: Routledge, 2009.
Russell, Bertrand. *The Philosophy of Leibniz*. London: Routledge, 1900.
Shields, Christopher. "Leibniz's Doctrine of the Striving Possibles." *Journal of the History of Philosophy* 24, no. 3 (1986): 343–57.
Spinoza, Baruch. *Ethics*, translated by Edwin M. Curley. New York: Penguin Books, 1996.
Stang, Nicholas F. *Kant's Modal Metaphysics*. Oxford: Oxford University Press, 2016.
Stekeler-Weithofer, Pirmin. *Hegel's Analytic Pragmatism*. Unpublished. Accessed online: http://www.sozphil.uni-leipzig.de/cm/philosophie/files/2012/11/StekelerHegelsAnalyticPragmatism.pdf (accessed September 25, 2018).
Stewart, John (eds.). *The Hegel Myths and Legends*. Evanston: Northwestern University Press, 1996.
Stiegler, Bernard. *Technics and Time, 3: Cinematic Time and the Question of Malaise*, translated by Stephen Barker. Stanford: Stanford University Press, 2010.
Strickland, Lloyd. "Leibniz on whether the World Increases in Perfection." *British Journal for the History of Philosophy* 14, no. 1 (2006): 51–68.
Taylor, Charles. *Hegel*. New York: Cambridge University Press, 1975.
Von Trier, Lars and Thomas Vinterberg. "The Vow of Chastity: Dogme Manifesto." 1995. Accessed online: https://ifsstech.files.wordpress.com/2008/06/the_vow_of_chastity.pdf (accessed September 25, 2018).

Warren, James. "Ancient Atomists on the Plurality of Worlds." *The Classical Quarterly*, New Series 54, no. 2 (2004), 354–65.

Whyte, Jessica. "I Would Prefer Not To: Bartleby and the Potentiality of the Law." *Law and Critique* 20, no. 3 (2009): 309–24.

Wieland, Wolfgang. "Bemerkungen zum Anfang von Hegels Logik." In *Seminar: Dialektik in der Philosophie Hegels*, edited by R.P. Horstmann, 194–212. Frankfurt am Main: Suhrkamp Verlag, 1978.

Wilson, Catherine. "Leibnizian Optimism." *Journal of Philosophy* 80, no. 11 (1983): 765–83.

Winfield, Richard Dien. *Hegel's Science of Logic: A Critical Rethinking in Thirty Lectures*. Lanham: Rowman & Littlefield, 2012.

Winfield, Richard Dien. "Negation, Contradiction, and Hegel's Emancipation of Truth, Right, and Beauty." Unpublished.

Witt, Charlotte. *Ways of Being: Potentiality and Actuality in Aristotle's Metaphysics*. Ithaca: Cornell University Press, 2003.

Žižek, Slavoj. *Tarrying with the Negative*. Durham: Duke University Press, 1993.

Index

actuality
  absolute 28, 109, 118, 128–30, 185
  expansion of 107, 118
  formal 109, 122
  immediate 110
  primacy 6–10, 117
  real 122, 124, 129, 145
ancient Atomists 4, 12, 14
Anselm 4, 163
apophatic 47, 55–7, 198, 200–3
  negative theology 55, 57, 201
Aristotle 2–4, 7–11, 13–15, 17–19, 54,
    82–3, 92–3, 106–7, 110–11, 128–9,
    131, 143
Aufhebung 33, 47, 52, 70, 80, 126, 139,
    141

Berlin, Isaiah 193–6
Borges, Jorge Luis 19, 173
Brandom, Robert 77–9
Buddhism 58–9
Burbidge, John W. 8, 113

compossibility 156, 161–3, 168–70, 176,
    182, 185
condition 8, 22–4, 27, 31–2, 60, 79, 86,
    105, 108–10, 114, 116, 118, 122–5,
    127–9, 134, 140, 142–6, 149–50,
    155, 161, 167, 173–6, 178–81, 187,
    191, 193–7, 199, 200–2
contingency
  absolute 29, 31, 38, 107, 109, 133,
    135–7, 155, 202–3
  formal 108, 113, 115, 118–21, 124
  real 128
contradiction
  and contrariety 92–4
  and death 98–9, 102
  and essence 77–8, 81, 94–8
  existence of 18–19, 26, 74, 77, 80, 92–3
  law of non- 13, 16–19, 73, 76–7, 79, 80,
    87, 89, 92–3, 113, 121–2, 127, 130,
    140, 143, 181, 197, 217
  and life 78–9, 81, 98–9, 100–2
  primacy of 73–5, 78, 80, 87–8, 95
  productive 24, 74, 102–3, 105
  and self-identity 79, 81
  and totality 70–1, 74

de Boer, Karin 79, 81, 105
Deleuze, Gilles 2, 6–7, 10, 17–19, 31–2, 138,
    155–7, 159, 161, 163, 165, 167–9, 171,
    173, 175, 177, 179, 181–8
  virtuality 17, 19, 173, 185
Derrida, Jacques 65, 201
Descartes, René 4, 42, 54, 63–4
Desmond, William 5, 37, 64–7, 69, 71
dialethism 80
Dick, Philip K. 174

Fichte, Johann Gottlieb 63, 193
Flint, Eric 174

Goethe, Johann Wolfgang von 30, 98

Hahn, Songsuk Susan 53–4, 78–9, 81, 98–9
Harris, Errol 10, 60
Hartmann, Eduard von 76
Heidegger, Martin 10, 54–5, 106
Henrich, Dieter 48–9, 51
Heraclitus 50, 58–9, 63–4
Hobbes, Thomas 179, 193
Houlgate, Stephen 50–1, 145

immanence 9
inaccessible 6, 23, 27, 29–30, 33, 127, 137,
    141, 144, 147, 155, 174–5, 178, 199
incompossibility 6, 32, 155, 157, 159,
    161–3, 165, 167, 169, 171, 173, 175,
    177, 179, 181, 183, 185, 187
  lawful interpretation 168–70
  logical interpretation 167–70

infinite 4–6, 12–16, 20, 22, 26, 28, 31–2, 55, 65, 67–71, 137, 144, 156–60, 162, 164, 168, 170–2, 174–6, 176, 182–5, 189–91, 196, 201

Kant, Immanuel 4, 10–12, 29, 54, 79, 154, 193
Kierkegaard, Søren 37, 50

Lampert, Jay 8, 99, 100–1, 114
Leibniz, G.W. 2, 4–7, 9–11, 14–17, 19, 31–2, 88, 132, 138, 155–77, 179, 181–3, 185, 187–93
Levinas, Emmanuel 37, 65, 201
Lewis, David 4, 15–17, 174
Lovecraft, H.P. 207 (endnote)

Maker, William 48–9
McDonough, Jeffrey K. 169–71
Megarians 2–4, 7, 9, 14, 16, 106–7
Meinong, Alexius 174
modal
   indeterminacy 2–8, 10–11, 13–17, 19–20, 24, 151, 162, 171, 176, 190
   optimism 5–6, 26, 28–9, 31–3, 107, 136–8, 177–9, 189–91, 194, 196–7, 200–1, 203
   priority 3–7, 9–11, 15–17, 20–1, 28, 117, 190
   transitivity 30, 141, 148, 151–3
Monad 162, 181–3, 187
Mure, G.R.G. 39

Nancy, Jean-Luc 105
necessity
   absolute 6, 28–9, 31–2, 38, 113, 130–3, 135, 137–8, 155, 157–9, 168, 176–8, 180, 188, 190, 192, 197, 199, 200, 202–3
   access model 6, 147, 178, 180
   as constraint 152–3
   formal necessity 121–2, 127, 153
   hypothetical necessity 6, 128, 156, 158–9, 168, 199
   production model 6, 147, 149–50
   real 127–8, 130, 175, 199
   and science 140
   Spinozistic necessarianism 155, 157–8

negative theology 55, 57, 201
Nietzsche, Friedrich 12

Ockham's razor 166

Parmenides 58
Perec, Georges 153
perfection 14, 17, 31–2, 155–7, 159, 163–7, 169–70, 174–6, 179
Phenomenology of Spirit 8, 10, 25, 33, 48–9, 52, 56, 65–6, 79, 101, 125, 139
Pippin, Robert 77–8, 81, 96–7
Plato 11–12, 54, 96–7, 200
Popper, Karl 76
possibility
   absolute 107, 178, 200
   as alternatives 20–4, 32, 115, 156, 172, 186
   both sides of 107, 109, 114–19, 121–2
   as a degree of quantity 20, 22–4, 32, 116, 156, 171–3
   dunamis 7, 9, 143
   formal possibility 110, 112–13, 120–1, 123, 143
   itself 6, 26–7, 32, 107–8, 114–25, 172, 196
   negative side of 25–6, 29, 105–7, 112, 118–20, 124, 175
   not to be 18, 105–7, 109, 112, 116, 118, 120, 123
   potentiality 2–4, 7–11, 102, 106–7, 115
   primacy 10, 117
   production of 153
   qua possibility 180
   real 22, 122–4, 127–8
   to be 18, 105–6, 108, 110, 112
   and totality 23, 105, 115, 117, 127, 134, 137
   and truth verification 105–8, 110
   unactualized 3, 5–6, 11, 26, 29, 117, 134, 158, 163, 165, 173–4, 186
possible worlds 4–6, 11–17, 19–20, 22–3, 31, 68, 96, 138, 155–65, 169–75, 189, 191
Priest, Graham 80–1

quantum mechanics 174
Quine, Willard Van Orman 174

reductio ad absurdum 74, 77
Rescher, Nicholas 15, 157, 166, 170, 174
Rick and Morty 13–14
Rosen, Michael 46, 56
Russell, Bertrand 76–7, 96–8, 174

Schelling, Friedrich Wilhelm Joseph 50
Schopenhauer, Arthur 12
simplest means for maximum ends 165–7, 175
Socrates 42, 64, 96–7
Spinoza, Baruch 14, 155, 157–8, 168, 171, 191
    Spinozistic necessarianism 155, 157–8
Stiegler, Bernard 107
substance 6, 8–9, 30, 57, 93, 99–100, 102, 108–9, 117–18, 128–31, 134, 136, 157–8, 162, 164–5, 169–70, 181, 186, 195
substitution 6, 74–6, 80–1, 90–9, 97, 98, 99, 102–3, 108, 118, 120, 122, 125, 170

teleology 79, 98–9
Thales 63–4
totality
    dialectical 5, 37, 39, 53, 60–5, 67, 70–1
    of form 26, 38, 112
    of possibility 23, 105, 115, 117, 127, 134, 137
transcendence 5–6, 11–12, 20, 25, 29, 61, 65, 69, 90, 174–5, 191
tree (oak tree) 7, 22, 27, 53, 90, 123, 125, 127–8, 146, 148–50, 198–200
Trendelenburg, Friedrich Adolf 50

vanishing 44–5, 75

Winfield, Richard Dien 63
world separation 3, 5–6, 10–11, 14, 17, 20, 28, 190

Žižek, Slavoj 105

www.ingramcontent.com/pod-product-compliance
Lightning Source LLC
Chambersburg PA
CBHW050327020526
44117CB00031B/1832